Metaphor Networks

Metaphor Networks

The Comparative Evolution of Figurative Language

Richard Trim
Université de Provence

© Richard Trim 2007

All rights reserved. No reproduction, copy or transmission of this publication may be made without written permission.

No paragraph of this publication may be reproduced, copied or transmitted save with written permission or in accordance with the provisions of the Copyright, Designs and Patents Act 1988, or under the terms of any licence permitting limited copying issued by the Copyright Licensing Agency, 90 Tottenham Court Road, London W1T 4LP.

Any person who does any unauthorised act in relation to this publication may be liable to criminal prosecution and civil claims for damages.

The author has asserted his right to be identified as the author of this work in accordance with the Copyright, Designs and Patents Act 1988.

First published 2007 by
PALGRAVE MACMILLAN
Houndmills, Basingstoke, Hampshire RG21 6XS and
175 Fifth Avenue, New York, N.Y. 10010
Companies and representatives throughout the world

PALGRAVE MACMILLAN is the global academic imprint of the Palgrave Macmillan division of St. Martin's Press, LLC and of Palgrave Macmillan Ltd. Macmillan® is a registered trademark in the United States, United Kingdom and other countries. Palgrave is a registered trademark in the European Union and other countries.

ISBN-13: 978-0-230-50751-7   hardback
ISBN-10: 0-230-50751-4   hardback

This book is printed on paper suitable for recycling and made from fully managed and sustained forest sources.

A catalogue record for this book is available from the British Library.

Library of Congress Cataloging-in-Publication Data

Trim, Richard, 1950-
　　Metaphor networks: the comparative evolution of figurative language / Richard Trim.
　　　　p. cm.
　　ISBN-13: 978–0–230–50751–7 (cloth)
　　ISBN-10: 0–230–50751–4 (cloth)
　　1. Metaphor. 2. Historical linguistics. 3. Language and culture. I. Title.

P301.5.M48T75 2007
415–dc22   2006052779

10 9 8 7 6 5 4 3 2 1
16 15 14 13 12 11 10 09 08 07

Printed and bound in Great Britain by
Antony Rowe Ltd, Chippenham and Eastbourne

In memory of Kitty
who first awakened my interest in language at the age of ten

Contents

List of Figures	x
List of Tables	xii
Preface	xiii
Acknowledgements	xv

Part I Synchronic Networking

1 The Role of Cognition — 3
- 1.1 Historical origins — 3
- 1.2 Defining metaphor — 9
- 1.3 The history of ideas on approaches to metaphor and cognitive science — 13
- 1.4 Prototype metaphor — 15
- 1.5 Metaphor scenarios — 21

2 Universal Trends — 28
- 2.1 Conceptual metaphor and linguistic form — 28
- 2.2 The body and universal metaphor — 30
- 2.3 The drugs metaphors network — 33
- 2.4 The cross-language dimension — 36
- 2.5 The universality of personification — 47

3 Culture-specific Conceptualisation — 49
- 3.1 Universals and culture — 49
- 3.2 The American cultural model of marriage — 50
- 3.3 Cultural transfer of metaphor — 51
- 3.4 Interaction between language and cultural environment — 53
- 3.5 Determining universal or cultural sources — 54
- 3.6 Colour metaphors — 56

4 Conceptual Equivalence and Translation — 63
- 4.1 Translation options — 63
- 4.2 Traditional views of translatability — 67
- 4.3 The BUSINESS CORPORATION = FAMILY model — 72

Part II The Diachronic Dimension

5 Cultural Patterns of the Past — 83
- 5.1 New perspectives from a diachronic viewpoint — 83
- 5.2 Diachronic cultural patterns — 84
- 5.3 Cultural history of the BUSINESS CORPORATION = FAMILY model — 86

6 Metaphor and Semantic Networks — 91
- 6.1 Semantic fields and polysemy in meaning change — 91
- 6.2 Vagueness and ambiguity — 92
- 6.3 Centralised meaning in metaphor networks — 95
- 6.4 Random polysemous features — 95
- 6.5 Chronological polysemy in diachronic change — 97
- 6.6 Regularity in change — 99
- 6.7 Unidirectional change — 102
- 6.8 Chaining in semantic fields — 104

7 Metaphor Paths in Base Concepts — 109
- 7.1 Diachronic conceptual networking — 109
- 7.2 The metaphor path of FLATNESS — 112
- 7.3 The metaphor path of SMOOTHNESS — 114
- 7.4 Binary concepts: TIGHT/LOOSE — 116
- 7.5 Complex systems: DRYNESS — 118

8 Germanic Influences in Old English — 122
- 8.1 Long-term metaphor — 122
- 8.2 Short-term Germanic influences — 125
- 8.3 Links to other Germanic languages — 130
- 8.4 Collocational interchangeability in Germanic origins — 133
- 8.5 Cultural influence and saliency — 137
- 8.6 Diachronic saliency — 138

9 Metaphor Death — 141
- 9.1 Problems of definition — 141
- 9.2 Patterns of metaphor death — 144
- 9.3 Regeneration of metaphors — 147

10 Historical Mindsets — 152
- 10.1 Similarities between time-specific and culture-specific models — 152
- 10.2 Attitudes towards imagery through time — 154

10.3	Changing attitudes in long-term models: Ancient Greece	156
10.4	Religious mindsets	160

Part III Historical Networks

11 The Evolution of Love Metaphors: a Case Study — 169
- 11.1 Exploring medieval metaphor — 169
- 11.2 The structure of emotions — 170
- 11.3 Concepts of love — 172
- 11.4 The historical networking of love metaphors — 175
- 11.5 Matches between Middle and modern English — 176
- 11.6 Medieval courtly love — 180
- 11.7 Time-specific saliency in English medieval metaphor — 185

12 Latinate-based Origins in English Medieval Metaphor — 190
- 12.1 Literature as a record of metaphor evolution — 190
- 12.2 Medieval French sources — 191
- 12.3 Medieval Italian sources — 193
- 12.4 Chaucer and Boccaccio — 194
- 12.5 Petrarch — 197
- 12.6 Latinate sources in Antiquity — 201
- 12.7 Metaphor links to the classical period — 204

13 Historical Models of Love Metaphors — 211
- 13.1 Literary paths in metaphor creation — 211
- 13.2 Long-term models of love — 212
- 13.3 Long-term models of love with variable cultural connotations — 214
- 13.4 Time specificity: models of diachronic saliency — 215
- 13.5 Conventionalised love metaphors — 216
- 13.6 Metaphor death in love — 217
- 13.7 The overall picture — 218

References — 222

Index — 229

List of Figures

1.1	The HABITAT classifier in Egyptian hieroglyphics	8
1.2	The *Akhet* hieroglyph: a horizon or solar eclipse symbol	8
1.3	Three-dimensional model of metaphor interpretation of cancer	17
1.4	Conceptual linking in the *mother* concept	19
1.5	Sub-images linked to a base PU component	20
1.6	Linear sub-images linked to a phraseological unit	21
1.7	Networking in the love metaphor scenario	26
2.1	Major phases in the drugs war scenario	35
2.2	Networking in the UP-DOWN model of drug effects	37
2.3	The container image viewed from different sections of society	39
2.4	Networking in the binary concepts of temperature, health and dirt	43
3.1	The cultural colour web	61
3.2	Colour overlapping and shifts	62
4.1	Translatability and cross-language equivalence in metaphor	66
4.2	Comparative networking in shared conceptual metaphors	70
4.3	Comparative networking in language-specific conceptual metaphors	71
4.4	Predominance in cross-language networking patterns	79
6.1	Trier's semantic field theory	92
6.2	Diachronic chaining in the semantic field PRIMATES = BRUTISHNESS	105
6.3	Networking in the semantic field BIRDS = FOOLISHNESS	106
7.1	The comparative evolution of metaphor paths	111
7.2	Diachronic networking in the FLATNESS concept	113
7.3	The diachronic network of SMOOTHNESS	115
7.4	Metaphor paths in the TIGHT/LOOSE binary concept	116
7.5	Secondary clusters in the DRYNESS model	120
7.6	Cross-language divergence in the DRYNESS model	121
8.1	Replacement by borrowing of the SWELL = ANGER conceptualisation in Old English	127

8.2	Changing evolution of cross-language metaphoric collocations	132
8.3	Collocational switching resulting in a change of metaphor paths	133
8.4	Diachronic network of comparative collocational metaphors in English and German	137
8.5a	Diachronic saliency in time-specific metaphors	139
8.5b	Fluctuating saliency in long-term metaphors	139
9.1	Relationship between literal and metaphorical meanings in dead metaphors	143
9.2	Variation in the perception of metaphor death	146
9.3	Death of the 'pedigree' metaphor	148
9.4	Regeneration in dead metaphors	149
9.5	Diachronic phases of live, dying and dead metaphors	150
12.1	Chaining of conceptual forms of love	204
13.1	Literary paths of English love metaphors with Latinate-based sources	212
13.2	The long-term diachronic network of the conceptual metaphor FIRE = LOVE	213
13.3	Variable connotations of the LOVE = PAIN metaphor	214
13.4	Fluctuating diachronic saliency in the pain model	215
13.5	Conventionalisation in the LOVE = UNITY model	217
13.6	Metaphor death and conceptual switching	218

List of Tables

3.1	The lexical legacy of humoral theory	56
4.1	Warfare ontology in business enterprises	72
4.2	Chronology of the family scenario	73
6.1	The diachronic model ANIMALS/BIRDS = STUPIDITY	107
6.2	The French model ANIMALS/BIRDS = STUPIDITY	107
8.1	Present-day collocations of *sharp* in English and German	134

Preface

Among the vast number of books which have been published on metaphor in recent years, it seems there is still a lack of studies concerning one major aspect: its historical evolution. Where do a lot of our metaphors originally come from? How do they evolve? How long do they last and where do they end? It is hoped that this book will help to answer some of these questions and fill the gap in our historical knowledge of metaphor evolution by proposing a fundamental process at work: the role of conceptual networking. Based on substantial empirical data, the book suggests that this cognitive process is responsible for the evolution of a large part of our present-day figurative language.

Although it is, of course, impossible to re-trace every figurative expression, whether they be metaphoric or metonymic features, proverbs, idioms, puns or other kinds of figurative structure, it can nevertheless be seen that many of our basic conceptual metaphors, together with their various linguistic derivations, do have specific models of evolution.

Much of our creation of metaphors depends on their links to related concepts and on what has gone before. In many cases, models cluster into groups and are linked to pre-existing ones. Our conceptualisation of the environment is linked to the images of previous generations and our metaphors can have a long history. Regular patterns develop in specific directions. There are a number of different ways in which they may evolve according to cultural and linguistic parameters. Some of these depend on cultural history or contact with other cultures, the nature of saliency at a given point in time or the complex area of conventionalisation and metaphor death. All these issues play a role in the types of long or short-term metaphor paths which are created in a given linguistic environment.

Despite the complexities and fluctuations in evolutionary paths, it appears that the same networking processes have been at work since time immemorial. The hypothesis is that the same kind of process operates in all cultures and regular patterns develop in specific directions due to underlying base concepts. A model of diachronic conceptual networking would appear to explain these patterns.

Part I looks at the general cognitive process of conceptual networking, as well as the implications of universal trends and their culture-specific limitations from a synchronic angle. Part II explores the diachronic dimension with reference to regular trends, saliency, metaphor death and historical attitudes towards metaphor in long or short-term paths. Part III looks more specifically at a case study of a historical network involving love metaphors, which are well documented in European literary works. With the aid of recent studies in the present-day metaphorisation of love, which are used for the purposes of comparison, these networks are traced back through time with corpus analyses of manuscripts from the Middle Ages and Antiquity. These analyses are discussed in conjunction with research into the pathways of literary ideas throughout European history.

This study grew out of a long-standing interest in comparative and historical linguistics. It took shape in conjunction with teaching university courses in both translation studies and the history of language, as well as with ongoing research in the field of metaphor. It is hoped that the book will therefore be of use to all those who are engaged in metaphor research and also to those with a general interest in language evolution.

I would like to take the opportunity of thanking the (anonymous) reviewer at Palgrave Macmillan for the useful comments and suggestions made on improving the first draft of the manuscript. Any outstanding errors or omissions are entirely my own responsibility. In addition, thanks are also due to Palgrave Commissioning Editor, Jill Lake, for all her assistance in preparing the typescript for publication.

I am also grateful to various colleagues and friends from different universities for their useful references, examples, articles and helpful suggestions in the making of this book. They include, in particular (and in alphabetical order): Jean Aitchison, Kathryn Allan, Jonathon Charteris-Black, Caroline Gevaert, Adrian Harding, Jean-Marie Merle, Joanny Moulin, Anita Naciscione and Jacqueline Percebois. Last but not least, a special word of thanks is due to artist, Anisa Caine, for designing and producing the painting specially for the front cover of the book.

RICHARD TRIM

Acknowledgements

Acknowledgements are due to the following publishers and authors for permission to reproduce illustrations and tables of data: to Cambridge University Press for including Figure 9.1 on the relationship between literal and metaphorical meanings in dead metaphors (Searle, 1979); to *History of Intellectual Culture* and Ulrich Teucher for reproducing Figure 1.3 on a three-dimensional model of metaphor interpretation of cancer (adapted from Teucher, 2003); to Mouton de Gruyter for permission to reproduce data with regard to the lexical legacy of humoral theory in Chapter 3 (Geeraerts and Grondelaers, 1995); Figures 6.2 and 6.3 on diachronic metaphor chaining in primate and bird images (Lehrer, 1985) and data on drugs metaphors in Chapter 2 (Trim, 1997); to Anita Naciscione for her models on phraseological units (Figures 1.5 and 1.6.); and to *UCREL Technical Papers* and Kathryn Allan for permission to reproduce Table 6.1 on a diachronic model of animal images (Allan, 2003).

Acknowledgments

Part I
Synchronic Networking

1
The Role of Cognition

1.1 Historical origins

Ever since the early days of Indo-European philology at the beginning of the nineteenth century, scholars have been trying to find regular patterns of evolution in language in order to draw conclusions on the mechanisms and diachronic theories involved. The search for principles of meaning-change and their origins proved to be a hard task. Research made relatively rapid progress with regard to more rigid structures in language such as phonetic systems. In the case of sound shifts, comprehensive theories were put forward such as Grimm's Law on the First Consonant Shift in early Germanic languages (Prokosch, 1938) and the Great Vowel Shift in Middle to Modern English (Jespersen [1909] 1939).

The field of semantics, however, appeared to be generally random. The problem is that the numbers of different senses that may be attributed to lexical items can be extremely varied and, at first sight, arbitrary in every case. Parallel to the search for laws in phonetic systems carried out in the nineteenth century, an attempt was made at formulating laws of semantic change in literal meaning. One of the only successful ones was proposed by Stern ([1931] 1968) who claimed that all English adverbs in the Middle Ages having the sense of 'rapidly' changed to 'immediately' after an intermediate stage. According to this finding, the semantic shift was for a limited period and did not operate after 1400 AD. Due to the failure to find other regular patterns, the search for laws based on this kind of model was subsequently abandoned. Although a large number of regular features can be found in Stern's law, it also reveals discrepancies in the chronological dating of examples due to the scantiness of Old and Middle English texts in the corpus.

The evolution of figurative language was hardly taken into consideration at all in these traditional approaches to historical linguistics.

However, it is this area of semantic change, or its role in causing general principles of change in literal meaning, which appears to offer more scope for finding regular patterns. More recent research puts forward strong arguments as to the existence of diachronic regularity and that metaphoric processes contribute towards such regularity (Sweetser, 1990; Traugott and Dasher, 2002). These mechanisms have been discovered with the help, in particular, of the relatively new field of cognitive linguistics which, compared to the former neogrammarian, structuralist and transformational-generative models, has opened up new avenues of research into historical linguistics. The following discussions will explore how this new approach has widened our understanding about the evolution of metaphor.

In any study on evolution, the first question which arises is: where did it all start? In this case, where do the origins of metaphor lie? One of the answers to this question can really be found in new metaphors being created today or, in fact, by looking at metaphors being created at any time in history. In other words, metaphor creation seems to be a timeless process, the same mechanisms operate today as they did thousands of years ago. Of course, new images used for metaphor come into play through the course of time because new scientific, social and cultural concepts appear regularly in any language community, and these vary across cultures synchronically; but a cognitive model of our conceptualisation of the environment in the creation of metaphor would suggest that similar processes are in operation all the time.

This idea can be tested by looking at very early forms of language to see what kind of resemblances exist between those early forms and the present day. If we go back in time, we may first think of early written languages such as Latin or Greek and then, if we go back further, we come across written language in pictorial or hieroglyphic form. An analysis of early forms of written language shows that mental mapping processes used at that time are in fact very similar to those of today. Very often, exactly the same images are used. A study of Egyptian hieroglyphics shows that this early form of sign language contains similar figurative images to those found in modern English. A hieroglyph with the symbol of a bull's head indicates the emotion of 'rage' (Goldwasser, 2003) in the same way as the expression 'a raging bull' is used in English today. A perusal of written texts at other historical periods suggests that the same image has been used again and again. A translation from Latin texts reveals the same mapping procedure of the concepts rage and bull:

Achilles raged at this, as a wild bull in open circus ... (Ovid, *Metamorphoses*, 12, 64)

As when two bulls for their female fight . . . with rage of love the jealous rivals burn (Virgil, *Aeneid*, 12, 697)

The image applied here is the same one as today, thousands of years later. A very large number of images in our common culture, which go back to Antiquity, have the same conceptual links. The image may not be exactly the same, as in the example of the bull, as degrees of interpretation vary according to the strength of the conceptual link. One of the metaphoric meanings of the concept *dry* in the Middle Ages meant 'withered' or 'thin' as in *dry arms* (*OED*). This requires a certain degree of interpretation since the metaphor may be construed as simply dry skin rather than thin arms, but we will see later that it is in fact conceptually linked to a vast historical network which has the same notion across the Indo-European field. The French term *sec* (dry), for example, also has the meaning of 'thin' in a conventionalised metaphor today.

Many individual metaphors form part of long-term cultural symbols that re-occur at different historical and literary periods. They constitute networks which may go back a long way in time. Animals linked to the notion of rage in our culture are conceptualised in the same way as other animals with specific attributes such as a lion being courageous. The present-day notion of *lion-hearted* is linked to the historical label of *Richard the Lionheart* and the symbol of a lion as a national emblem in British heraldry. This symbol was incorporated into British heraldry because of its more general image of a crusading warrior which may have been related to Roman times when lions would have first been brought into Europe for the amphitheatres. The suggestion here is that the symbol of courage demonstrated by lions in amphitheatres was adopted by British heraldry.

The Lion as a symbol of bravery can also be seen during later historical periods, such as in Chaucer:

But been a leoun bothe in word and dede ('The Knight's Tale', *Canterbury Tales*, 1.917; Hieatt and Hieatt, 1976: 84)

As well as individual figurative items involving one-to-one mapping procedures, metaphoric processes often form part of a larger system which reflects the way in which the members of a given culture conceptualise experience. This experience may, for example, have formed part of European civilisation since the times of Antiquity. Lakoff and Turner (1989: 9) categorise such systems as *general conceptual metaphors*, rather than the actual metaphor itself. An example is the LIFE IS A JOURNEY image (metaphor models are often capitalised in this way in cognitive linguistics), which has occurred at different periods of literature. The beginning of Dante's *Divine Comedy* offers such an example:

In the middle of life's road
I found myself in a dark wood
(*Divine Comedy, Purgatorio*, I, 1–2)

If we go back further in time to the Classics, the same conceptual metaphor occurs, suggesting that the image had been passed down to Dante's mode of conceptualisation in the Middle Ages:

... spirits are assigned to less burdensome bodies on the journey of life
(Boethius, *Consolatio Philosophiae*, 3, 19)

Now your house is left without a friend, and Charon's boat awaits your children to bear them on that journey out of life, without return ...
(Euripides, *Heracles*, 430)

It can thus be seen that the journey metaphor is one which has been used throughout the history of literature, and it has been suggested that, in many works, it involves a process by which the hero of the story leaves the ordinary world, enters the world of the supernatural in which he has to fight all those intent on his destruction, and then returns to his own world to try and help his people with the knowledge he has gained. This has been summed up in the following way: 'If the story of *Odyssey* is humanity's story of loss and rebirth leading to transformation, so is *War and Peace* in a 19th century Russian context, and so is the *Star Wars* movie trilogy in a 20th century American one' (Gibbs, 1994: 188).

There are, of course, variations on this journey theme in the different works cited above. Dante's journey, leading from the ordinary world into the dark, supernatural region of Hell is a symbol of punishment from which the main evil characters of history are not to return. The more wicked the protagonists are, the longer the journey is, and the worse Hell gets. One of the worst journeys is reserved for Pontius Pilate who ends his journey deep down in Hell, hanging upside down and frozen solid.

The LIFE IS A JOURNEY conceptual metaphor can be seen in numerous examples of everyday speech in modern English, one being the conceptualisation of friendship as a journey:

> Their friendship has come a long way
> Their friendship has travelled some rough roads
>
> (Kövecses, 1995: 336)

The abundance of this model would therefore suggest that these systems of conceptualisation have a universal nature and have followed the same paths since Antiquity.

Underlying mental processes generate lexical forms in the language that are conceptually linked to the base mapping procedure. The term 'journey' does not necessarily appear in the actual expressions 'come a long way' or 'travelled some rough roads', but they are generated from the basic journey image, that is, from the same conceptual metaphor. Many figurative parts of speech thus follow the same paths of cultural experience.

One of the reasons why different historical periods produce large numbers of items from similar conceptual metaphors is due to the way we perceive our environment. The very essence of our forms of perception appears not only to be figurative in nature but also inevitably so: 'no sooner is a form seen than it *must* resemble something: humanity seems doomed to analogy' (Silverman and Torode, 1980). In the oft-quoted words of Lakoff and Johnson (1980: 3), 'our ordinary conceptual system, in terms of which we both think and act, is fundamentally metaphorical in nature'. This is not actually a new idea; Vico (1744) also considered metaphor to be essential and pervasive throughout human language in general.

Our expression of images comes not only in the form of written language but also in the field of semiotics: symbols, painting, photography, film and so on. If we turn on the computer and access the internet, we are confronted with a vast number of figurative symbols or icons representing a specific activity: a rubbish bin, a printer, a letter and so on. More sophisticated visual imagery is found frequently today in the world of advertising. One airline commercial used a pair of consecutive shots to compare the flight of a bird with that of an aeroplane. The picture of a bird landing is accompanied by the sounds of an airport control tower and a braking plane, implying that a flight with the airline in question is a very smooth one (Forceville, 1996: 203).

8 *Metaphor Networks*

Signs and symbols were often integrated in early forms of writing. These were used to develop later complex forms of written language as in Egyptian hieroglyphics. A basic symbol used as a [HABITAT] classifier in early Egyptian scripts is represented by a very simple box-type symbol with a small opening (Figure 1.1).

This symbol is a basic representation of a dwelling with four walls and a door. The symbol can be modified in different ways to signify various habitats in which either humans or animals live. Some modifications of the habitat classifier are quite clear while others are less so. Among the more evident symbols are, for instance, the addition of a bird symbol by the side of the box to indicate a nest or a rectangle with turrets to represent a fortress.

More complex mapping processes were also used. The juxtaposition of images in the airline commercial can also be seen in different representations of the (simplified form) of a hieroglyph known as *Akhet* (Figure 1.2).

Traditionally, the *Akhet* symbol embodies a straightforward representation of the horizon with the sun setting behind the mountains. However, some Egyptology scholars claim the symbol represents a solar eclipse and that the ancient Egyptians believed the solar eclipse to be the heavenly abode for the sun (Ibrahem, 2000). The metaphor model would thus be in the form of a SOLAR ECLIPSE = HEAVEN. Figurative symbolisation in hieroglyphs was therefore complex at this time, suggesting that our infinite way of creating analogies has not changed. The historical beginnings

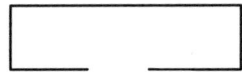

Figure 1.1 The HABITAT classifier in Egyptian hieroglyphics
Source: Goldwasser (2003).

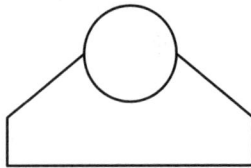

Figure 1.2 The *Akhet* hieroglyph: a horizon or solar eclipse symbol
Source: Adapted from Ibrahem (2000).

of figurative language are the same as creative processes today, a fact which would contribute towards similar patterns of evolution.

The differences between images across time and languages are mainly related to cultural ways of thinking, which change with the time dimension. One form of conceptualisation of evil in hieroglyphs was through the equation of evil with small, represented by a bird symbol (Goldwasser, 2003). Smallness in modern-day English would be equated with weakness rather than evil. The attributes of the word *puny*, meaning small and weak, would be an example. Ancient Egyptian culture therefore had a different way of viewing smallness. However, the same mental mapping processes existed in early forms of language and we can therefore assume that not only did metaphor exist at the beginning of human communication but that the same creative processes were involved.

The source of this ongoing, timeless and regular nature of metaphor creation must therefore be found in the way the human mind perceives the environment. The arrival of the *modern* approach to cognitive linguistics – the word 'modern' is stressed here since cognitive science itself is not new – helped to shed new light on the structure of figurative meaning.

1.2 Defining metaphor

The new approach brought in a number of interesting innovations with regard to how linguists define metaphor. Lakoff and Johnson (1980) introduced the idea that metaphor has a ubiquitous nature and that it is fundamental to our way of thinking. Such is the effect of a concept like the journey metaphor which produces endless new metaphors in all kinds of domains. The journey metaphor is therefore fundamental – at least to Western society – and it structures our very thought processes.

In discussions on the historical evolution of metaphor this is an important point, since it determines when we think a metaphor still exists or if it has really disappeared. The definition of metaphor thus depends on the notion of *conventionalised* or *dead* metaphors at any given point in time. This aspect will be dealt with in more detail later from a historical point of view, but suffice it to say that there are very many conventionalised metaphors in our language that started off with a metaphoric origin but would not normally be considered today as metaphors. To make matters more complicated, apparently conventional metaphors may vary considerably in their degree of *metaphoricity*, that is, there is often a gradation of how metaphoric each metaphor might look in a given conceptual cluster. Another aspect of the journey metaphor may highlight the problem of metaphoricity.

In a discussion of the ubiquitous nature of metaphor, Gibbs (1994, 148 ff.) cites Lakoff and Johnson's (1980) examples of journey metaphors in the domain of love:

(1) Look how far we've come
(2) It's been a long bumpy road
(3) We're at a crossroads
(4) We may have to go our separate ways
(5) Our marriage is on the rocks
(6) We're spinning our wheels

As Gibbs points out, there is a tight mapping between entities in the domain of love (the lovers, their common goals, the love relationship and so on) which corresponds systematically to entities in the domain of a journey (the traveller, the vehicle, the destinations and so on). This invariant, recurring mapping motivates the tight correspondence between source and target domains. However, a large number of ordinary language users, as well as metaphor theorists, would not consider these expressions to be metaphoric, but rather literal in nature.

To a certain degree, this is understandable, but if we look at these examples more closely, an everyday speaker may suggest, on reflection, that there are definitely some expressions which appear more metaphoric than others. For example, 'look how far we've come' looks very literal, while 'we're spinning our wheels' looks far more metaphoric. There is definitely a separate image of a wheel in the process of spinning which portrays a specific state of a love relationship.

All these expressions, however, come from the same underlying conceptual metaphor of a journey and are therefore related. Expression (1) may not look metaphoric, but it has certainly come from a metaphoric origin; in cognitive linguistic terms, it would be termed a conventional metaphor. There are very many metaphors of this kind in everyday speech such as the conduit metaphors developed by Reddy (1979: 284–324) and discussed further by Lakoff and Johnson (1980). Reddy analyses expressions such as the following:

(1) Try to *get* your *thoughts across* better
(2) None of Mary's *feelings came through to me* with any clarity
(3) You still haven't *given me* any *idea* of what you mean

It can be seen from these examples that entities are passed from one person to another (the notion of *conduit*). In the words of Lakoff and Johnson: 'the speaker puts ideas (objects) into words (containers) and sends them (along a conduit) to a hearer who takes the ideas/objects out of the word/containers' (1980: 10).

To the ordinary language user it would probably appear that the speaker is using a number of verbs and prepositions common to everyday speech: of a very literal character and with nothing metaphoric about them. What is metaphoric about the prepositions *across* and *through*?

A conceptual analysis nevertheless shows that, taken together with their counterparts in the entire expression, there is a process from a metaphoric origin to conventionalisation. In other words, 'to get across' would be an example of this process. To some, these are no longer metaphors or are simply regarded as *dead* metaphors – another possible bone of contention. A significant problem in metaphor definition is therefore ascertaining which items are actually metaphoric, and this has developed into a very controversial point among linguists today.

A further problem relates to terminology. Terms vary not only between different fields of linguistics, they vary within the same field of linguistics and through time. Very often, the problem also concerns the aspect of conventionalisation. For example, Newmark (1985: 93) makes the distinction between dead, cliché, stock, recent and original metaphors, the first four broadly covering the conventional category. More recent studies have concentrated on the differences between metaphor and metonymy. The distinction of a metonym, as compared to a metaphor, can be seen in the example given by Lakoff and Johnson (1980: 35):

The *ham sandwich* is waiting for his cheque.

The context here is a waiter in a snack bar informing another waiter that a client who has ordered a ham sandwich wishes to pay. In this case, the 'ham sandwich' is being used to refer to an actual person and is not being 'likened' to the client in question. This should also be differentiated from personification, since human qualities are not being imputed to the ham sandwich. Gibbs suggests another way of differentiating the two:

A convenient way of distinguishing the two types of figurative trope is to apply the '*is like*' test. Figurative statements of the *X is like Y* form are most meaningful when X and Y represent terms from different conceptual domains. If a non-literal comparison between two things is meaningful when seen in a *X is like Y* statement, then it is metaphorical; otherwise it is metonymic. For example, it makes better sense to say that **The boxer is like a creampuff** (metaphor) than to say **The third baseman is like a glove** (metonymy).

(Gibbs, 1999: 36; emphasis in the original)

Along these lines, a definition put forward by Barcelona (2000: 3–4) claims that metaphor is widely felt to be a process whereby one experiential domain is partially mapped or projected onto a different experiential domain, so that the second domain is partially understood in terms of the first one. Metonymy, on the other hand, is a conceptual projection whereby one experiential domain is partially understood in terms of another experiential domain which is included *in the same common experiential domain*.

However, other metaphor theorists suggests that the situation is more complex. Goosens (1990; 2000) claims that there is not always a clear demarcation between metaphor and metonymy. Some figurative items could be both a metaphor or metonym according to the context so that the two concepts may then become intertwined. This point of view has led to the term *metaphtonymy* being coined.

The suggestion is that there are also several categories of intertwined concepts. As an example, one of these is a group referring to 'metaphor from metonymy'. In this case, we get metaphors which are linked to a metonymic origin. The 'donor domains' of many proverbial expressions are claimed to be metonymic as there are often different related concepts in the same domain. According to Goosens, the expression, 'to talk with one's tongue in one's cheek', that is, to 'say something and mean the opposite, especially in an insincere or ironic way', would have a metonymic base. The metonymic aspect is equated with the literal notion of the speaker pushing his tongue into his cheek while saying something he does not mean. As soon as it is projected onto the 'target scene' to imply insincerity, it becomes metaphoric (1990: 332). The two notions of metaphor and metonymy are therefore linked to the same expression.

Many different terms could be cited from studies carried out over the last two or three decades. However, this would probably be confusing, particularly as some are fashionable only for a short period of time and others never really come into fashion.

In a large part of the literature, 'metaphor' has often been used as a form of umbrella term to cover a wide variety of figurative items. It has been suggested that conceptual metaphor, a term which itself often requires a definition, appears in similes, analogies, personification, synaesthesia, zeugma, as well as expressions in the forms of idioms and proverbs, (Steen, 2002: 21). To facilitate our understanding of these changing attitudes to metaphor definition, we shall look at a brief overview of historical approaches to the question.

1.3 The history of ideas on approaches to metaphor and cognitive science

Traditional views of metaphor were based primarily on the idea of fixed meanings. A great deal of the groundwork in our understanding of metaphor was carried out within the framework of these traditional views but the fact that these theories lacked the component of flexibility in meaning has been the subject of much debate. Lakoff (1987), for example, goes to great lengths to reject any pre-cognitive approaches to figurative meaning which involve what he terms 'the objectivist paradigm' or 'a God's eye view' of meaning.

His basic idea is that meaning cannot be defined outside the mind, in other words, meaning definition is related to individual perception of the environment and not to a totally independent and fixed notion of semantics. He feels, nevertheless, that this latter notion is still held to be true today by a large range of linguists, philosophers and psychologists.

At the beginning of the most widely known scholarly work on metaphor, Aristotle defines metaphor as an implicit comparison, whereby the name of one entity is applied to another. It is thus termed the Comparison Theory, implying that the common ground of metaphor shares a set of features or common category memberships (Aristotle: *Poetics*, 1927: xxi, 7 ff.; *Rhetoric*, 1932: III, ii, 7 ff.).

The Comparison Theory was reformulated by Richards (1965: 174) with metaphoric labels known as the tenor, which is 'what is to be said' and the vehicle 'the way of saying it'. Other variants developed from this viewpoint. Some comparativists stressed the importance of similar attributes between tenor and vehicle. Others have emphasised the relevance of dissimilar attributes, a so-called Anomaly View. The implication here is that metaphor is viewed as a mistake or absurdity since it conflicts with literal meaning. Consequently, special procedures are needed to account for anomalous sentences, such as interpreting metaphor in a literal sense first and then setting up special rules or ignoring violated rules (Harris, 1976). Yet another variant was the interactionist view, first introduced by Richards, which places equal emphasis on both similarity and dissimilarity. The implication of this approach is that the tenor is regarded in a new way, an important point since the features of the vehicle cannot be directly applied to the tenor and are often only shared metaphorically.

Among the drawbacks of such traditional theories were the fact that (a) literal and figurative meaning were often to be viewed as natural and deviant language, respectively, and that (b) figurative language was consequently viewed from a literal-meaning position. The anomaly theory automatically assumes a degree of deviance. For a long time, metaphor was measured in terms of truth conditions which are supposed to make up literal senses. The traditional definition of meaning is usually based on factors outside the thought processes of individuals. Mathematical formulae are used to fix references of meaning and these in turn are used to define what is true or false in words or sentence constructions. The fixed-reference approach thus made the understanding of metaphor structures very rigid. The interactionist view did at least recognise that metaphoric mapping is more complex than simply comparing similar attributes. In many ways, this led the way to more comprehensive models which introduced the essential argument that fixed meaning could not be part of metaphor creation. The evolution in this trend was also seen in the field of generative semantics of the 1960s. Reddy (1969) likewise emphasised the gestaltic nature of metaphor and the role of context and imagination.

A new approach was adopted in psychology in the 1970s in which the perception of our environment was focused primarily on the workings of the mind rather than on defining the actual form of entities around us. A number of scholars came up with some interesting views on the importance of unclear boundaries between semantic categories. Labov (1973) demonstrated how certain objects may have a transitional stage between one category and the next. A group of items having this aspect are utensils such as cups, bowls, vases and so on, which may not be easily identifiable as one or the other. If the idea of 'fuzziness' (Johnson-Laird, 1983) in semantic boundaries is accepted, it then solves the problem of previous fixed-meaning theories which tried to account for a number of 'sufficient and necessary' conditions constituting a meaning definition, as in checklist theories of framework semantics (Fillmore, 1975). This definition of meaning claimed that a given concept had to have a fixed number of attributes, for example, a square had to have four necessary conditions: (1) a closed, flat figure; (2) four sides; (3) all sides equal in length; and (4) all interior angles being equal (Smith and Medlin, 1981). However, it is clear that it is difficult, if not impossible, to define all necessary conditions for a large number of objects. The utensils example is a case in point since the same precise conditions cannot be applied to a vase or bowl. The new approach in cognitive studies nevertheless helped to overcome many of the problems involved in the theories of meaning definition.

It should be emphasised again, however, that the notion of cognition was not entirely new. John Locke, in his important work, *An Essay Concerning Human Understanding*, published in 1690, represented an early model of cognition. In many ways, he was one of the precursors of an early form of cognitive science. His model was based on two general categories of sensation and reflection, the first concerning the way in which perception of the environment enters the mind and the second the way in which this perception is subsequently processed. Sensation tends to be a passive process whereas reflection may be either active or passive and may have an influence on sensation.

The outcome is the categorisation of ideas which also fall into two categories: simple or complex. The first refers to concepts which may not be broken down further into other sub-categories such as hot, cold and so on. The second refers to ideas which are produced by various interpretation processes of simple concepts such as comparing or uniting the ideas.

The subject of cognition had therefore been broached several centuries before in a different form. Locke's general principles were made more flexible by other aspects he raised, such as *will*. He was of the opinion that human activity was basically geared towards achieving pleasure or, on the other hand, avoiding pain: 'pain has the same efficacy and use to set us on work that pleasure has, we being ready to employ our faculties to avoid that, as to pursue this' (1690: 161). He also felt that religion had a role to play in this process, although he tended to be ambiguous about the subject, and was not clear about the dividing-line between striving for pleasure or avoiding pain.

In the 1970s, a new breakthrough appeared with regard to meaning classification. Originating in psychology, it came in the form of prototype theory which was to determine the future direction of cognitive analyses of language.

1.4 Prototype metaphor

Rosch's 'Cognitive representations of semantic categories' (1975) was the first major empirical account of human categorisation within the modern framework of cognitive linguistics which offered a different view from some of the traditional hypotheses of fixed meaning. The findings showed that perception can vary from one individual to another and that meaning can also exist in a graded form. Objects often have good or bad examples in each semantic category and internal structure affects individual perception (Rosch, 1975: 225). This discovery led to the foundation of prototype theory which claimed that many concepts have a core meaning that is typical of the category and other attributes which become less typical towards the boundary. One of Rosch's examples is the bird category which, in a given culture, has a typical image of a robin as being a bird, whereas an ostrich would be less typical. The boundary area represents the fuzzy edges of meaning. Fuzzy edges are not only found in word-category membership but also in less clearly-defined expressions such as 'strictly speaking', 'so-called' and so on, termed 'hedges' by Lakoff (1972).

Prototype theory of literal meaning was a useful tool for understanding the flexible nature of metaphor creation. The interpretation of the two entities matched in the metaphor process varies along a scale within and between two entire conceptual domains. An example of interpretation within prototype metaphor was proposed by Tourangeau and Sternberg (1982) in their domains-interaction theory. Their empirical experiments included the collection of data on what people thought were typical examples of different categories matched with the concept of power and aggression on one scale and prestige on the other. Two conceptual domains were analysed: on the one hand, land mammals, which included weasels, gorillas, tigers, lions, horses, antelopes and squirrels and, on the other, world leaders at the time including Amin, Castro, Brezhnev, Carter, Giscard, Callaghan and Miki. These two categories varied considerably according to the variables of power/aggression and prestige.

A typical image of a horse in American culture is perceived as prestigious but not aggressive whereas a weasel is much lower on these two scales. Similarly, the typical image of informants regarding Carter was an aggressive and prestigious one, whereas the former Japanese leader, Miki, tended towards the opposite. The importance of these findings is that the interpretation of concepts in the formation of metaphor is a flexible one in accordance with prototype theory. Interpretation may be graded along a scale. Furthermore, flexibility is enhanced by other factors. The findings represent a snapshot of one group of informants in a given culture at a given point in time.

The notion of a gradation in metaphor interpretation has also emerged in recent studies which do not mention the concept of prototypes. Teucher (2003) carried out a detailed empirical analysis of metaphors referring to cancer. By using informants to elicit opinions on the meaningful relationships between cancer metaphors, he established three-dimensional constructs from the results of interpretation surveys. The dimensions involved internal/external, intangible/tangible and static/dynamic axes with metaphor clusters being represented along these axes by means

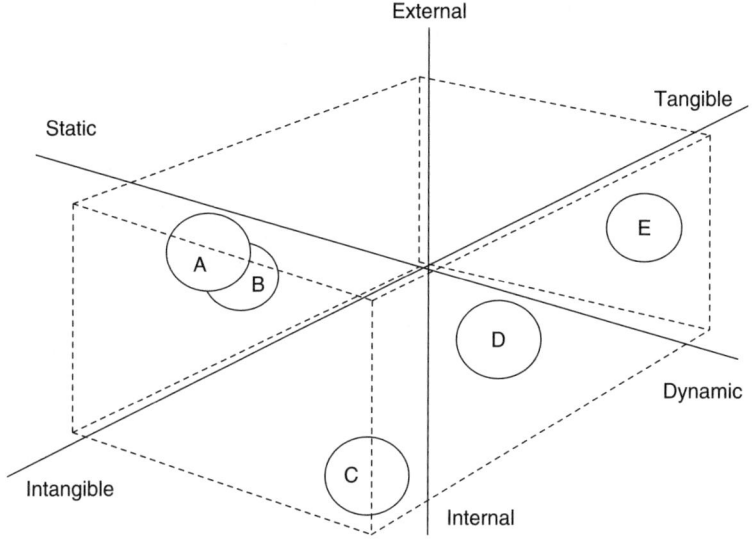

A: Oppressive surroundings
B: Obstacles
C: Growth inside
D: Intrusion
E: Invasion

Figure 1.3 Three-dimensional model of metaphor interpretation of cancer
Source: Adapted from Teucher (2003).

of spheres. One such model included clusters of invasion, intrusion, oppressive surroundings, obstacles and growth inside (Figure 1.3).

The overall pattern is a CANCER = WAR projection. Many metaphors represent cancer as being a constant battle in life. Metaphor clusters A and B, represented as oppressive surroundings (images such as a dark scary cave, overhanging cloud and so on) and obstacles (a stone wall that blocks my road) are more static, intangible and external concepts. Cluster C, representing the image of growth inside (for example, a parasite; being eaten from the inside out) is logically more internal as well as having the impression of being intangible and tending towards being dynamic. Cluster D, intrusion, (cancer as a 'thief that steals one's time'), is naturally internal but more tangible than C and without a specific tendency towards either dynamic or static. Finally, cluster E, invasion (as in opponent, battle and so on), is clearly tangible, dynamic and tending towards the external. In all cases, it can be seen that there is a degree of flexibility and a notion of gradation in the interpretation of these types of metaphors.

The problems of prototype theory have been much debated (Geeraerts, 1989). It does, however, offer a starting-point in understanding how basic metaphor structures are extended to new metaphor creation. The idea of typicality and category membership contributes towards regularity in conceptual extension. As we have seen, the whole nature of human conceptualisation appears to be based on analogy. Perception of one entity recalls another entity. In order for this to happen, conceptual links have to be set up. In the case of many metaphors, links evolve from a central, or typical image. Lakoff (1987: 79 ff.) developed the notion of radial categories in his discussion of the *mother* concept. First, the interpretation of a typical mother varies according to whether she is a *housewife mother* or a *working mother*. The first category traditionally represents the stereotypical type of mother with the second type forming a subcategory of the first, although this may be changing with time as there are more and more mothers who go out to work. A number of other models converge on the central concept of the *housewife mother* such as the *adoptive mother* who did not give birth but is the legal guardian of the child, the *foster mother* who did not give birth either but is being paid by the state to provide nurturance and, as laws change, the *surrogate mother* who has contracted to give birth and no more. There are other types of mother in non-figurative meaning which are also less typical than the *housewife mother* and that may also be created according to new social situations. The main process involved is one of conceptual links which represent a process of networking around a core concept, visually represented by radial categories. The same happens in figurative concepts, each new item being linked to the base. This may involve the same base lexical item as in the *mother* example to form a lexical chaining network, or it may simply involve a concept linked to the core without the original term. The *mother* model may be visually represented as in Figure 1.4.

The figurative component implies a MOTHER = BIRTH mapping in which the concept is linked to the time the person was born. *Mother tongue* represents the language you are born with or *mother country* the place you were born. In the history of European civilisation, the core person has often been represented by either parent so that *father* has also been used in the past with the same connotation. In Latin, both concepts were used: *Terra Mater* (mother earth) and *patria* (literally: land of our father), hence the use of *patriotic* and so on. This has led to the second

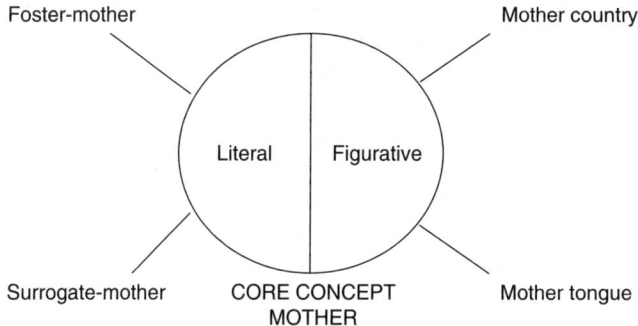

Figure 1.4 Conceptual linking in the *mother* concept

option of using the symbol of *father* in some European languages, such as *Vaterland* (father country) in German. Both terms, *father* and *mother*, are conceptually linked in the base concept and have produced similar networked items.

There are very many concepts which follow radial patterns and a large proportion of metaphors are created through conceptual networking. If this approach is accepted, it follows that a large part of metaphor creation is determined by conceptual links which are not haphazard. A base concept will produce metaphors in a clearly-defined conceptual direction. On the time scale, the etymology of the *mother* model in English shows that linked concepts were added at different times along the same conceptual path: *mother tongue* (fourteenth century) and *mother country* (sixteenth century) (*ODEE – Oxford Dictionary of English Etymology*).

Most figurative concepts are in some way conceptually linked to others. They appear at different levels: one-word or multiple-word metaphors or metonyms, a short idiomatic phrase or proverbial expression, long passages of personification or extensive areas of experience involving the conceptualisation of a single mapping base. In the case of the first category, exemplified by the mother network, this model of conceptualisation has been referred to by different terms in cognitive linguistics. Lakoff would refer to this network as an idealised cognitive model, or ICM, which we will discuss in more detail below. It represents a structure whereby we organise our knowledge of the environment and where prototype effects are by-products of that organisation (1987: 68). Hence, the mother network in literal meaning concepts is a structure which has more or less typical category members as in *foster mother* or *surrogate mother*. Other scholars such as Langacker have preferred terms such as 'cognitive domain' for structural models of experience (1988: 385–6) and suggest that linguists beforehand had envisaged similar constructs under terms such as the *frame semantics* theories (Fillmore, 1982) or the term *script* (Schank and Abelson, 1977).

The networking process can also be clearly seen when extensions occur in either the single-word figurative items or longer idiomatic expressions. Not only do a number of images occur in a base unit such as 'let the cat out of the bag', the images may be extended in subsequent discourse. Naciscione (2004: 2–13) refers to this process as instantial stylistic use of phraseological units. Many cognitive skills are used in this process such as metaphor, pun, zeugma, allusion and so on, and can take on a number of structural extensions. Some of the main patterns described by Naciscione include: (a) one or several sub-images going back to the same base component; (b) strings of sub-images; (c) extension of several notional base components; (d) replacement of a metaphorical component; (e) concurrent use of metaphor; and (f) phraseological saturation which results in the blending of metaphors.

Two of her examples illustrate how the networking process is extended in discourse (Naciscione, 2004: 4–5). The linking of one or more sub-images to the same base component can be seen in the phraseological unit (PU) *blind alley*:

> It proves only that the religions that men have accepted are but *blind alleys* out into an impenetrable jungle and none of them leads to the heart of the great mystery.
>
> (W.S. Maugham, *The Summing Up*)

This would represent the simplest type of extended metaphor, remaining the focus of the whole extension and linking sub-images such as *an impenetrable jungle* and *the heart of the great mystery*. It may be illustrated as in Figure 1.5.

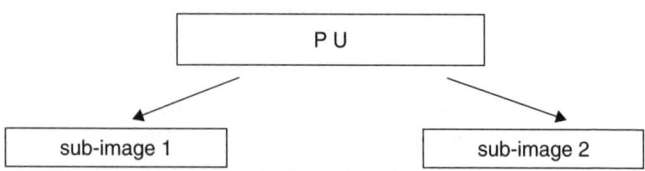

Figure 1.5 Sub-images linked to a base PU component
Source: After Naciscione (2004).

Another kind of extended phraseological metaphor involves a linear development of sub-images without change in the base structure of the PU. A chain reaction sets in whereby each sub-image initiates a subsequent one. The following example of the idiomatic expression *a new broom sweeps clean* demonstrates the linear structure:

> Wonderful what a lot of virtues she managed to have in a hurry. Though she wasn't at all *a new broom*, she swept the dust from pillar to post, and left everybody spitting, till some poor devil got the dustpan and collected the dirt.
>
> (D.H. Lawrence, *Mr Noon*)

Linear sub-images such as *swept the dust, dust-pan* and *collected the dirt* are set off in a chain reaction, as illustrated in Figure 1.6.

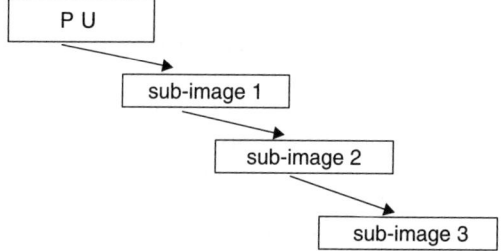

Figure 1.6 Linear sub-images linked to a phraseological unit
Source: After Naciscione (2004).

It can therefore be seen that phraseological units in all forms of idiomatic expressions may be extended in spontaneous discourse, forming creative extended metaphor networks. The extension of networks, however, attain their greatest size in what Lakoff defines as a metaphor scenario. Although such structures vary enormously in their extent, they can cover vast areas of human experience. Since the hypothesis here is that a large majority of metaphors are created by networks, we shall look in more detail into this 'hyper-construct' which, we shall argue, can be linked together in groups in the same way as vast entities such as galaxies are linked in rotating groups in space.

1.5 Metaphor scenarios

Scenarios have been described in great depth with considerable varieties of examples. We first need to look into theoretical constructs of cognition to find out how linguists came to the idea of scenarios as a mental model. Much of this work is illustrated in the approach by Lakoff (1987) and embodied in the term 'idealised cognitive model' (ICM) mentioned above.

Lakoff bases ICMs on mental models which accommodate problems of categorisation with regard to semantic attributes and real-life knowledge. As a result of different prototype effects, the human mind sets up all kinds of ICMs which fit real-life conditions to a greater or lesser degree. Some cognitive models correspond very well to our knowledge of the world, others not so well. As Lakoff claims, the outcome of how appropriate the ICM may be, when applied to the real world, results in a gradience structure, that is, incorporating a basic prototype effect. For example, the term 'bachelor' applies to all males who meet the normal conditions of bachelorhood. This ICM refers to a particular type of society but not to the existence of priests, homosexuality, Moslems who are permitted four wives and only have three, long-term unmarried relationships and so on.

This particular problem has led to criticism of how ICMs can actually deal with prototype effects. One of these points of criticism is that we are not sure of idealised conceptual knowledge in certain types of concepts such as focal colours. Another problem area is that many ICMs are probably too large to deal with as one cognitive unit. For example, idealised knowledge of bachelors does not automatically link the typical notion of a bachelor to the pope, not because of the attributes of bachelorhood (adult, male, never having been married), but due to the special circumstances of the papacy (Langacker, 1988: 386).

Despite the problem areas, Lakoff has defined four main types of ICMs, ignoring, for the sake of convenience, a fifth category of symbolic ICMs which links conceptual to linguistic structures. These four categories are (1) propositional, (2) image-schematic, (3) metaphoric and (4) metonymic. Johnson and Henley (1988) suggest that these four groups may be reduced to two main types since two of the models create the other two. In their view, propositional and image-schematic models represent the basic ICM groups. Metaphoric and metonymic models are either mappings from these two basic types from one domain onto another, respectively, or models in which one part of the model stands for the whole. We shall first look at image-schematic ICMs and then the propositional model which embodies scenarios responsible for large-scale networking.

Lakoff's idea of image-schemas appears to cover primarily orientation. He does, however, refer to another category in the form of basic-level structures which includes concepts such as natural kinds and neurophysiologically determined entities such as colours. With regard to orientation, there is conceptualisation of a direct kind on the one hand, and a less direct kind on the other. The direct kind includes spatial orientation in what he terms 'The Spatialization of Form Hypothesis'. This gives a comprehensive overview of orientational image schemas (1987: 283):

- Categories (in general) are understood in terms of CONTAINER schemas
- Hierarchical structure is understood in terms of PART-WHOLE and UP-DOWN schemas
- Relational structure is understood in terms of LINK schemas
- Radial structure in categories is understood in terms of CENTRE-PERIPHERY schemas
- Foreground-background structure is understood in terms of FRONT-BACK schemas
- Linear quantity scales are understood in terms of UP-DOWN and LINEAR ORDER schemas

The principle is that physical space is mapped onto 'conceptual' space, whereby spatial structure is mapped onto conceptual structure. Mental interaction with the environment is therefore dependent on physical interaction and corresponds to Johnson's proposition of 'putting the body back into the mind' (1987: xxxvi). Image-schematic structures derived from our bodily experience are developed by means of our powers of imagination.

To illustrate how metaphor derives from these constructs, we can take examples from Lakoff and Johnson's (1980) orientational metaphors such as 'happy is up' or 'sad is down':

My spirits *rose*
You're in *high* spirits
I *fell* into a depression
My spirits *sank*

Examples of CONTAINER schemas would be:

He's *out of* the race now
How did you *get into* window-washing?

Not all of these metaphors may be universally considered metaphoric. Their origins as conceptual metaphors, however, are definitely metaphoric. They form a part of everyday expressions and show how basically metaphoric our language can be. In the same way, Reddy's (1979) examples of the *conduit metaphor* discussed above are also based on a spatial paradigm of passing entities from one person to another. The more indirect form of orientation covers models such as SOURCE-PATH-GOAL, BALANCE, COMPULSION, LINKS and SCALARITY. The first covers the time dimension, the others form metaphors based on our everyday perception of space, shapes, forces and so on.

Image schemas are very often incorporated into propositional ICMs and for this reason the distinction between the two is not always very clear in Lakoff's definitions. However, as far as scenarios are concerned, one of his clearest definitions is the following: 'the overall structure of the proposition is thus characterized by a *part-whole* schema, where the proposition = the whole, the predicate = a part, and the arguments = the other parts . . . A scenario consists fundamentally of the following ontology: an initial state, a sequence of events, and a final state. In other words, the scenario is structured by a SOURCE-PATH-GOAL schema in the time domain' (1987: 285).

Perhaps a more precise explanation is given by Johnson (1987: 3–6) who classifies propositions as follows:

(a) statements
(b) representations using finitary predicate symbols and a number of argument symbols
(c) a state of affairs
(d) (i) a function from possible worlds to truth values
    (ii) a function from possible situations to facts
(e) finitary representations using elements and relational elements among those elements
(f) a continuous, analog pattern of experience or understanding, with sufficient internal structure to permit inferences

He argues that (a) to (e) are finitary and therefore purely propositional; (f) does allow image schemas to operate, for example, in the case of the compulsion schema, whose internal structure may enter into transformations and other cognitive operations. Compulsion, in Johnson's view, is the cognitive perception of compulsion analogous to its role in physical forces. A person may feel under pressure from peers to join a particular association in the same way as continental plates move according to tectonic pressure.

We have seen that metaphors can develop as single lexical items as in the radial chaining of MOTHER and they can develop into longer structures such as the phraseological units of idiomatic expressions. Furthermore, large or very extensive mental models in the form of propositional ICMs, to use Lakoff's term, can lead to extensive chaining of metaphors in the time dimension. In the next chapter, however, it will be suggested that metaphor scenarios do not necessarily represent purpose, as in the SOURCE-PATH-GOAL schema, but also consequences of a series of events. In addition, due to the different chain reactions which occur in society, scenarios can often be seen as forming stages themselves. In other words, there may be sequences of interlinking scenarios covering a specific aspect of society. This will be discussed in more detail with regard to universal metaphor trends in the drugs war outlined in the next chapter. We shall first look at standard scenario models which have been developed according to Lakoff's theories.

Areas which were explored in early studies included, in particular, the field of emotions. One aspect of emotions was the different scenarios of love in Western society (Kövecses, 1988: 56–83). These include ideal, typical, non-prototypical or alternative models in modern English. Kövecses explains how metaphoric thought portrays a natural development of emotions. The ideal model based on associated metaphors is one of romantic love. Among the many examples cited, the following metaphors would fit into this scenario:

1. True love comes along, for example, the unity metaphor: *She has found Mr Right*
2. The intensity of the attraction goes beyond the limit point: *She just melted when he looked at her*
3. There is a state of lack of control: *He had her hypnotised*
4. The experience of physiological and behavioural effects which result in happiness: *She had been high on love for weeks*

If we accept that there is a natural development of models, which may in this case follow in rapid succession, we can also claim that there are conceptual links between core concepts, as in the radial pattern of the mother concept, which contribute to an even greater network (Figure 1.7).

This ideal scenario is modified in different ways; a more typical scenario would involve the following stages:

1. True love comes along: (*Mr Right*)
2. An attempt to control emotions: *She tried to fight off her feelings of love*
3. The effort is unsuccessful: *She lost her grip on her feeling of love*
4. A lack of control: *Her love got out of hand*

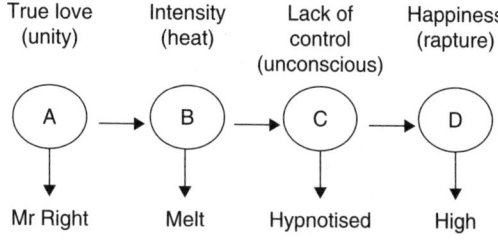

Figure 1.7 Networking in the love metaphor scenario
Source: After Kövecses (1988).

5. Marriage: *Love is a flower which turns into fruit at marriage*
6. Love's intensity decreases and turns into affection: *There was a warm glow inside*

The main differences between the two are therefore the addition of phases 5 and 6 of the typical scenario which varies with our common notion of romantic love. However, a large number of variants may be added to the typical scenario in the form of non-prototypical or alternative cases. Some of these include:

Love is war:	She *fought* for him, but his mistress *won out*
Love as hunting:	She *snared* him
Love as fishing:	She *hooked* a rich husband
Love as a game:	She *plays hard to get*
Love as a structured object:	This is a *working* relationship

All of these models probably represent long-term conceptualisations of love in English-language culture with the exception of the last. The idea of love as a working relationship may be relatively new, reflecting present-day concepts of partnerships consciously working together to make it last. However, a large number of apparent innovations regarding the love scenario may be found in Lakoff and Johnson's lists (1980: 140) of non-conventional or creative metaphors such as:

Love requires a shared aesthetic
Love needs funding

Love cannot be achieved by formula
Love is an expression of who you are
Love reflects how you see the world

This makes up quite complex networks in the field of emotions and adds to the wide variety of core concepts which may form part of a given scenario. The result is that not only are there single-base concepts such as the mother model which may create a large variety of networks, they may also be linked together in a long scenario which in turn produces a vast complex of linked images. Among the metaphors which are not produced, a huge number of *potential* creations also exist. A core concept could potentially produce metaphors which do not in fact come into existence.

So far we have seen that the role of cognition has opened up new opportunities in finding regular patterns of metaphor creation. Prototype theory has changed our views on the structure of meaning and the way in which the interpretation of concepts in our environment depends more on the way we perceive those objects than on fixed definitions involving a number of attributes. This is an important aspect regarding the way in which figurative language is produced. Metaphor, as a central part of figurative language, develops chaining systems from core concepts. These may be relatively compact, as in the example of radial chaining from the base *mother* concept, or far more extensive, as in the phraseological units of idiomatic expressions. Even more extensive are the features of metaphor scenarios involving different areas of human behaviour and activity. This leads us on to the assumption that a large part of metaphor creation must be subject to conceptual networking processes.

We have been looking primarily at various examples from English, and we have seen that a core concept has the potential to produce metaphors which do not actually come into existence. We may wonder whether a potential metaphor, that is not present in English, may nevertheless arise in another language. In fact, do similar kinds of networking patterns develop across other languages and cultures? If we accept the general role of cognition in metaphor creation, we may work on the assumption that this is the case. But are the same kinds of images also being networked? The next chapter suggests that, in many cases, this is actually happening. We shall now look at what kinds of images tend to have a cross-language structure.

2
Universal Trends

2.1 Conceptual metaphor and linguistic form

In this chapter, we shall first be looking at what kinds of conceptual capacities create metaphors with universal trends. We shall then examine how similar metaphors have developed in a group of West European languages. This study concerns the field of drugs, an area rich in figurative language. Although there is undoubtedly a certain amount of borrowing, there appear to be similar conceptual systems which produce the same kinds of networking patterns and images. Hence, a number of parallel internal processes seem to be at work. Before looking at this study, several issues of metaphor analysis need to be clarified in order to avoid areas of confusion in the discussion of cross-language patterns. The first involves the metaphors themselves and the structures behind figurative innovations.

In any discussion of metaphor evolution, a fundamental distinction which has to be made is the line between the underlying processes which contribute towards the creation of a metaphor and the actual word produced in the language. A common definition used by cognitive linguists is the term *conceptual metaphor* for the former domain and *linguistic forms* for the words which appear in different languages (compare Charteris-Black and Ennis, 2001: 251 ff.). Taking one of the examples of love in the preceding chapter, it could be said that the word *melt*, as in *she just melted when he looked at her*, would represent a (surface) linguistic form, while a conceptual metaphor HEAT = PASSION would be the underlying process which created the word itself.

This distinction is an important one when trying to determine whether the same processes of metaphor creation are occurring in all languages. We can put forward the theory that there are probably three main combinations of these two basic forms: (i) two languages share the same linguistic form; (ii) two languages share the same conceptual metaphor but not the same linguistic form; and (iii) two languages share neither, that is, one conceptual metaphor may exist in one language with no equivalent in another or they have two different conceptual metaphors to convey the same figurative meaning.

There are a number of variations in this simplified pattern. In their analysis of English and Polish metaphors, Deignan et al. (1997) add a further category whereby words and expressions with similar literal meanings but different metaphorical meanings may exist in two languages. In addition, there are variations in the linguistic form. One language may not have the same morphosyntactic features in a metaphor which can produce, for example, problems in finding the right equivalent in the translation of metaphor. Variation in morphosyntactic features may produce different semantic attributes.

A further dimension may be added in the discussion of universal trends which involves the distinction between language and culture. These two notions may mean the same, but not necessarily so. There is, of course, a considerable cultural difference between two languages such as English and Swahili. If we consider two languages such as English and French, a preliminary analysis of cross-language networks involves practically the same culture. A closer metaphoric analysis of these two languages, however, can actually reveal a considerable number of cultural differences so that, except in the case of bilingual communities in the same country, a two language/one culture combination is probably rare or non-existent.

It is likely that there is a relationship between cultural distance and the types of underlying conceptual metaphors. The greater the distance between cultures, the more likely there are differences in conceptual metaphors between two languages. This, in turn, will produce a greater variety in the linguistic form. The starting point for exploring universal trends must therefore be in the underlying structures of conceptual metaphor. We are at once confronted with a major dilemma in this respect given the number of cultures and languages around the world. Considerable progress has been made in the English language and in the Indo-European field in general, but data on other languages tend to be much more scanty. New research findings are, however, being published on a wide variety of the world's language families (for example, Haser, 2000) which should greatly improve our knowledge on metaphor universals.

A number of hypotheses have been put forward regarding universality in conceptual metaphor. Much of this work has been produced by

Lakoff (1987), Johnson (1992), Sweetser (1990), Traugott (1989) and Traugott and Dasher (2002). Lakoff and Johnson's work concerns synchronic universals, Sweetser and Traugott's findings are more related to diachronic patterns. We shall first examine synchronic trends and relate them to networks in metaphor scenarios.

2.2 The body and universal metaphor

Lakoff's first category of being a likely candidate for universals is what he terms the basic-level concept. In line with the prototypical analysis of categories (Rosch, 1975), the basic level tends to be an intermediate one which is easier to discern than superordinate and subordinate items in a category. Major category types are more conspicuous than more finely graded items. Basic-level concepts comprise objects, actions and properties:

> we have basic-level concepts not only for objects but for actions and properties as well. Actions like *running, walking, eating, drinking*, etc. are basic-level, whereas *moving* and *ingesting* are superordinate, while kinds of walking and drinking, say, *ambling* and *slurping*, are subordinate. Similarly, *tall, short, hard, soft, heavy, light, hot, cold*, etc. are basic-level properties, as are the basic neurophysiologically determined colors: black, white, red, green, blue and yellow.
>
> (Lakoff, 1987: 271)

The other two major categories of universals that Lakoff and Johnson (1980) propose are in many ways linked: those constructs they term simply metaphorical concepts and the image schemas outlined in the previous chapter (Lakoff, 1987; Johnson, 1992). These two categories, together with basic-level concepts, form a general division of metaphors known as potential universal physiological features. They are related to processes involved in our bodily experience of the environment.

The body as a focal point in Lakoffian theories is also extended to parts of the body being used for metaphor creation. Many examples from languages around the world highlight this fact. As Heine (1997: 143) points out: 'the ability to use the human body as a structural template to understand and describe other objects can be assumed to be universal; hence, we may expect this to be reflected in all languages'.

It seems to be a basic instinct in the creation of new languages such as in pidgins and creoles. Body parts are extended to metaphoric concepts of the natural environment (Aitchison, 1996: 124). The English pidgin

Tok Pisin, for example, has extended different body parts to natural phenomena. The head (*het*) is used for the top of an object:

| *het bilong diwai* | 'top of a tree' |
| *het bilong maunten* | 'top of a mountain' |

The hand (*han*) is used for extensions of an object:

| *han bilong diwai* | 'branch of a tree' |
| *han wara* | 'tributary of a river' (hand-water) |

Indeed, Heine (1997: 141) claims that the head is a body part which lends itself naturally to the areas of spatial orientation or intellectual ability. He feels that some parts of the body are more likely to be used for specific domains and other parts are less likely, or even unlikely, to be used in this way. A comparison between the head and the liver makes this point clear.

Lakoff and Johnson's term 'metaphorical concepts' embodies the type of relationship between our physiological sensory perception and the environment. Orientation, for example, plays an important role in the structure of metaphors; 'HAPPY' means to be 'UP', 'SAD' means to be 'DOWN'; having force means to be 'UP', being subject to force means to be 'DOWN'. Particular notions are attached to specific orientational images, and orientations such as these, whether they are spatial or non-spatial, are probably used by all cultures. Exactly how they are used depends on the values of the culture or sub-culture. English appears to use a great deal of up-down orientation but other cultures seem to use the notions of balance or centrality more in their formation of metaphoric language. Likewise, the non-spatial, active-passive dimension may be valued more. Different dimensions are likely to be used by all cultures but the importance of their role varies from one culture to another (Lakoff and Johnson, 1980: 24).

Lakoff (1987: 380 ff.) discusses in detail a metaphor scenario which is linked to presumed universal physiological features: the human emotion of anger. He proposes that the anger ontology consists of two types of constitutive metaphor: on the one hand, basic-level metaphors such as hot fluid, fire and so on, which are more directly linked to experience and are rich in mental imagery and, on the other, superordinate concepts such as intensity, force, control and so on, which are more abstract. The first category helps us understand what anger is, the second how to control it. In a reference to studies carried out by Ekman et al. (1983),

Lakoff maintains that our concept of anger, in the form of these two groups of constitutive metaphors, is thus directly related to our physiology. Factors such as pulse rate and skin temperature correlate with particular emotions. As anger becomes more intense, pulse rate and skin temperature increase. A central metaphor referring to increasing anger involves the HEAT OF FLUID IN A CONTAINER image as the source domain (Lakoff, 1987: 384–5):

1. The intensity of anger increases, the fluid rises: *his pent-up anger welled up inside him*
2. Intense anger produces steam: *she got all steamed up*
3. Intense anger produces pressure on the container: *he was bursting with anger*
4. A variant involves keeping the pressure back: *he managed to keep his anger bottled up inside him*
5. The container explodes: *she blew up at me*
6. When a person explodes, parts go up in the air: *she flipped her lid*

This example represents one part of the overall scenario. As in the love metaphor, the complete anger ontology can have variants. A prototypical scenario would be: (a) there is an offending event; (b) anger; (c) attempt at control; (d) loss of control; (e) act of retribution. Non-prototypical cases would, according to the situation, involve different types of anger, for example, insatiable anger – it does not disappear; frustrated anger – revenge is not possible; redirected anger – frustration is taken out on another person; cool anger – the victim remains in control, and so on.

Cross-language studies of anger reveal that similar models appear in very different cultures. The HEAT OF FLUID IN A CONTAINER concept can be seen in Japanese (Matsuki, 1995: 140 ff.):

atama kara yuge ga tatsu	'Steam rises up from the head'
haha wa toutou bakuhatsu shita	'My mother finally exploded'
harawata ga niekurikaeru	'The intestines are boiling'.

Chinese has a similar image except that the container symbol has a slight variant with hot gas rather than a fluid to illustrate anger (Yu, 1995: 67 ff.):

bie ba feigei qi zhale	'Don't burst your lungs with gas'
bie qi pole dupi	'Don't break your belly skin with gas'

According to Draaisma (2000: 9), this type of physiological image applies to other types of emotions, such as the libido, also described by Lakoff.

Freudian metaphors derive from liquid exercising pressure which can overflow or drain away into a reservoir. The *id* is compared to a pot full of seething excitement and represents a precarious balance between pressure and counter-pressure.

The heat metaphor in this case is also supported by empirical studies of cross-language emotions involving the libido. Emanatian (1995: 163–82) suggests that English and the culturally very different language of Chagga, a Bantu language of Tanzania, have parallels in their conceptualisation of sexual desire. Heat (and consequently fire metaphors) can be seen in expressions such as:

kyambuya riko lilya	'Look at that oven' = Look at that sexy woman
ngi woni mtsu	'I see smoke' = I can tell she's sexually exciting
nekeokya	'She roasts' = She is sexually desirable

This domain also reveals other physiological models which may have a universal trends. Emanatian suggests that the activity of eating, as in English, is often equated with sexual desire:

ngi'ichuo njaa ia mndu mka	'I feel hunger for a woman' = I'm desirous of a woman
ngi'kémméria mara	'I swallow saliva for her' = I really desire her

This corresponds to such expressions in English as 'I hunger for her touch'. Studies on cross-cultural models therefore suggest that physiological metaphors are likely to have universal trends.

We shall now have a look at a study of similar, cross-language trends in a very extensive networking scenario in the drugs field. In this way we shall be able to see how some of the processes outlined above fit in with parallel patterns across languages.

2.3 The drugs metaphors network

One metaphor scenario which shows that the same networking processes are taking place across different languages is the contemporary conceptualisation of drugs in Western society (Trim, 1997). The following discussion will propose a slightly modified version of the scenario outlined in both the 1997 version of this data as well as the traditional Lakoffian literature of scenarios. Chained events of metaphor creation leading to particular scenarios can also be based on the fact that the events do not necessarily follow a specific goal but are related to each other by chain reactions. One phase causes another rather than the initial phase having a goal. Emotions are concerned with the mental and physiological states of the individual. There are other types of metaphor scenarios which develop, such as social events that can lead from one phase to another. These are not based purely on physiological features and the overall event therefore tends to be a cultural phenomenon. However, if one type of society, say Western society, develops in an area in which a large number of languages are spoken, the cross-language conceptual metaphors used tend to be relatively uniform. The differences are found more at the level of linguistic metaphors. Such is the case of the drugs war scenario.

This semantic field is extremely fertile in metaphor creation and provides an excellent basis for studying potential universals and language-specific items. Although the same types of European society are involved, and there could very well be greater discrepancies if very different cultures were compared, it does show that European languages follow similar patterns. A brief outline of the background to this scenario will first be given.

For different reasons, drug-taking became a popular social habit which, nevertheless, led to certain risks in the physical effects obtained. Because of the exciting but dangerous effects which were experienced, various social attitudes developed according to whether the person involved was situated inside or outside the drugs scene. The consequences of these developments led to a 'war' against drugs.

A campaign against the proliferation of drugs originating particularly in the South American continent and, to a lesser extent, South-East Asia, was set up by the first Bush (senior) administration of the 1980s. Attempts at controlling the use of drugs go back much further in time but it was at this particular period that a large number of new metaphors were produced in English. The fight against drugs also involved Europe and many of these items were loaned or calqued into European languages in general, either in the form of conceptual or lexical metaphors. English is often a major source but there is a certain amount of calquing from Spanish.

Consequently, a degree of uniformity has been established, particularly at the conceptual metaphor level; but since the same types of cognitive processes are operating across all European languages in this field, the same also applies to a large number of lexical items. In this survey, data were collected in a comparative study of English, French, German and Italian from the European and North American press. Press reports were analysed in relation to a ten-year period covering the 1980s and involving some of the major newspapers and magazines of the countries

Figure 2.1 Major phases in the drugs war scenario

concerned such as *Le Monde, Le Figaro, L'Express* (France), *Der Spiegel, Die Welt* (Germany), *La Repubblica, L'Espresso* (Italy) and *Time* and *International Herald Tribune* (United States).

In line with this chronological order of events, a linked mapping procedure has developed a three-stage scenario, illustrated in Figure 2.1. Since the whole scenario is particularly extensive, even though related, we could almost speak of *interlinked scenarios*. The first one is based on physiology, the second and third on social forces.

Physical effects phase

The distribution of drugs to the consumer has varying physical effects which also lead to a variety of names for drugs according to the types of sensations experienced. These effects can give a very pleasant sensation but they very often finish with extremely unpleasant effects.

Social attitudes phase

The dangers involved in these physical effects have led to various attitudes being adopted by conventional society and the consequent prohibition of drug consumption.

Drugs war phase

This involves the linked ontologies:

- The production of drugs: illegality creates an enormous potential for money to be made so that drugs are mass produced
- Transportation: different ways are found to transport and smuggle drugs
- Distribution: the North American and European black markets are the major geographical areas involved
- Wealth: the returns on drugs via money laundering leads to immense wealth
- Power: wealth makes drugs bosses extremely powerful
- War: their power is used in the war against Western governments

The use of war metaphors in politics does not appear to be new. As Gibbs puts it: 'Another central metaphor in political discourse is POLITICS IS WAR.

When politicians must be portrayed as ruthless or treacherous, speakers usually resort to military metaphors' (1994: 143). The war metaphor was used by the Bush (senior) administration to help convince the public that the government was taking a tough stance against the drugs trade.

A vast network of metaphors has been created and linked to this basic scenario. Each stage has produced a variety of mapping procedures using different concepts in our environment. If we examine the first two stages of physical effects and social attitudes, theories of universals proposed by Lakoff and Johnson, such as orientation, do display similar features in different European languages.

UP-DOWN spatial orientation

The HAPPY = UP and SAD = DOWN pattern, for example, can be seen in equivalent positive and negative features. Kövecses (2000: 44) suggests that this is the most general dimension along which the emotions are classified. The basic notion produces a number of semantically linked metaphors. The UP = POSITIVE and DOWN = NEGATIVE feature of spatial orientation can be seen in the following:

> UP = POSITIVE
> The severe depression that follows a cocaine-induced *high*
> The euphoric *lift*, the feeling of being confident and *on top of things*
> Coke *picks you up*

Linked to the UP dimension is a rocket image:

> Sniffing cocaine produces a quick, short *boost*.
> *Ignition* can occur in various ways. 'Snorting', or sniffing the white powder, ensures absorption of the drug into the bloodstream through the mucous membranes.

2.4 The cross-language dimension

These models occur regularly in other European languages and reveal a considerable degree of cross-language uniformity. If we take a look at German, for example, the rocket image appears with a reference to a sniff of cocaine between business meetings. The original language will be inserted in each case to give a more precise comparative analysis of the cross-language dimension:

> *Als 'Zwischendurch-rakete' im Büro oder vor einer wichtigen Geschäftsbesprechung*

(As an 'in-between-rocket' in the office or before an important business meeting)

In contrast, networking takes place in the following metaphoric concepts of the DOWN dimension:

Cocaine abusers are using heroin to ease the postcrack *low*.
In a fit of rage accompanying a *'down'* period, he snapped off two teeth.
The *'crash'* from coke, the *letdown* when the drug wears off, is grim.

If we examine another European language such as Italian, the notion of 'to fall' (*cadere*) has a related negative sense of becoming addicted (falling into the world of addiction):

Anche l'attegiamento psicologico del giovane è tranquillo si è bucato ma, nella maggioranza dei casi, è convinto di non 'caderci'
(The psychological state of the youth is also calm when he injects a drug but, in most cases, he is convinced he will not *fall* (become addicted))

The networking cluster of the UP-DOWN model can be illustrated as in Figure 2.2.

Many basic concepts appear in the form of a binary structure such as UP-DOWN. Three other universal trends involving physiological binary metaphors in the drugs war scenario can be found in attitudes towards drugs in the third phase of social attitudes, once again in spatial orientation: INSIDE-OUTSIDE-PERIPHERY (containers) and the others relating to HOT-COLD and DISEASE-HEALTH. This at least appears to be

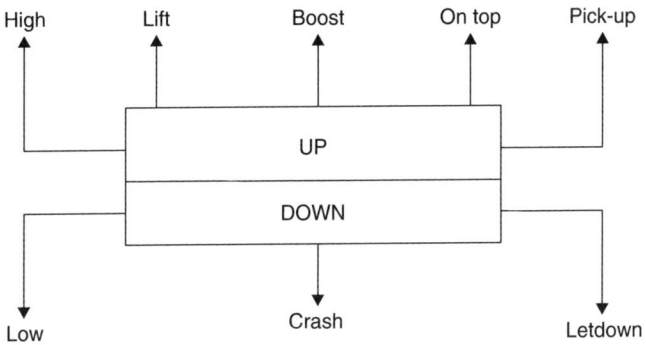

Figure 2.2 Networking in the UP-DOWN model of drug effects

uniform across European languages and probably within Western society as a whole.

CONTAINER images

Taking a closer look at these models, the container image can be seen in the traditional notion of the 'underworld' being outside the conventional society of the 'normal' world. The notion of DOWN = NEGATIVE is also represented in this concept. Likewise, an incomplete container is not the conventional norm, as in 'demi-monde'. Different European languages reveal the same trends:

> Barco appeared on national television to announce a fresh crackdown on the cocaine *underworld*

A similar concept found in a German example:

> *Die 'Halbwelt' unter der Peitsche der Drogen*
> (The 'demi-monde' under the scourge of drugs)

The notion of being outside the container can also be illustrated in the concept of 'exile' from conventional law-abiding society:

> *Die Drogenszene zwischen den Grachten bietet vielen Fixern 'Asyl', die vor der Fahndung der Polizei in den Nachbarstaaten nach Holland geflüchtet sind*
> (The drugs scene between the canals are an *exile* for many fixers who have fled from neighbouring states to Holland as a result of police searches)

Someone on the fringe of a container, represented by society, is usually already on the outside. In French, *un marginal* is someone who is close to being a 'drop out'. The 'Messia' in the following example is a person known to the police in the drugs world:

> *'Le Messie' est un 'marginal' du milieu*
> ('The Messia' is a person on the *fringe of society*, being from the drugs scene)

The notion of inside, however, can also be used to indicate someone's 'home ground' which may be outside conventional norms. This reinforces the idea that similar metaphoric structures are the result of the same conceptualising processes operating from different viewpoints.

The conceptual metaphor can be found in Italian and German but is probably a less widely distributed offshoot of the central core metaphor. In Italian, the notion of an 'integrated person' (*integrato*) is used for someone in the drugs scene:

> *Perchè se il tossicodipendente è sempre più una persona normale che rifiuta le vecchie ideologie di rivolta e 'buca' o 'sniffa' da 'integrato'* . . .
> (Because if the addict becomes more and more normal, rejecting the old ideologies of rebellion or 'fixing' and 'sniffing' as an 'integrated person' . . .)

In German, the idea of 'entry drugs' (*Einstiegsdrogen*) would not have the same concept as English 'conditioning drugs':

> *Ebenso wie bei den 'Einstiegsdrogen' war es die Neugier, die sie auf Heroin umsteigen liess*
> (In the same way as *conditioning drugs*, it was also curiosity which made them turn to heroin)

The differing spatial views of conventional society can be illustrated as in Figure 2.3.

We have already seen in the previous chapter that anger in modern English is frequently based on a model which involves the HEAT OF FLUID IN A CONTAINER. On the basis of an analysis of the conceptualisation of anger in four very different cultures, English, Hungarian,

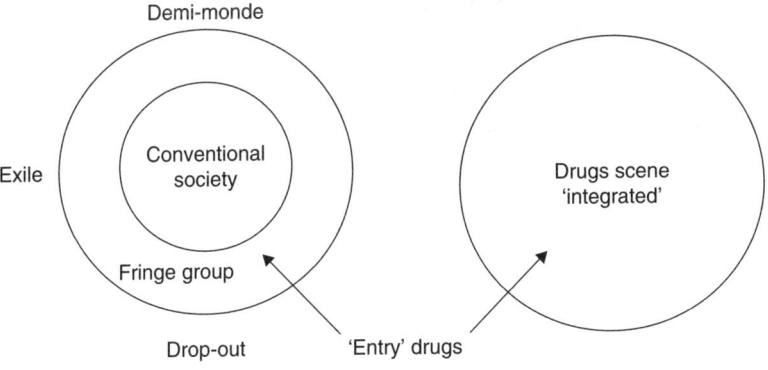

Figure 2.3 The container image viewed from different sections of society

Chinese and Japanese, Kövecses (2000: 146 ff.) suggests that the CONTAINER image is indeed a construct with universal trends:

> English   He was filled with anger
> Hungarian   *Tele van dühvel* (He is full of anger)
> Chinese   *Man qiang fen nu* (To have one's body cavities full of anger)
> Japanese   *Ikari ga karadajyu ni jyuman shita* (My body was filled with anger)

Although, of course, there may not be the same image in all languages in other fields, the metaphorisation of anger as a CONTAINER in this particular concept is a sign that completely different cultures do create similar underlying conceptual metaphors.

The heat image

The physiological binary concept of hot-cold is somewhat similar to Lakoff's notion of heat being associated with an increase in emotion, as in the anger model. The concept of heat in drug effects signifies intense feeling:

> Extreme cocaine dosages light a kind of *fire* in the brain

However, the notion of cold does not necessarily imply lack of intensity, but rather extremely negative feelings:

> I was into heroin, I cooked it up and shot it into a vein. A few minutes later my whole body was going *cold*. It felt like I was going to faint or was getting seasick.

In the case of social attitudes towards drugs, heat is associated with drug-related entities. In the same way as English 'hot spot', which may involve not only drugs but any area of social conflict in the world, similar metaphors have developed in different European languages:

> French: *Les quartiers 'chauds' du trafic de la drogue à Marseille*
> (The *hot* districts of drug-trafficking in Marseilles)

Networked linguistic forms include the concept of Italian *bruciato* (burnt) implying a drug-related district:

> *Mentre la zona di piazza Euclide, nel quartiere Parioli, sembre essere una piazza 'bruciata'*

(While Euclid Square, in the Parioli district, seems to be a *'hot square'* (burnt square))

The health-disease concept

The physiological model of health-disease in social attitudes logically refers to the association or not with drugs. Different disease terminology is networked with reference to drugs as in:

> If the price stays low, coca paste could become *epidemic* here too
> We are committed to getting rid of the *cancer* that would destroy our very existence as a nation
> Latin Americans have come to question the Reagan administration's commitment to fighting the drug *blight*

These terms are found across European languages, including the opposite concept of health which refers to legality or the notion of drugs-free, as can be seen in the following French examples:

> *La Banco de la Republica permet, sans aucun contrôle, de transformer des dollars d'origine douteuse en pesos parfaitement 'sains'*
> (The Banco de la Republica allows, without any control, the changing of suspect dollars into perfectly *healthy* pesos)
>
> *La mère de Julien, 15 ans, a pris des renseignements dans trois lycées parisiens avant d'inscrire son fils dans un établissement réputé 'sain'*
> (The mother of 15-year-old Julien made inquiries among three Parisian schools before putting her son's name down for an institution reputed as being *healthy*)

The models described so far represent physiological metaphors which, even if there is a certain amount of borrowing from English and Spanish, are likely to represent universal trends in underlying conceptual bases with a number of variant offshoots in surface linguistic forms.

The dirty-clean image

The dirty-clean binary concept is also represented in all the European languages investigated with similar meanings. However, it stems from visual perception rather than physiological conceptualisation and is therefore normally open to more variation. In this case, it is highly likely that the model is a less divergent one in visualisation, with more universal characteristics of dirt being negative and clean positive.

Thus in English, dirt refers to an association with drugs or illegality and cleanliness the opposite:

The cocaine trade is *dirty* and dangerous
A torrent of *dirty* dollars
It will be more than drug money we come up with, and what happens when we stumble over a really major company and hold up its *dirty* linen?

These attitudes are also found in French:

Mme Bhutto, parce qu'elle ne voulait pas être impliquée dans cette 'politique sale', venait de refuser l'offre faite par un 'baron' de la drogue
(Since Mrs Bhutto did not want to be implicated in such *dirty politics*, she had refused an offer made by a drug baron)

The opposite occurs frequently in different European languages in common expressions such as 'money-laundering' and related concepts:

In Bolivia and Peru, where the cocaine trail begins, governments have made considerable progress toward *cleansing themselves* of corruption
There would be many more judges and probation officers to make sure that criminals did their time and *stayed clean* afterwards
In a *wash cycle* that often takes less than 28 hours, the drug-smugglers can turn coke-tinged $20 and $100 bills into squeaky-clean assets

Italian: *Mi sono 'ripulita'* (I have cleansed myself = I have given up drugs)
French: *Eduardo Martinez Romero, un 'mini-narco', un spécialiste du 'blanchiment' des dollars de la cocaïne, a été extradé vers les Etats-Unis*
(Eduardo Martinez Romero, a 'mini-narco', a specialist in *laundering* dollars made from cocaine, was extradited to the United States)

The health-disease (unhealthy) and clean-dirty models as POSITIVE-NEGATIVE are reflected in other forms of human emotions and behaviour. They can be seen, for example, in manifestations of desire (Deignan, 1997: 36–9). The following examples are cited from the press and fiction:

HEALTHY DESIRE = POSITIVE
She had her sights firmly set on a career and, despite a healthy interest in boys, concentrated on training as a State Enrolled Nurse

UNHEALTHY DESIRE = NEGATIVE
[This behaviour] is tailor-made to induce teen infatuation, unhealthy sexual fantasies and pandemonium at gigs.

The concept of CLEAN, not usually associated with desire in English, can generally be seen, apart from the political field, as a positive quality:

CLEAN = POSITIVE
Written and produced by John Hughes . . . the film is good clean family fun.

However, DIRT is very often associated with negative desire and can be found in numerous English expressions:

DIRTY DESIRE = NEGATIVE
He was a filthy pervert. God knows how many women he molested.

Given the rich variety of these expressions across European languages in the political field, further study would probably reveal the same patterns in desire and so on having similar universal trends in other areas of human life.

To demonstrate the conceptual links in metaphor creation, the last three binary concepts in the drugs war can thus be illustrated as in Figure 2.4. This is an illustration, in fact, of a synchronic pattern in networking since networks can take on a spatial dimension across Europe at a given point in time.

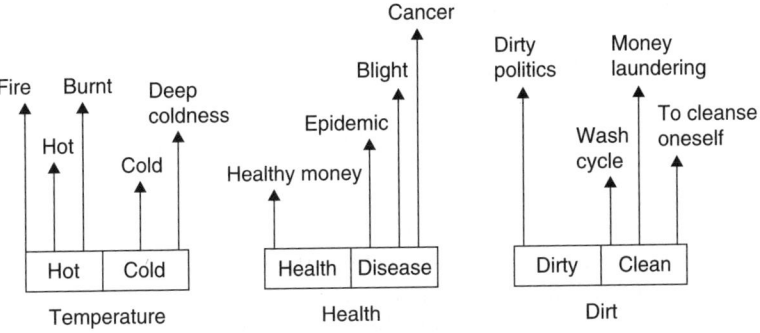

Figure 2.4 Networking in the binary concepts of temperature, health and dirt

The last phase of the network, the actual drugs war, tends to have a more cultural aspect, even though the languages surveyed have very similar metaphors. The languages are situated in the same cultural sphere of Western society and therefore display similar social ordering, visual perception, activities and so on. Included in this phase could be the actual production of drugs since this aspect, together with its transportation, forms part of the drugs war.

Starting with the production stage, some English examples will be listed here without giving large numbers of translations in other languages. Suffice it to say that most of the metaphors are found in some or all of the four languages examined:

PRODUCTION = COOKING
A large range of cooking metaphors are linked to production:
Cocaine powder is *cooked* into rock-hard crack
Any chemistry student can *cook* 'angel's dust' for a dealer's price.
The first delivery of crack for American syringes was *baked* in a kitchen of the former British colony
He produced a hashish *cookery book*
At *kitchen labs* dotted around the country, coca leaves brought in from all over the Andes are distilled into a paste
They *boil the brew* until a whitish lump, or freebase, is left

TRANSPORTATION = PLANES, SHIPS, ANIMALS, INSECTS and so on
The Bahamas, known among drug-runners as our *aircraft carrier*, serve as a transshipment point
Small dealers, in the trade jargon 'mulas' (*mules*), swallow it in plastic bags shortly before take-off
Cocaine is not like heroin which can count on an army of *ants* each carrying two to three kilos

DISTRIBUTION = WATER
All metaphors really signify a large quantity, but the following have been listed approximately according to the quantity of the source concept of flowing water:
This is called the Colombian Connection . . . though the Mafia is starting to move in on this *stream* of gold
The US government has tried to choke the *river* of drug money
The crackdown has made a major dent in the *flow* of grass
The cocaine *wave* . . . is spilling into Western Europe
The man I'm working for now . . . seems to have a *waterfall* of money from banks in Luxembourg and Amsterdam

In drug-trafficking, the new white *tide* . . . is invading the United States
A *torrent* of dirt dollars
The volume . . . is believed to be only a small percentage of the tons *flooding* the US
Indeed, the city's banks have been embarrassingly *awash* in cash, much of it cocaine profits
A forum for chastising Latin leaders about their failure to curb the *tidal wave* of cocaine
The *sea* of drugs

DISTRIBUTION = STORMS
The weather, particularly different types of storms, are used for the large impact of drugs distribution on society representing the major clients:
The crack *hurricane*: the new American plague
We see coke sales in suburbs, in recreational centers and in national parks. It is an unrecognised *tornado*
A new heroin *cyclone* is coming
Largely unchecked by law enforcement, a veritable *blizzard* of the white powder is blowing through the American middle class

WEALTH = GOLD
These usually refer to types of drugs or geographical areas in which they are produced or distributed:
A luxurious marijuana of heady strength known as *Santa Marta Gold*
Panamanian traffickers are trying to relocate and turn Guatemala into a '*golden bridge*' for their goods
Commanders of the Afghan resistance who are opium producers in the *Golden Crescent*
A heroin tycoon in the *Golden Triangle*

POWER = NOBILITY
A range of noble titles have been chosen including the term 'don':
Colombia's six-month-old crackdown against the *drug barons*
Colombia's *kings* of cocaine
Austria is a favourite port of call for Middle East *drug princes*
The *cartel lords* set up . . . the largest cocaine factory in the world
Some of the Colombian *drug dons* have been forced out of their homelands

WAR = MILITARY TERMINOLOGY
Stemming from the drugs 'war' term, apparently coined by President Nixon at the beginning of the 1970s, this area represents a vast

network of metaphors, some of them being represented by the following:

The Colombian Connection . . . owns an *armada* of ships and has recruited an *army* of bush pilots

Vice President George Bush, head of President Reagan's South Florida *Task Force*

Bush's *drug czar* Bennet

His *commander-in-chief* Bennet defined the aims of the war

The *anti-drugs-squadron* stormed the village

The federal anti-drug effort was establishing its first *beachhead* in Miami

One is his reputation as a hard-line antidrug *warrior*

It has become conventional wisdom in the drug war's *high command*

Though he *sounded a call to arms* soon after taking office, the President too has turned his attention elsewhere

He announced the big *crusade* in the war against cocaine

The US wages its frustrating domestic *offensive* against cocaine

It was in fact in this clean city, territory *conquered* by drugs

We have been under *siege* for almost two years by drug dealers

The list of war metaphors is almost endless, covering every aspect of the military from battle strategies to ordinary foot soldiers. All these metaphors have developed in a structured way since they are dependent on social causes and events. The nobility model, for example, would not have been created if drugs had not produced great wealth. There would not have been a war if the drugs trade had not created certain risks for consumers, and so on. All metaphors are conceptually linked in the scenario as a result of the political environment.

The different types of models used in the actual physical effects of drugs also come from varying domains but have a rich variety of networked items in each group, a majority of them covering the areas of voyages, rockets, explosions, spatial location and orientation, falling, immobility, colours, temperature, death and drugs personification. Likewise social attitudes have vast networked clusters, although the fields they draw on tend to be less extensive than in the other two stages of the scenario, the main ones being dirt, heat, disease, prestige and spatial orientation.

The analysis demonstrates the enormous power of metaphoric networking. An almost endless list of additional linked concepts could be given. It proves that similar networking processes are at work in different languages and producing related images. These images may be borrowed across languages, particularly in a field which is highly dominated by the media, but borrowings also fit into the conceptual patterns of each language. The same basic concepts related to theories of universals generate extensive networks and the production of similar metaphors. It can therefore be assumed that networking theory is a universal process.

2.5 The universality of personification

To finish this discussion of networking in the drugs field, a number of other figurative processes lend themselves to universal trends in metaphoric creativity. One such aspect is personification which can be transmitted from one culture to another. It also appears to be a human cognitive process in Western civilisation since time immemorial: 'From the earliest poetry, personification is a basic feature of Greek imagination and language' (Padel, 1992: 157). Sometimes the symbols of personification can be culture-specific although the passages of extended metaphor translate easily into other languages. One personification of death in English is an old man reaping corn. A suggested reason for this symbol is that, in the same way as the reaper is taking away the corn in a field, he also takes our life away. This results in other metaphoric expressions such as 'death cut him down' or 'death took him from us' (Lakoff and Turner, 1989: 78). It is unlikely that this particular symbol is used in all cultures, since not every country grows corn, but similar personification symbols of death are likely to be universal.

A final, lengthier passage on drugs metaphors will therefore be taken from the Italian magazine *L'Espresso* which depicts the personified power of cocaine and death in a very poetic way and shows how a large number of metaphors may be networked in discourse, similar to the types of extended phraseological metaphors we have seen. In many European press reports, cocaine, as a symbol of death, is not viewed as a male figure but rather as being female. She is represented as the queen of all drugs. The Italian version is as follows:

> *Una mossa dopo l'altra e la cocaine si è cucita adosso il suo falso vestito . . . Nella seconda metà del secolo scorso il trono della regina era già edificata. Ma la Regina, come tutte le regine, non si lasciava avvicinare facilmente; costava carissima e quindi a godere dei suoi favori erano in pochi: i ricchi, i nobili, gli intellettuali . . . Che male c'era se i potenti e quelli baciati dal genio invitavano la Regina nei loro salotti dorati e chiusi? . . . Forse si è mai visto un ricco vagolare per la città come un spettro commettendo piccoli e grandi reati per procurarsi i tesori da deporre ai piedi della Signora?*

An approximate translation would be:

> One movement after the other and cocaine stitched together her fake clothing . . . In the second half of the last century the Queen's throne had already been erected. But the Queen, like all queens, could not be approached easily; she cost a lot and there were therefore few people who could take advantage of her favours: the rich, noblemen and intellectuals . . . What harm was there if those in power or gifted intellectually were able to invite the Queen into their gilded and closed salons? . . . Perhaps a rich man was seen now and again wandering through the city like a spectre, committing small or larger crimes to procure enough money to lay at the Lady's feet?

There is obviously no problem in translating the personification aspects of the Italian passage into English. We can thus conclude that there are different elements in the structure of metaphor which appear to be similar across languages. Apart from features such as personification, we have seen that a large part of this similarity stems from physiological models. In the case of European languages, they undoubtedly produce similar metaphoric mapping processes. Since all human bodies have certain physiological characteristics and conceptualisation processes in common, such as the perception of gravity and spatial orientation in general, it may be assumed that the types of images produced by these processes may very well have universal trends across a large number of different cultures.

If we go deeper into our analyses of cross-language metaphor patterns, a closer look at some types of metaphor nevertheless reveals that a direct linguistic or conceptual equivalent may actually be missing. The networking process can be easily modified by cultural parameters. What kinds of figurative language, however, tend to be culture-specific? We shall now move on to the world of culture in metaphor.

3
Culture-specific Conceptualisation

3.1 Universals and culture

It is clear that not all cultural and linguistic systems view the world in exactly the same way. Individual conceptual systems must also be responsible for cross-language variation in metaphor. In the following discussion, we shall look at a number of major issues on the relevance of culture in metaphor creation before looking at culture-specific networking. We shall examine how linguists have tried to set up definitions of cultural models, the types of misunderstanding which may occur between different cultural metaphors, the interaction between language and cultural environment and claims about the underestimated role of cultural sources in so-called universal models. Finally, in order to highlight cultural contrasts, we shall also explore the fascinating world of colour conceptualisation. These different issues demonstrate the powerful role of culturally-defined metaphoric language in contrast to the kinds of universal trends discussed in the previous chapter.

There are naturally a large range of straightforward examples of culture-specific concepts such as the obvious customs of a country, particularly in areas such as eating and drinking. Typical figurative expressions in British English include 'it's not his cup of tea' or 'it's a strange brew' coming from the customs of brewing tea and beer. But the dividing-line between a universal and culture-specific model can be a very complex one.

The distinction between universals and cultural systems has often led to a considerable amount of debate and controversy. Some scholars prefer to emphasise the importance of culture in metaphoric structures although it has not always been clear what constitutes a cultural model. Quinn and Holland (1987: 32 ff.) believe that cultural models are indeed based on prototypical structures as outlined in cognitive science. However,

Quinn (1991: 93) claims that it is not clear what the underlying structure of a cultural model is, whether it be image-schematic or even metaphoric at all. She goes further, in contrast to Lakoff and Johnson, by claiming that there is more to culture than just metaphor and that metaphor, an assertion disputed by cognitive linguists such as Gibbs (1994: 203 ff.) and Kövecses (2000: 114 ff.), plays a comparatively minor role in constituting our understanding of the world. However, when metaphor is used, cultural understanding is a basic premise.

There are all types of cultural models in societies across the world, including forms of marriage and political concepts as well as the field of emotions which we have referred to already. Let us first look at marriage.

3.2 The American cultural model of marriage

One aspect of Quinn's work which has caused a considerable amount of controversy is her analysis of the American model of marriage (1987: 173–92). A brief overview of Quinn's study reveals the proposal of eight models of marriage in American English. The following notions of marriage are supported by comments made by informants in her marriage surveys to portray their conceptualisation of the subject:

MARRIAGE is

(1) ENDURING: our relationship just gets more solid all the time
(2) BENEFICIAL: we've kind of meshed in a lot of ways
(3) UNKNOWN AT THE OUTSET: falling into marriage like king pins at the bowling alley
(4) DIFFICULT: the uphill stretches or the rocky road of marriage
(5) EFFORTFUL: you need to learn and work hard to make the first marriage stick
(6) JOINT: being cemented together/tied to each other
(7) MAY SUCCEED OR FAIL: the marriage worked out
(8) RISKY: there's so many odds against marriage

The suggestion, in a nutshell, is that the totality of these conceptual equations makes up a general cultural model of American marriage. Although this probably does give an overview of a typical model, it has been subject to a considerable amount of criticism. The first concerns the empirical data.

Gibbs (1994: 202) feels that Quinn's arguments are of an intuitive nature and claims that cognitive psychologists are generally sceptical about hypotheses of human conceptual knowledge based on intuition. This is a distinction between what Kövecses (2000) calls the 'folk versus expert theories of emotion'. The former refer to theories based on a shared, structured knowledge derived from examples of everyday language. The latter refer to theories that experts such as psychologists and philosophers develop to account for a given area of experience. A name which comes to mind in this respect would be, for example, Darwin.

In addition, Quinn claims that the American conceptualisation of marriage is based on literal thought processes and that metaphor may or may not come out of it. Both Gibbs and Kövecses reject this notion by maintaining that the concept of marriage is metaphorically constituted.

A more serious criticism perhaps is that the large range of comments from informants which have been used in the study tend to indicate that Americans do not have a single cultural or cognitive model of marriage. It is more likely that our understanding is far more complex and has the tendency to change over time. Experience of marriage can change people's attitudes and hence change a model. This could equally imply that cultural models in general are probably heterogeneous within a given society and that time can modify them.

With regard to marriage, it is indeed likely that people have different ideas about what marriage should be. From a cross-cultural point of view, however, a glance at Quinn's list above does suggest certain unifying characteristics which contribute towards one particular model. It gives the impression that the two partners in a marriage are desperately trying to make it work, a notion which probably did not exist to that extent in times past. Difficult, effortful, risky are all adjectives which portray marriage as a huge task. This would contrast very much with marriages in, for example, the Middle East, India or medieval Europe where marriages are, or were, usually arranged beforehand. There was no question that there would be a break-up, even though partners were often not satisfied with the arrangement.

Other cultural models involve areas such as politics which use metaphoric images that are not so easily understood between cultural spheres. In order to promote understanding between political leaders, images have been known to be changed, and this represents another feature of the powerful distinctions between metaphoric systems.

3.3 Cultural transfer of metaphor

In the field of translation, interpreting or the media in general, for example, cultural metaphors may be transferred from one language to another by changing the metaphoric image to fit the target culture. Even though political rhetoric in present-day Western society is, to a large extent, becoming international in nature due to mass media, this process may be required to avoid political embarrassment, confusion or even conflict. Schäffner (1997) develops this point with reference to the metaphor 'a common European house', coined by the Soviet leader Mikhail Gorbachev in the mid-1980s. The metaphor, EUROPE IS A HOUSE, was to represent the idea of all European states living in peaceful coexistence, whether located East or West of the Iron Curtain (Gorbachev, 1988).

The problem with this idea was that Gorbachev's image was based on typical Russian dwellings, which led to confusion in the conceptualisation of peaceful coexistence. The prototypical house in large Russian towns is a multi-storey apartment block with a number of entrances and in which several families live. This can be very different to typical dwellings in a country such as Great Britain in which the prototypical house may be detached, semi-detached or terraced. Hence, this could potentially lead to misunderstandings in political dialogue between Britain and Russia.

Gorbachev's concept of a 'common European house' was not, in fact, very welcome in the West but it was accepted in political discourse by changing the conceptual features of the metaphor model. Thus, in Britain, it took on the features of a typical British house. Which 'state' would live in which corridor or front yard was changed to references using fences, detached houses, rooms and so on. This therefore represents an example of a concept being transferred from one language to another and the metaphoric image changed to fit the target culture.

The metaphor also had problems in other West European countries such as the Federal Republic of Germany at that time. Speakers from different countries and cultures may have different *intentions* when using the same metaphor. Schäffner (1997: 59–60) illustrates this through a discussion between Gorbachev and the then German federal president, Richard von Weizsäcker. Their conversation with regard to the 'European house', taken from Gorbachev's book *Perestroika* (1988: 185) in which 'home' and not 'house' is used in the English translation, went as follows:

> Richard von Weizsäcker: It is a reference-point which helps us visualize the way things should be arranged in this common European home. Specifically, the extent to which apartments in it will be accessible for reciprocal visits.

Mikhail Gorbachev: You are quite right. But not everyone may like receiving night-time visitors.

Richard von Weizsäcker: We also aren't especially pleased to have a deep trench passing through a common living-room

It became clear in this discussion that the extended metaphor of 'night-time visitors' was a reference to Gorbachev's idea of trust and security, whereas von Weizsäcker's extension using 'a deep trench through a common living-room' revealed that he had the possibility of German reunification in mind.

The cultural transfer of metaphor can thus have a number of repercussions. One of these is that the original metaphor may not be properly understood due to the cultural environment of its source and has to be adapted to fit the target culture. Another aspect is that speakers of the same metaphor may actually have different goals or concerns in mind, particularly in the field of politics.

Further discussions on the role of culture-specific features have, in particular, involved the extent to which they are more powerful than language or whether linguistic structures themselves may alter cultural thinking. It would be worth also investigating this aspect as the controversy on this topic has been going on for a long time and continues to do so.

3.4 Interaction between language and cultural environment

The debate on language-specific conceptualisation has taken on very different approaches in the past. Whereas cultural models today are usually discussed in terms of the cultural environment, it has also been suggested in the past that cultural-specific thought processes are actually determined by the structure of the language employed. Does the environment structure our thought processes or is this role performed by the language itself? For those who have read about this particular aspect, the name of Whorf immediately springs to mind. The controversial Whorfian hypothesis suggests that language determines cultural thought processes. A relevant issue here is the concept of time.

Whorf states that 'the concepts of "time" and "matter" are not given in substantially the same form by experience to all men but depend upon the nature of the language or languages through the use of which they have been developed' (1956: 158). He based these conclusions on evidence gathered from his well-known study of the North American Indian language, Hopi. A major finding concerning the time concept was that Hopi has no way of linguistically expressing time since it has no tense systems. This lack of time structure influences the way in which the speakers of the language conceptualise their environment.

If we accept that there are both more general and language-specific trends, the problem which arises is how can the dividing-line be drawn between the end of potential universals and the beginning of cultural influence? A number of theories have been put forward in this respect. One of these involves what Lakoff defines as the distinction between system and capacity. We have seen that the basic experiences such as kinaesthetic images arising from physiological effects are among the likely candidates for universals. These are what Lakoff would term conceptualising capacities. These, in turn, may produce different conceptual systems. The first group is influenced by pre-conceptual experience, but since experience does not determine a conceptual system but only motiv-ates it, the same experiences may provide equally good motivation for two different systems (Lakoff, 1987: 310). In Indo-European languages, for example, the heart is often considered as the physiological centre of feeling. Lakoff suggests that there is a different conceptual system in Japanese in which the belly (Japanese 'hara') represents the locus of thought and feeling.

This is supported by empirical evidence provided by Matsuki (1995: 144 ff.). When a person gets angry in Japanese, *hara* is said to rise up:

Hara ga tatsu   'Hara rises up'

In English, when someone tries to 'bottle up' anger to attempt to get rid of it, Japanese uses the *hara* image by trying to keep anger in the belly. The belly is therefore the equivalent container image of 'bottle'. This produces slightly different metaphors such as:

Hara ni osameteoku   'Hold it in *hara*'

Or when a person is unable to control his or her anger:

Hara ni suekaneru   'Cannot lay it in *hara*'

3.5 Determining universal or cultural sources

In many ways, this would help explain the different variations of conceptual systems found across languages. There has, however, been some criticism of certain features which Lakoff presumes to represent universal mechanisms in emotions. A case in point is the ANGER = HEAT model outlined in the previous chapter. A cultural analysis of this model suggests other possible options. Some scholars have put forward arguments about anger not only being cultural-specific but that its metaphoric representations can be retraced to its cultural heritage. It would be worth examining this example in order to highlight the potential cultural role in metaphor creation.

Geeraerts and Grondelaers (1995) claim that, without totally rejecting the physiological aspects, the source of metaphorisation in anger in English and other European languages is motivated to a large extent by the reinterpreted legacy of humoral theory. This school of thought goes back to Hippocrates in Ancient Greece and became a dominant way of thinking in the Middle Ages. It was a common belief before the advances made in science after the medieval period that the four humoral fluids of the body regulate characters and emotions. Geeraerts and Grondelaers maintain that the conceptualisation of humoral theory continued to exist in language after such claims were only finally rejected by scientists in the nineteenth century, and in particular, Rudolf Virchow's *Die Cellularpathologie* in 1858.

The choleric temperament (anger) is determined by the amount of yellow bile, the melancholic temperament by an excess of black bile. A phlegmatic personality is linked to an excess of phlegm in the mucous membranes of the respiratory passages and the sanguine temperament (passion and enthusiasm) is due to aspects of blood circulation. Such common beliefs were reinforced in both art, as described in Cesare Ripa's *Iconologia* (1593) and in Elizabethan literature:

> I tell thee, Kate, 'twas burnt and dried away,
> and I expressly am forbid to touch it,
> for it engenders choler, planteth anger;
> and better 'twere that both of us did fast,
> since, of ourselves, ourselves are choleric
>
> (Shakespeare, *The Taming of the Shrew*, IV.i.157–61)

Furthermore, Geeraerts and Grondelaers give examples of the lexical legacy of humoral theory; Table 3.1 gives examples from English and French.

On the basis of this evidence, it is suggested that anger metaphors in present-day English are a result of culture-specific patterns found in humoral theory and that they fit in with a lot of Lakoffian examples of universal trends. Using counter-arguments, Kövecses (1995) claims that

Table 3.1: The lexical legacy of humoral theory

Humoral concept	English	French
1. phlegm	*phlegmatic* ('calm, cool, apathetic')	*avoir un phlegme imperturbable* ('to be imperturbable')
2. black bile	*spleen* ('sadness')	*mélancolie* ('sadness, moroseness')
3. yellow bile	*bilious* ('angry, irascible')	*colère* ('anger')
4. blood	*full-blooded* ('vigorous, heart, sensual')	*avoir du sang dans les veines* ('to be spirited')

Source: After Geeraerts and Grondelaers (1995).

if this were the case, humoral theory probably originally comes from physiological effects. This would then assume a more universal nature in their origin. However, in order to carry out this type of research, it is clear that an investigation would have to go back a very long way in time to pre-Ancient Greece, since Hippocrates formulated the beginnings of the doctrine. This would probably mean trying to retrace patterns as far back as the time of the Egyptian hieroglyphics.

It is sometimes necessary to dig deeply into different cultures in order to find possible explanations of specific images. Yu (1986: 82–3) suggests that the choice of a GAS concept in Chinese rather than the English FLUID for the container model of anger is due to the underlying culture of *yin* and *yang*. The former, which is associated with fluid substances, is linked to cold temperatures and the latter linked to gaseous substances and therefore heat. Anger and heat are thus associated with gas rather than fluid. This is an oversimplification of the theory but illustrates how traditional philosophies may influence cultural-specific metaphor.

We shall now turn to the field of cultural models and colour. It is interesting to see how individual languages have developed metaphoric colour patterns and these offer yet another illustration of well-defined cultural models.

3.6 Colour metaphors

The table of humoral concepts outlined above, with *yellow bile* and *black bile* invoking sadness and anger, bring to mind the issue of cross-cultural specificity in colour and its corresponding metaphors. Indeed, comparisons of both close and widely different cultures raise the question as to whether or not there are universal trends in colour metaphors.

Evidence for cultural differences abound. A starting-point in such an investigation is that a differentiation already exists in (literal) colour categorisation around the world. In the traditional literature on the subject, a number of well-known non-correspondences exist in different languages: it is claimed that Russian has no real word for blue: *goluboy* denoting 'light, pale blue' and *sinij* a 'dark, bright blue' which are not different shades of the same colour; French has no single equivalent to English brown with variants in *brun* and *marron*, while the oft-cited Welsh *glas* translates into English blue, green or even grey (Taylor, 1989: 3). One of the problems with these traditional analyses is that they have been analysed from one particular cultural viewpoint, usually in English and, as Wierzbicka (1992) points out in emotions analysis, cross-cultural comparisons really require a form of independent metalanguage.

One of the standard works on the cognitive analysis of colour categorisation involved a prototype theoretical study of basic colour terms (Berlin and Kay, 1969). Within the literal perception of colour, they claimed that there are a number of generalisations and perhaps these could be regarded as universal trends. A major point of the findings was that central members of basic colour categories seem to have the same universal structure. This theory would then support prototype theory which advocates a more typical centre within semantic categories. A basic category has a number of attributes which are thereby more common to the language user: (a) it has to be well-known, for example, *yellow* as opposed to *saffron*; (b) it should not be restricted to a small number of objects; (c) it has to consist of a short, one-morpheme construct such as *red* rather than *dark-red*; and (d) it should not be contained within another colour category such as *scarlet* within *red*.

Berlin and Kay proposed eleven basic categories for English: *black, white, red, yellow, green, blue, brown, purple, pink, orange* and *grey*. However, as it turns out, not all languages appear to have these basic categories. This presents a primary problem in trying to find cross-language equivalents among culturally very different languages, in the same way as the colour variations in the European languages described above. There seems to be a hierarchy of the most common categories, as seen in the following list, which can be extended as more basic categories are added:

black, white
red
yellow, green, blue

brown
purple, pink, orange, grey

In other words, some languages have only black and white and if they have a third colour it will be red. If they have additional colours, they will be taken from yellow, green, blue and so on according to the hierarchical list. This type of cross-cultural variation in colour combinations appears to increase when the figurative dimension is applied. We shall first take a look at widely different cultures and then at variation within European languages. An interesting case is the difference between English and Chinese.

We would normally assume that the first basic colours on the hierarchy, black and white, should have some universal features similar to the dirt/clean image of the drugs scenario. Within the drugs field in European languages, there are, in fact, some common trends since the colours *black* and *white* are often associated with darkness and lightness. As can be imagined, darkness tends to have a negative connotation whereas white is positive. This can be seen particularly in metaphors concerning the physical effects of drugs (taken from *Time* magazine):

> With higher doses and chronic use, the alertness and exhilaration so prized by coke's connoisseurs quickly turn into *darker* effects, ranging from insomnia to full-fledged cocaine psychosis

The colour *grey* has the same effect as *black*:

> The whole world was going *gray*, everybody in the room getting real distant. I was going limp and lifeless, and the only thing I could think about was to concentrate on my breathing

This negative pattern can be found across European languages. An English/Chinese comparison, however, reveals similarities but also distinct differences. According to Li (2005), the colour *black* can be found in both languages as in *blacklist, black market, black magic* and so on. Further study in this field may, however, reveal that they have been borrowed from English or other European languages. As far as *white* is concerned, both languages also have the symbol of 'purity'. Nevertheless, this colour in particular illustrates some fundamental differences in philosophical thought. *White* is the colour for funerals in traditional Chinese custom, as opposed to English *black*. The reason is that the Chinese traditionally consider death as a happy occasion.

In the same way, the colour *red* is used for weddings in China, as opposed to *white* at a traditional English marriage. *Red*, in fact, is a very important colour in Chinese custom and, apart from marriages, is also the symbol of revolution, communism and socialism. *Yellow* tends to be negative in English, as in the sense 'cowardly', in Chinese it is associated with nobility and the aristocracy and thus symbolises wealth. *Blue* is apparently always positive in Chinese but in English it often mixed with negative overtones: *the blues, blue joke* and so on.

The result is that patterns of colour symbolisation can be arbitrary and therefore very often culture-specific. Within European languages there are more correspondences due to a common cultural heritage and they may follow certain common trends at any one period of time. One example is the colour *green* with reference to political parties.

We have referred to *red* being associated with politics in China and colours are frequently used for all kinds of political groups. *Green* was originally associated with the ecological party in Germany during the 1970s and was quickly calqued into other European languages as the 'Greens'. Further networks were developed in Germany such as the '*red-green coalition*', meaning collaboration between a leftist party and an ecological one. The link with nature here is an obvious one but a historical comparison of *green* between English and French, for example, shows that this colour has been symbolised in very different ways, despite a common cultural heritage, and its origin is more difficult to trace.

In English, metaphor models using *green* have been largely pejorative with connotations such as gullibility, immaturity, inexperience and simplicity, as in '*he is green for his age*'. In French they have been largely positive with associations of strength and youth, for example, '*un vieillard encore vert*' ('an old person who is still green' = strong). In English, presumably, greenness symbolises youth but with the association of inexperience in a young person; in French, it also symbolises youth but in an old person this would be a positive feature.

Similar trends in colour metaphors are therefore often hard to distinguish, even between culturally related languages. Sometimes, certain features may display similarities. For example, *red* in European languages is usually associated with positive features but *yellow* is often linked to negative symbolisation, including *green* in some cases. Whether it is because these two colours are close together on the colour spectrum, *yellow* being situated between *green* and *red*, is a speculative question. However, *yellow* and *green* appear to have correspondences in some European languages.

In French, there is the expression *un rire jaune* (a yellow laugh), meaning 'a forced laugh'. There does not seem to be a corresponding English colour metaphor for this feature of wryness. However, Dutch has one, in *hij lacht groen* (he laughs greenly). Dutch therefore swaps *yellow* for *green*. Although this is a standard expression in Dutch, it should also be pointed out that there is also a fixed expression, *groen en geel* (green and yellow), listed by the Robert and Von Dale dictionary, which is used to reinforce an emotion. It can be seen in a number of different emotions, including envy, discussed below. Examples are: *hij werd groen en geel van nijd* (he became green and yellow with envy = really envious), *zich groen en geel ergeren* (to become green and yellow with anger = really angry), *het wordt hem groen en geel voor de ogen* (it became green and yellow before his eyes = he became really dizzy). First of all, this must mean that the two colours in Dutch have been fused into a fixed idiomatic expression. Without exploring the details of its history, the status of a fixed expression may lead to the assumption that it has also probably been in existence for a considerable period of time. Second, the fact that this fusion has taken place also implies that the two colours are conceptually very close together, at least in the field of emotions.

With regard to emotions, green in English signifies 'envy' as in *to be green with envy*. The interesting point about this expression is that, according to etymological dictionaries, English actually adopted the colour *yellow* a long time ago and the use of the metaphor YELLOW = ENVY only died out in the seventeenth century. Diachronically, there has thus been a switch between these two colours. The conclusion is that the two do seem to be historically related and interchangeable. Either there is a shift, as in English, or they may become fused in a fixed expression, as in Dutch.

Does this mean that there are, after all, trends and patterns in the creation of colour metaphors? In the case of *yellow* and *green* it is very hard to say without a great deal more research into this aspect of European cultural history. There could be a link to some visual aspect such as the colour of the face which can turn 'green' or 'yellow' in ill health and therefore has a pejorative effect in emotions. This could be regarded as parallel to the visual aspect of bile in humoral theory. In Ancient Greek symbolism, yellowish liquids in the innards are apparently associated with negative emotions. They are not identified with the blackening emotion of anger, but with fear, like facial pallor (Padel, 1992: 26). Again, Greek humoral theory may account for some present-day colour metaphors in the emotions.

Some regular trends may therefore exist, particularly in linked cultures, otherwise it looks as if colour metaphors have very much a cultural-specific characteristic. Once the conceptual colour metaphor has been established in a specific culture, other linked metaphors, and particularly linguistic ones, are networked to the base concept. We have seen, in the case of black, *black market* and so on. Other colours produce the same radial chaining as in the positive values of Chinese *white: white hope* (a person who aims to be successful in a group), *white hat* (a good person in general), *white-handed* (honest), *white list* (a list of acceptable people), *white-haired boy* (a favourite person). *Red* in Chinese is also usually positive with the connotations of profits for a company (contrasted with *in the red* in English), honour and beauty, but also, equivalent to *green* in English, envy in Chinese is associated with *red* (Li, 2005). There is thus no link with the yellow or green part of the spectrum for this emotion. The reason can probably be explained by the fact that, as well as looking ill as a result of envy, the face could display anger and thus become red.

If we look again at the hierarchy of basic colour categories outlined above, we can see that different conceptual metaphors are linked to the various colours and that this tends to vary across languages and cultures. Figure 3.1. illustrates this pattern with some of the cultural conceptual metaphors in the first three levels of the basic colour hierarchy.

Two extra points can also be summarised and illustrated with regard to this pattern: the first is related to synchronic overlap due to borrowing and the second is colour proximity resulting in synchronic overlap of colours themselves.

The colour metaphors in Figure 3.1 refer to conceptual metaphors rooted in the history of the cultures concerned. A considerable amount of borrowing can also occur in the form of lexical units such as the *blacklist*, *black magic* and *black market*. Without investigating the precise etymology of the items, it is highly unlikely that lists such as these would have originated separately in the two cultures in question. There is evidently a

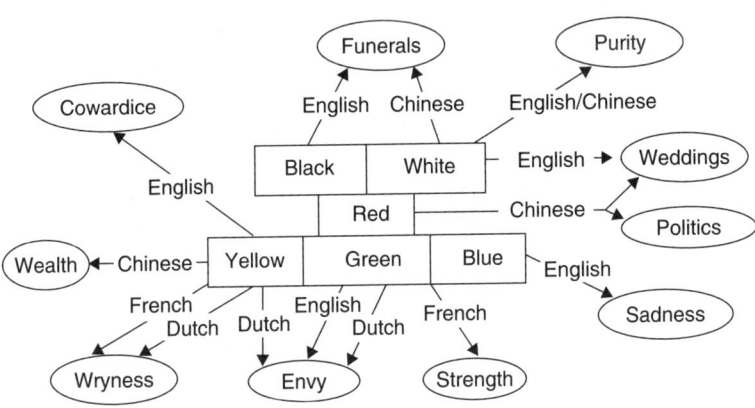

Figure 3.1 The cultural colour web

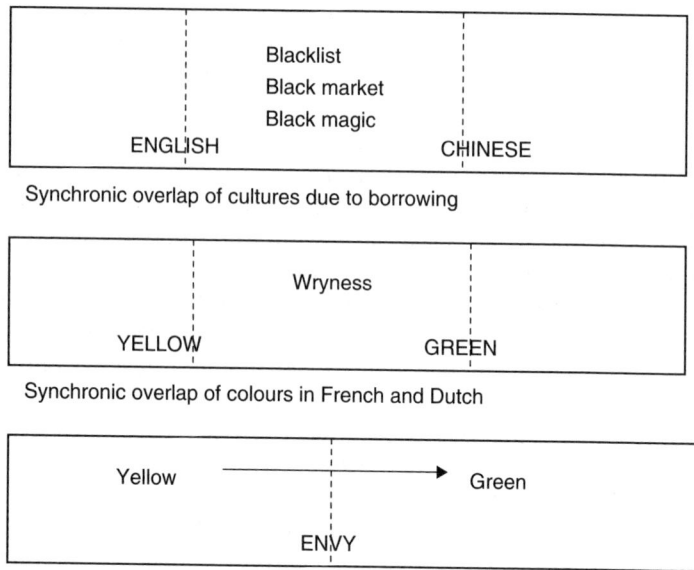

Figure 3.2 Colour overlapping and shifts

case of borrowing and colour metaphors are often transferred easily in specific expressions, particularly in the world of economics.

The second point is that it is perhaps not coincidental that two colours such as yellow and green are at the same level in the basic colour hierarchy. The conceptual proximity of these two colours appears to encourage both synchronic colour overlap and diachronic colour shift. Figure 3.2 illustrates the overlapping and shifts of colours which, yet again, tend to make category boundaries fuzzy. It is likely that yellow and green underwent a transitional stage of overlap in the diachronic shift of envy.

We can conclude that colour definitely represents culture-specific features in metaphor. The kinds of issues we have been discussing in this chapter, such as the form of cultural models, cross-language misunderstanding and colour metaphors all point to the fact that figurative language is also entrenched in different cultural systems.

This aspect is further highlighted by the field of translation. The attempt to translate figurative expressions from one language to another can be a challenge. The test of cultural specificity in translation is the subject of the next chapter and demonstrates the variation which can occur in the individual networking patterns of the languages concerned.

4
Conceptual Equivalence and Translation

4.1 Translation options

Imagine we have the task of translating a novel. If we accept the cognitive view that a large part of our language is metaphoric, we will have to translate figurative language almost immediately in our work: probably within the first paragraph or two. Some metaphor scholars interested in translation issues point out that many standard textbooks on translation make very little mention of metaphor (for example, Naciscione, 2006: 103). This does in fact appear to be the case. Many textbooks devote only two or three pages to the problem. In a book of 200–300 pages, this would only make up 1 per cent of translation strategies. Why is this the case? There could be a number of reasons but the obvious one is that translation theorists may not consider figurative language to be a major problem and that there are more important aspects to discuss, such as terminology, collocations or general stylistic problems.

One point is clear, however: translation does clearly illustrate the different types of cross-language equivalence which exist in figurative language. The following discussion on translation strategies in metaphor is not to be considered as a problem-solving debate for translators but as a means of showing how the medium of translation represents one way of establishing such conceptual equivalence. In this way, we are able to establish which metaphors are more culturally specific than others. The process of translation is able to highlight culture-specific metaphor in even very closely related languages. Furthermore, we are able to establish where predominant metaphor networks are operating.

A perusal of French translations of classical English literary works reveals that a number of strategies are employed in the case of metaphoric expressions. We shall look at just two or three examples from the French translation (*Loin de la Foule Déchaînée*, 1980) of Thomas Hardy's *Far from the Madding Crowd*, in order to illustrate the kinds of equivalence which may be involved.

If it is difficult finding a metaphoric equivalent, the simplest strategy in translation is, of course, to leave out a metaphoric expression entirely. This is particularly the case if the structure is not essential to the meaning of the passage in question. This may detract from the poetic content of the passage but it is a sign that the translator may have considered it too difficult to produce a figurative equivalent in the target language. An example can be seen in the following translation:

> On a day which had **a summer face and a winter constitution** – a fine January morning, when there was just enough blue sky visible to make cheerfully-disposed people wish for more . . . (p. 62)
> . . . *Par une belle matinée de janvier, alors que le ciel montrait un coin bleu juste assez grand pour en faire désirer davantage*

The original English expression, *a summer face and a winter constitution*, representing a conceptual metaphor of BODY PARTS = SEASONS, has been completely left out in the translation. This could mean that the same metaphor might have sounded strange in French to the translator. At the other end of the scale, there is obviously no difficulty in translating the following passage relating to the HEAT = PASSION conceptual metaphor:

> Oak belonged to the even-tempered order of humanity, and felt the secret fusion of himself in Bathsheba to be **burning with a finer flame** now that she was gone . . . (p. 70)
> *Tel était le cas chez notre fermier, et son secret d'amour pour Barbara **brûlait d'une flamme plus ardente** que jamais*

In line with our discussions above on universal trends, it would appear that this kind of physiological model represents no particular translation difficulties regarding metaphoric equivalents. In between these two strategies of either leaving out a translation entirely or finding an exact equivalent, there are all kinds of approaches linked to differing levels of translatability. This is ultimately related to saliency in the language in question. The notion of saliency is fundamental to metaphor interpretation and one which will be dealt with more fully in Part II. However, it does appear that language-specific saliency also plays a major role in cross-language equivalence and cultural models. Its importance tends to vary according to the type of text involved but in literature it is probably more flexible due to the wide interpretative notions of poetic licence. This flexibility would be reduced in texts requiring more standard expressions such as in the natural sciences, law or even journalism. Not only may a translator use non-conventional metaphor in the target text, the source text may also contain metaphors which sound strange to the everyday language-user. The translations of creative innovations vary enormously and usually lie somewhere on the scale between high and low translatability. This depends on the ability to interpret and transfer the source-language metaphor (SLM).

The SLM may fit into the target language (TL) without any problem, as in the HEAT = PASSION metaphor above. On the other hand, the SLM may be readily understood but it may sound strange in the TL. In other words, the expression is on a lower level of saliency in the TL. This is the case of the *summer face and winter constitution* metaphor. The term *dry carcases of leaves* in the following example represents a similar situation, even taking the poetic style of the context into account. The translator has also decided to leave out the *carcases* image:

On the higher levels the dead and **dry carcases of leaves** tapped the ground as they bowled along helter-skelter **upon the shoulders of the wind** (p. 77)
*Sur la grande route les feuilles mortes **chassées par le vent*** (=chased by the wind)

Indeed, the translation *carcasses sèches de feuilles* (dry carcases of leaves) would probably sound odd in French even in a poetic style. However, the second idiomatic expression, *upon the shoulders of the wind*, has been translated. In this case, a conventionalised metaphor has been used in French with the symbol of CHASING: *chasser* (to chase). The translator has decided to avoid the English BODY PARTS conceptual metaphor since the French *sur les épaules du vent* (on the shoulders of the wind) would equally sound strange. The result thus represents the translation of a creative metaphor without the same image. This pattern occurs frequently and suggests that either the translator wishes simply to be free in the choice of options, which may not necessarily have the same metaphor, or there is a degree of variation in cross-language equivalence and language-specific saliency which imposes constraints. It can be observed that it is the latter area which often plays an important role in translation options.

It will not be our aim in this discussion to attempt to quantify translatability and cross-language equivalence. Suffice it to say that translatability follows a scale from almost complete freedom to use similar metaphors in universal features to considerable constraints in fixed-language and cultural-specific expressions. Creative innovations appear to fluctuate between these two points. The level of equivalence thus varies accordingly (see Figure 4.1).

Creative innovations are thus dependent on TL saliency. Various criteria may be observed at the lower end of the translatability scale. These may include not only cultural-specific structures but also fixed language-specific expressions. However, these features can sometimes fluctuate since they may be found in more than one language due to cultural overlap (see Newmark's examples below). In addition, regional and time-specific variants may arise in translation. How can dialectal metaphors be translated to portray the fact that standard language is not being used? Should a present-day translation of a nineteenth-century novel reflect the language of that time in order to capture the cultural atmosphere of life as it was then? Both regional and time-specific variants embody the source culture. Should such a text, on the other hand, be modernised to make it more comprehensible to the modern reader? These strategies vary from one translator to the other. In many cases, translators appear to play safe and translate metaphoric expressions with either conventionalised, target-language metaphors or with standard non-metaphoric structures. The following passage illustrates these points:

> Be as 'twill, she's a fine handsome body as far's looks be concerned. But that's only the **skin of the woman**, and these **dandy cattle** be as proud as Lucifer in their insides (p. 79)

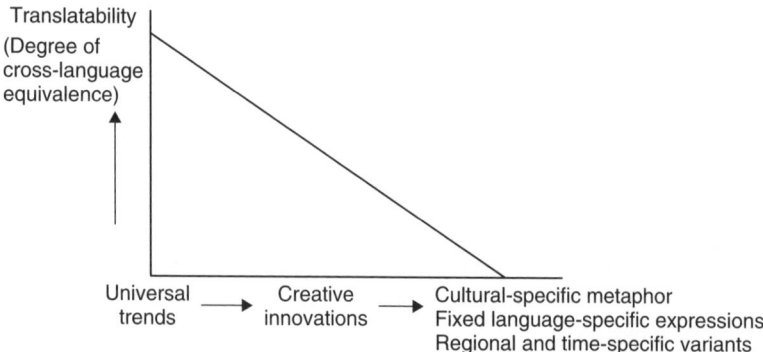

Figure 4.1 Translatability and cross-language equivalence in metaphor

*En tout cas, autant qu'on en peut juger, elle est bien belle. Je ne parle que de l'**extérieur de la femme**, et ces **beautés-là** sont ordinairement pleines d'orgueil, comme Lucifer lui-même*

The first example of *skin of the woman*, with the sense of outward or physical appearance, sounds a bit strange as it stands. In English, there are standard variants of the SKIN = EXTERIOR conceptual metaphor, such as *to have a thick skin*, meaning to be insensitive, but the expression above appears to be more of an individual creation. There is a further possibility that this expression was current in Hardy's time or common in his particular dialect of Wessex. A clear case of a dialectal metaphor is *dandy cattle*, translated by the French *beautés* (beauties). It is obvious that this latter example cannot use the same metaphor image. Furthermore, the skin metaphor has not been translated literally and the translator has opted simply for the term *extérieur* (exterior). Regional (and, as the case may be, time-specific) metaphors therefore naturally tend towards the lower end of the translatability scale, but they are useful in enhancing the source culture in translation.

There are numerous reasons why translation strategies of figurative language can be problematic and influence cross-language equivalence. Many other variations could be added here. However, we shall now look at some traditional theories on translatability before discussing how translation also reveals language-specific networking.

4.2 Traditional views of translatability

Some attempts have been made to assess the translatability of metaphor by means of the level of informational content. The suggestion is that translatability is in inverse proportion to the quantity of information manifested by the metaphor and the degree to which this information is structured in the text. The less information conveyed by a metaphor and the less complex the structural relations into which it enters in a text, the more translatable this metaphor will be, and vice versa (Van den Broek, 1981: 84).

Others have analysed the degree of translatability according to the classification of types of figurative language (Newmark, 1985: 320–3). Since cross-cultural idioms, puns, proverbs and the like may also carry a considerable amount of information, the correlation of information and classification with translatability is not always satisfactory. As we have suggested above, a great deal depends on whether metaphoric expressions contain more universal, basic concepts or more culture-specific ones. The former increase translatability and the latter reduce it, unless there is cultural overlap. This phenomenon implies that two languages have been in contact and that exchanges of figurative expressions are likely to have taken place as in *his life hangs on a thread* which has an equivalent in French *sa vie ne tient que d'un fil* or German *sein Leben hängt an einem Faden* (Newmark, 1985: 304). This involves a combination of several concepts whose parallel creation would not only be less frequent than single-concept metaphors, but whose conceptual structure contains images which may not be predominantly 'universal' as in *thread* or *hanging on a thread*. Translatability of such culture-specific metaphors increases among languages which exchange images of this kind within an area of cultural overlap, but decreases outside the given area.

The idea of overlap in cross-language equivalence is important since it also involves the notion of conceptual sharing as well as equivalence at the linguistic level. However, differentiation also appears to exist in closely-related language families. Conceptualisation of the qualities in animals varies considerably within European languages. According to Newmark (1985), a horse is strong in English, healthy and diligent in French and hard-working in German. These all represent positive qualities but this aspect may also vary within the same animal or bird. Newmark suggests that ducks are affectionate creatures in English but they can be lying rumours in French and German. It should be pointed out that the interpretation of such images can vary a little between native speakers' views on the subject but it is clear that there is cross-language variation.

Again, in the field of emotions, Wierzbicka (1992) maintains that Polish does not have a word corresponding exactly to the English word *disgust*. She rejects the claim that there are a number of fundamental emotions, as listed by Izard and Buechler (1980), which include interest, joy, surprise, sadness, anger, disgust, contempt, fear, shame/shyness and guilt. She feels that one of the problems in describing cross-cultural or universal trends in human conceptualisation is that linguists are forced to establish descriptive analyses according to the conceptual framework of the language being used. A Polish linguist may have set up a different list to Izard and Buechler. As we have seen above in the discussion on colour metaphors, it is almost as if a 'language-independent semantic metalanguage' (Wierzbicka, 1992: 134) is required for the analysis of conceptual systems.

This has often been the criticism in the past of the overwhelming amount of research described in English on universals or culture-specificity. However, conceptual variation in human emotions has been a major point in the work of American linguists such as Lakoff who also points out that there is variation in the emotion of sadness. The Tahitian language apparently has no word for this concept but the Tahitians experience sickness, fatigue or the feeling of being attacked by an evil spirit as an equivalent (Lakoff, 1972).

Wierzbicka suggests that the problem is that emotions have many similar sub-groups and that the exact boundaries between related feelings are language-specific (1986: 590). If we again take the word *disgust*, there are a number of related feelings such as distaste, revulsion, repulsion, repugnance and so on. The boundaries of these emotional fields thus vary between English and Polish. Polish has a number of translation equivalents such as *niesmak* (approximately, 'distaste'), *wstret* (roughly, 'revulsion'), and *odraza* (roughly, 'repulsion'). A rough translation of 'disgust' would be *obrzydzenie* but Wierzbicka points out that even the purist Polish writer Jan Lechon, writing his diaries in America, repeatedly used the English loan *dyzgust* since he felt that there was no exact Polish equivalent.

Some linguists feel that basic emotional terms should not be a rigid concept but that some terms tend to be more basic than others (Kövecses, 2000: 3). He feels that more basic terms in English would be *anger, sadness, fear, joy* and *love*. Less basic ones would be *annoyance, wrath, indignation* and *rage* for anger and *terror, fright* and *horror* for fear.

The idea that the notion of 'basic emotions' is not very satisfactory and that some terms seem to be more basic than others is supported by Ortony et al. (1988: 26 ff.). They feel the term is unacceptably vague. Some emotions are a mixture of two or more into 'dyads' or 'tryads'. There are many factors which may play a role in considering one emotion more important than another. Some 'basic' emotions, such as anger or fear, may be important for the organism and may actually play a role in survival. Saliency may also contribute towards 'basicness'. It is suggested that some emotions appear at an earlier stage in life than others, anger being clearly evident at four months of age.

The whole spectrum of ideas which go into defining cross-cultural conceptualisation is therefore complex and is often reflected in the process of translation. If we consider more specifically cross-language equivalence in the translation of figurative language as a whole, Newmark defines 'conceptual metaphor' as being basic and universal, the indispensable key to thought-processes, and including human activities such as manufacture, trade, life/birth, health, disease, sex, copulation, death, valuation, play, struggle and communication, in addition to logical, spatial and temporal dimensions (1985: 320).

A crucial distinction in equivalence, however, concerns the notion of conceptual metaphor compared to linguistic form as discussed in

Chapter 2: the extent to which languages share both. The drugs model in the last chapter shows that, despite the universal trends portrayed by the underlying conceptual models of, for example, heat, dirt and health in European languages, there are a considerable number of different linguistic expressions on the surface such as Italian *bruciato* (burnt) with the meaning 'associated with drugs' which does not appear to exist in English. Despite a common cultural heritage, European languages reveal a distinct cleavage in the second phase of the drugs scenario.

A common distinction which occurs in the translation of metaphor is therefore whether two languages share the same conceptual metaphor, and if they do, which items of linguistic form they also share. Problems arise where there is not an equivalence. The level of equivalence does tend to be flexible in figurative language but there are definitely some items which sound strange in one language but not in another. It is often up to the translator to decide whether the item is acceptable in the target language. Two of the main models which emerge may be illustrated in the following way. Figure 4.2. depicts a situation whereby meaning X is present in two languages L1 and L2 in the form of a conceptual metaphor Y. However, each language produces different linguistic forms from the same underlying concept: L1a, L1b, L1c on the one hand, and L2a, L2b, L2c on the other. In the case of an underlying concept HEAT, as opposed to COLD, a number of linked images are generated associated with a general notion of intensity referring to danger, emotional feeling and so on. The Italian linguistic form *bruciato* may be construed as originating from the same underlying concept of HEAT, as in English *hot spot*, but with a different linguistic form and, in this case, meaning.

The other common type of language-specific metaphor items is illustrated in Figure 4.3. A common meaning X is represented by two conceptual metaphors Y and Z in languages L1 and L2. As pointed out earlier,

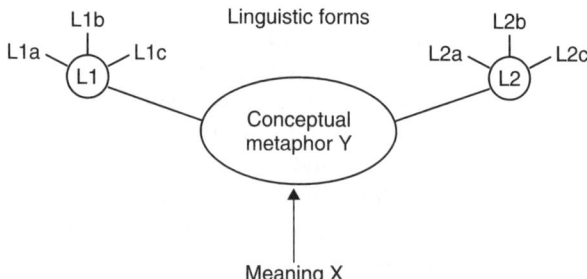

Figure 4.2 Comparative networking in shared conceptual metaphors

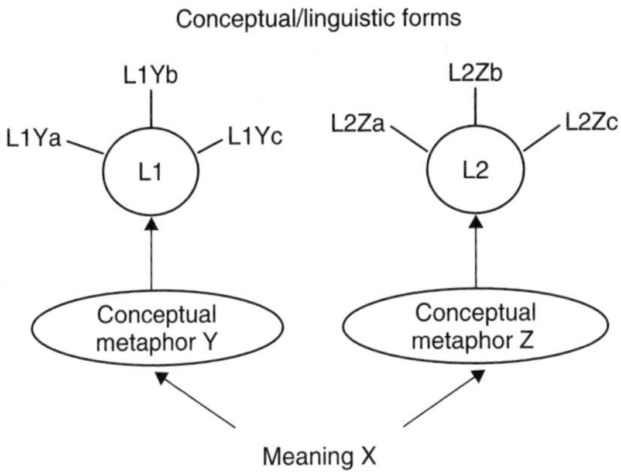

Conceptual Equivalence and Translation 71

Conceptual/linguistic forms

```
        L1Yb                          L2Zb
L1Ya  \  |  / L1Yc        L2Za  \  |  / L2Zc
       ( L1 )                    ( L2 )
         ↑                          ↑
   ┌───────────┐              ┌───────────┐
   │ Conceptual│              │ Conceptual│
   │ metaphor Y│              │ metaphor Z│
   └───────────┘              └───────────┘
          ↖                    ↗
               Meaning X
```

Figure 4.3 Comparative networking in language-specific conceptual metaphors

the common meaning X may only produce one conceptual metaphor in one language but in this case we shall be examining the development of two parallel metaphor systems and their equivalents in two languages. Cross-language differences in this model thus take the form of conceptual/linguistic forms of L1Ya, L1Yb, L1Yc in one language and L2Za, L2Zb, L2Zc in the other.

In this particular situation, we may have two different types of images for the underlying conceptual metaphor such as the notion of spatial proximity for being well-organised in one language and balance in another. This can occur in colloquial language as in the case of 'he's a very together guy' in English (spatial proximity) or '*c'est un mec très équilibré*' (he's a 'well-balanced' guy) in French. Both models can occur in one language but their choice may depend on context. For example, German has both in the sense of English 'pull yourself together' (German: *reiss dich zusammen*), but German cannot use the same expression 'he's very together' (**er ist sehr zusammen*) and would use the balance image *ausgeglichen* (balanced) as in French *équilibré*. (The asterisk is a conventional sign often used in linguistics for an incorrect or reconstructed sentence, particularly in historical linguistics.) The result is that a number of different conceptual and linguistic metaphor items are produced in various languages. The proximity image in English has produced other colloquial expressions in the same semantic domain as in 'spaced-out', 'strung-out' and non-standard 'untogether'. This binary feature is also present in other languages but can have semantic offshoots. French *déséquilibré* (unbalanced) has the meaning 'insane' rather than 'disorganised' and it is in this new semantic domain that the balance image can come into play in English: 'he is unbalanced' (psychologically disturbed). The result of the different cross-language combinations is that each culture follows the same networking principles but can come up with varied conceptual and linguistic combinations which depend on either their existence in the language or on contextual and stylistic criteria which account for their actual usage.

4.3 The BUSINESS CORPORATION = FAMILY model

One of the main hypotheses proposed here is that, due to the evolution of different scenarios and systems, networking patterns are set up which appear to encourage metaphor groups to become predominant in specific languages. Where predominance occurs, there seems to be a snowball effect. This may arise from set patterns in cultural thinking. On a synchronic level, we shall first examine a comparative metaphor model based on a BUSINESS CORPORATION = FAMILY equation in contemporary English and French economic texts taken from the present-day press.

The business corporation has, in fact, been analysed metaphorically from a number of different viewpoints. The warfare ontology has been applied to business enterprises as in Table 4.1 which gives a brief summary of metaphoric mapping in a business scenario (Resche, 2006; citing Santamaria et al., 2004):

In a discussion of Darwinism in socio-economic systems, Resche (2005; citing Hodgson, 2002: 260) points out such systems have also been likened to living beings (chronic deficit, endemic inflation, financial injection, market cure, infant industries, teething problems and so on) or to the mechanical world (leverage, market mechanisms, financial instruments, overheating, fine-tuning, macroeconomic tools and so on).

In many ways, the BUSINESS CORPORATION = FAMILY model fits into Newmark's ideas on the definition of conceptual metaphors as the model includes concepts such as birth, death and so on, as well as family

Table 4.1: Warfare ontology in business enterprises

	Warfare	Business
Mission/goal	Seize an objective	Gain market shares
Step 1: Observe	Reconnaissance	Market study
Step 2: Orient	Intelligence	Environmental scan
Step 3: Decide	War games	Scenario planning
Final step: Act	Action	Action

Source: After Resche (2006).

relationships which take place in all societies. It also involves the second type of 'deep/surface' combination in Deignan's (1997) categories.

A chronological pattern in the family scenario can be seen in the two languages in Table 4.2.

Any of these stages can occur in the scenario. The model is predominant in French so that a comparison will be made from French to English with contextual information and translation possibilities. The scenario thus starts with examples taken from the birth image:

1. *Birth*

    Dernière-née *des méga-fusions du secteur bancaire nippon, Mizuho holdings est la première banque mondiale pour la taille de ses actifs*
    (**The last born** (the latest) giant merger in the Japanese banking sector, Mizuho holdings represents the first world bank for the size of its workforce)

In this case, although the metaphor is understood in English it would probably not be used in this particular translation although it could perhaps be used in an expression such as 'a company was born'.

2. *Christening*

    *'Mizuho, une banque pour un monde de solutions', clamait la publicité de Mizuho lors de son lancement **sur les fonts baptismaux**, le 1er avril*
    ('Mizuho, the bank which solves all problems', was Mizuho's publicity claim during its **christening** (inauguration) on the 1st April)

A literal translation of *lancement sur les fonts baptismaux* as 'christening' (literally: its launch at the baptisal font) would obviously not fit here in

Table 4.2: Chronology of the family scenario

French	English equivalent
1. Naissance	Birth
2. Baptême	Christening
3. Mère/père	Parent
4. Parrain/marraine	Godfather/godmother
5. Cousin(e)/soeur	Cousin/sister
6. Mariage	Marriage
7. Divorce	Divorce
8. Mort	Death

English and has to be replaced by a term such as 'inauguration' or simply 'launch'. A similar problem can be seen in the following example:

> *Chaîne d'information en continu de Canal+, i-télévision, créée en novembre 1999 et restructurée recémment, s'est entièrement mobilisée l'après-midi du mardi 11 septembre. 'C'est notre **baptême du feu**', déclare Bernard Zekri, directeur de la rédaction*
> (Canal+'s non-stop news channel, i-television, which was founded in November 1999 and recently restructured, went into action on the afternoon of Tuesday 11th September. 'It was a **new start** for us', according to chief editor, Bernard Zekri)

The term *baptême du feu*, 'baptism of fire', is an expression which exists or has existed in English for a long time. Its general meaning refers to the start of an event which is characterised by notions of difficulty. Again, a more neutral term such as 'new start' would be needed in this translation.

3. *Parent*

The closest family members associated with a birth are the parents themselves which are projected on to the founding company. There is a divergence here between English and French in that the former is usually limited to the term 'parent company', while the latter has opted for the 'mother company' (*maison mère*), often being combined with the symbol of a house:

> *Selon nos informations, la **maison mère** peut compter sur un financement autour de 2 milliards d'euros*
> (According to our information, the **parent company** will be able to count on a financial plan amounting to around 2 thousand million euros)

Variation of the underlying concept is common in European languages, such as the German *Tochtergesellschaft*, 'daughter company', meaning a subsidiary company.

4. *Godfather/godmother*

Other common family memberships in French include *parrain*, 'godfather', and *marraine*, 'godmother', in the sense of sponsors. The former can be used in specific texts in English, such as indicating the head of a Mafia clan, but the two family members are commonly used in business texts in French, with the normal term *parrainage* for sponsorship which can also be seen in free variation with the English loanword:

Elle emploie près de trente-cinq professionnels, compte une dizaine de **sponsors**... deux **parrains** importants (la DATAR et l'INA) et une **marraine** de choix en la personne de Jacqueline Baudrier
(It employs a staff of thirty-five professionals, includes about ten **sponsors**... two big **sponsors** (DATAR and INA), and a **sponsor** of its own choice: Jacqueline Baudrier)

French thus has more variation here with both the male and female versions of godparents being used. The symbol of 'godfather' is a more neutral term, as seen in the reference to companies or sponsorship in general, but where the person is clearly female, a 'godmother' metaphor can be chosen.

5. *Cousin/sister*

A question which arises here is whether this variation in gender can be seen in other family members. The answer is probably that it is the case, as can be seen in the example of the female counterpart of 'cousin': *la cousine*, with reference to a related company. Here again, there tends to be variation between languages concerning the lexical item of the shared underlying concept. English may be more likely to opt for 'sister company', which is also shared by French *société soeur*, rather than a cousin:

Comme sa **cousine** luxembourgeoise, ce produit a pour vocation d'investir sur des 'grosses valeurs moyennes'
(Like its **sister company** in Luxembourg, the aim of this product is to invest in 'high mean values')

Gender, however, may often be related to syntactic features rather than symbolic ones, since the 'cousin' example can also be masculine if used with a masculine noun such as *auditeur*, 'auditor' or feminine when referring to the lexical item *société*, 'company':

Un changement d'identité coûteux, mais dont les consultants se félicitent a posteriori: ils échappent aujourd'hui au discrédit qui frappent leurs **cousins auditeurs**
(A costly change of identity which consultants were nevertheless pleased about afterwards; they have not now fallen into disrepute in the same way as their **sister company of auditors**).

> *En attendant, Andersen a perdu 90 gros clients aux Etats Unis ... les* **cousines** *du reste du monde ont préféré se rendre à la concurrence*
> (In the meantime, Andersen has lost 90 major clients in the United States ... **sister companies** in the rest of the world have preferred to become competitive)

6. Marriage

A very common metaphor found in the merger of companies is the marriage concept, an underlying metaphoric construct found in English with similar conceptual ideas but used in different contexts. The following example concerns the merger of two leading Spanish banks, Banco Santander and Banco Central Hispano, and also includes the BIRTH model described above:

> *Ce* **mariage** *donnera naissance au huitième établissement bancaire de la zone euro*
> (This **merger** will launch the eighth largest banking institution in the euro area)

The interesting point about this example is that the marriage metaphor has no doubt encouraged the birth metaphor in the same sentence which makes the latter even more appropriate in French, as in the following example:

> *La deuxième banque espagnole, Banco Bilbao Vizcaya Argentaria,* **née** *fin 1999 du* **mariage** *de BBV et d'Argentaria, paie un lourd tribut à la crise argentine*
> (The second-largest Spanish bank, Banco Bilbao Vizcaya Argentaria, **a product of the merger** between BBV and Argentaria at the end of 1999 is paying a high contribution to the Argentinian crisis)

The marriage metaphor in English, however, needs to be replaced by a term such as 'merger' which would make a subsequent birth metaphor even more unlikely. The French term is used in a number of syntactic and lexical variations. The term *marier*, 'to wed', can be used in the sense of linking up business partners as in the case of self-employed persons working for different companies:

> *Freelance.com* **marie** *indépendants et entreprises*
> (Freelance.com **forges links** between the freelance and company sectors)

The idea of creating a link in business via the marriage metaphor is also used in French with the preliminary stage of 'flirting' which may lead to marriage, as in the following example:

> *C'est ici que l'Icann sort de son rôle technique pour venir **flirter** avec le marketing, la culture, la politique*
> (In this case, Icann leaves its technical expertise to one side and **tries its hand** in the marketing, cultural and political fields)

The metaphor has no exact cross-language equivalence in English in this context, another expression would fit better in English such as 'to try its hand'.

The following passage, with a direct translation of the marriage metaphors, illustrates the number of expressions which may develop from the core metaphor concept:

> *Accueillant, Michel Pébereau offre aux dirigeants des banques **'un repas de mariage'**. La banque dirigée par Michel Pébereau veut éviter, pour **réussir son mariage**, de commettre les mêmes maladresses que les équipes de la Société générale . . . Ayant tourné, non sans regrets, la page de son projet de **mariage à trois**, la BNP concentre ses forces sur la réussite de la fusion avec Paribas*
> (As a welcoming gesture, Michel Pébereau invited the bank managers to a **'wedding feast'**. In order to **make a success of its marriage**, the bank's manager, Michel Pébereau, wants to avoid making the same mistakes made by the staff at the Société Générale . . . Having turned the page, not without some regrets, in connection with his project involving a **three-way marriage**, the BNP is concentrating its energy on making a success of its merger with Paribas)

Once the chain of expressions related to the core concept of marriage has started, it is easy to create new metaphoric structures in the same context which would be increasingly difficult to translate literally if the beginning of the chain does not fit into the target language. In English, the translator would probably have to opt for a neutral expression in the first link by translating the 'wedding feast' metaphor with a paraphrase such as 'an invitation to a business lunch marking the beginning of a new partnership'. The marriage metaphor is therefore firmly established in French but would sound strange in English in certain contexts. For example:

> *George Bush et 'Schwarzy' ont fait un **'bon mariage'***
> George Bush and 'Schwarzy' made a **good marriage**

referring to the political affiliation between the President of the United States and Arnold Schwarzenegger who was elected Governor of California.

7. Divorce

As a follow-on to the marriage concept, the symbol of divorce is also very common in business texts:

> N'est-ce pas lié à une volonté de se développer rapidement après le **divorce** d'Andersen Consulting et les fusions annoncées par vos concurrents?
> (Isn't it due to the fact that they wished to expand quickly after the **split** between Andersen Consulting and the mergers announced by your competitors?)

Although this metaphor has been found in the English press, it is a rare one and would probably require another more general term such as 'split'. The presence of the DIVORCE metaphor in this context is also probably due to the fact that it is well-established in French in a number of similar contexts referring to politics and institutions in general:

> La gauche et les artistes: histoire d'un **divorce**
> (Artists and the left: a case of **splitting up**)

> Les textes proposés aggraveront . . . le **divorce** entre le pays et ses institutions
> (The proposed texts will worsen . . . the **split** between the country and its institutions)

In the latter example, other translations of 'divorce' could obviously be used according to the style of the text, such as 'divide', 'gulf' and so on which might also fit in better with a verb like 'to worsen'.

8. Death

Finally, the core concept of death terminates the family relationship in business with French terms such as *mort* (dead) as in the following example of the television channel Canal+ restructuring its workforce. Although the death symbol could perhaps be used in translation, other renderings may stylistically be better:

> La vieille garde de Canal+ sera donc **morte comme elle a vécu**
> (The old guard of Canal+ will then **disappear as it has come** = 'be dead as it has lived')

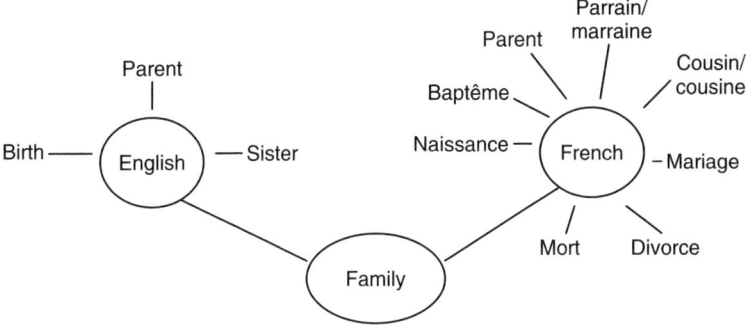

Figure 4.4 Predominance in cross-language networking patterns

Figure 4.4 shows that the network has a pattern in which secondary clusters develop from the core concept of the family image, such as parent, sister and so on. These secondary clusters may represent the actual linguistic item, as in 'parent company', or form another base concept to which related linguistic items are linked, as in French *'mariage'* or *'baptême'*. The former has produced the linguistic items of *mariage à trois, repas de mariage* and so on, the latter *baptême du feu, fonts baptismaux* and so on.

Although French and English share a large number of metaphoric concepts in the family network, the model appears to be more entrenched in French. To fully understand why this is the case, a diachronic analysis is essential to investigate where the differences are coming from. Recent studies on cross-language equivalence suggest that the time dimension highlights the patterns of changing semantic components of closely-related concepts. This can give the translator greater insight into a multitude of senses present in two synchronic cross-language terms, as in the case of cognates (Dury, 1999: 485–6).

Our investigations so far have shown that metaphor networking, from a synchronic point of view, is governed by universal trends and cultural-specific patterns. The first unifies cross-language models, the second encourages divergence. The synchronic aspect, however, only tells half the story with regard to how networks are created. We also need to go back into the past to find out how and why these patterns have taken on their current forms. We shall now start exploring the time dimension to see how networking evolves in relation to the universal/cultural divide.

Part II
The Diachronic Dimension

5
Cultural Patterns of the Past

5.1 New perspectives from a diachronic viewpoint

If we look at a range of mountains or a field strewn with large pebbles, we cannot really understand why the mountains are there or have a certain shape, or why all the pebbles happen to be in the field, unless we go back into the past. Only the past geology of the rock formations will give us a clear idea as to why such landscape features exist. In many ways, the same applies to language and, in particular to metaphor. In this chapter, we shall look at how cultural metaphor models may fluctuate in the past in one language and, using the illustration of the BUSINESS CORPORATION = FAMILY model outlined in the previous chapter, consider how they may fluctuate from a cross-linguistic viewpoint. This can help explain how even closely related languages may diverge or converge and can account for synchronic variation. At the same time, we are able to see how many of our present-day metaphors are networked to the past with the same images. The diachronic perspective is able to explore the origins of our conceptualisation.

The historical dimension is also an important one as it can often uncover unexpected findings or hypotheses on the origins of long-term models. The discussion in Chapter 3 on Geeraerts and Grondelaers's (1995) debate about the historical influence of humoral theory on cultural aspects of the anger model is a case in point. A purely synchronic analysis may take certain aspects for granted but a diachronic approach invites us to reflect on the wider issues of the universal/cultural divide.

In Chapter 3, we also mentioned the name of Whorf and his claims that language influences thought processes. Some of these claims were in fact based on his own historical research. Whether there is some truth in this hypothesis or not, it leads to some interesting views on our subject of the historical evolution of metaphor. Whorf (1950) proposed a number of theories on pathways of evolution.

First, he made some (rather wide) claims on differences between what he called SAE languages ('Standard Average European'), in which he appeared to include non-Indo-European languages in Europe, as well as the North American Indian language of Hopi which formed a major part of his linguistic research. Metaphoric trends in SAE are from spatial to non-spatial, or 'objective' to 'subjective', a movement which began in Ancient Hebrew and Latin, for example *educo* (to lead out), *religio* (to tie back), and set the trend for later languages. The language-culture partnership 'limits free plasticity and rigidifies channels of development in the more autocratic way' (1956: 156). In Hopi, on the other hand, the reverse trend of objective/subjective can take place with the concept 'heart' representing a late formation from a root meaning of think or remember.

Whorf's theories are very speculative, particularly as he described the heart concept as a late formation and then claimed that we would find a different type of language in Hopi history, *if we could read it*. The lack of written historical evidence makes such theories difficult to substantiate. However, he did make one important claim: there are channels of metaphoric development along the diachronic scale, even though these would not be considered rigid today. To what extent linguistic labels given to metaphors influence the continuation of metaphor paths is not clear. Certain aspects of Whorf's claim that language influences cognition have been supported to a limited extent in empirical research. It has been shown that linguistic differences can affect performance in choosing which sets of colours are most differentiated (Kay and Kempton, 1984). Likewise, in the case of learning a language, many linguists and anthropologists might support the hypothesis that learning a word for a culturally important category can linguistically reinforce the learning of the category itself (Sweetser, 1990: 7). This would suggest that each language is likely to follow similar patterns of metaphor creation based on lexical categories linked to the language's culture.

5.2 Diachronic cultural patterns

It is quite clear, however, that culture can also influence linguistic structures as far as metaphor is concerned, a fact which can also be substantiated if a diachronic perspective is taken into account. It could be stated that cultural variation can be seen synchronically across cultures and diachronically within a single culture. As Draaisma puts it: 'metaphors as literary-scientific constructs are also reflections of an age, a culture, an ambience. Metaphors express the activities and preoccupations of their authors.' He goes on to say that 'metaphors are guide fossils, they help the reader to estimate the age of the text in which he finds them' (2000: 4). The changing historical role of culture in metaphor creation can be seen in a study carried out by Smith et al. who analysed conceptual categories underlying figurative usage in American English from 1675 to 1975 (1981: 911–35). They concluded in a study of twenty-four American authors during this time period that different cultural domains correlate with varying degrees of metaphoric activity through time. Their investigation revealed, for example, that the domain of religion as a source of metaphor (labelled social aspects in their study) has steadily declined in American literature since the seventeenth century, whereas the domain of nature (the natural environment) reached its highest level of activity in the twentieth century.

The percentage of categories was based on analysis of six source domains – psychological, body, cultural, qualities (including general objects, space and time), nature and social aspects. These were compared along the time axis, broken into six historical periods, between 1675 and 1975.

It appears that the significance of metaphors in social/religious life, for example, played an important part in the beginnings of American literature, while nature took on a major role in the later works of writers such as Cooper, Emerson, Twain, Frost and Hemingway. These writers questioned human relationships to natural events and objects, following the period of westward expansion in the nineteenth century which involved coming to grips with the American wilderness. Early writers such as Matthews, Bradstreet, Edwards and Franklin, living in settled parts of the New World such as Boston and Philadelphia, did not have to come to terms with nature to this extent and therefore turned to the more dominant religious issues of the time (Smith et al., 1981: 933–4). The role of philosophical, social, religious and environmental issues have therefore played a major role in forming the trends of metaphor paths.

Such diachronic paths apparently have their own cultural 'energy' as regards establishing and maintaining metaphor models over a considerable period of time. Cross-language patterns vary since one language/culture may embody a base conceptual metaphor in the conceptual thought processes of the language's speakers to a greater extent than the speakers of another language. To investigate the reasons why one language has a predominance of conceptual or lexical metaphors while another may not, a search into the past can reveal some valuable information as to variational distribution in cross-linguistic patterns. A starting-point in this avenue of research would be to have a closer look at the data of the family model in the preceding chapter and to examine the language history of the items involved.

5.3 Cultural history of the BUSINESS CORPORATION = FAMILY model

Unequal distribution or language-specific lexical metaphors in a shared model are often due to a diachronic conceptual networking process which depends ultimately on cultural and historical aspects of the languages involved. In the case of English and French, the two languages have, for centuries, shared the same metaphoric projections about family relationships symbolising different types of links. However, it appears that French has retained many of the links which English has lost. This can be demonstrated by examining dictionary attestations of a selection of four of the models in the network described above: the baptism, marriage, divorce and godparent metaphors.

In all four models, attestations reveal a close link between the two languages with regard to underlying core concepts, particularly in the early stages of their evolution, with minor fluctuations in linked lexical items. In more recent times, there has tended to be more substantial divergence. In all cases, it can be seen that historically there has been a weakening in the English models which has been responsible for divergence in cross-language equivalence.

The underlying concept of baptism conveying the sense of a new start is portrayed in the religious ceremony of 'immersing a person in water, or application of water by pouring or sprinkling, as a religious rite, symbolical of moral or spiritual purification or, (Christianity), initiation into the Church', attested in texts dating back to the Middle Ages (*Oxford English Dictionary – OED*). The start thus refers to entry into a new spiritual world and was extended in the cultures of both languages to the blessing and naming of ships and bells during the sixteenth century: 'They upon their foundation have builded the **baptism of bells and ships**' (attest. 1585 – OED). In addition to other expressions which were added in French through the course of time, for example, *baptiser du vin/lait*, 'to baptise wine/milk', with the sense of adding water to wine or milk (*Grand Larousse de la langue française – GRL*), both languages subsequently developed the sense of entering martyrdom: '**the baptism of blood in martyrdom**' (attest. 1860 – OED) and *baptême du sang* 'baptism of blood' (attest. 1704 – *Dictionnaire historique de la langue française – DHLF*). In this case, water is symbolically replaced by blood.

It appears that the nineteenth century witnessed the first major lexical split in the underlying model. An interesting dictionary attestation using coincidentally both the terms 'maiden' and 'baptism' show that the former is used in the sense of 'young', 'early', 'first': 'those maiden showers which by the peepe of day do strew a **baptime o'er the flowers**' (attest. 1860 – *OED*). By the early twentieth century, the term 'maiden' was being used in expressions such as 'maiden voyage', 'maiden flight'. In French, however, the term *baptême* continued to be used in this sense, such as *baptême de l'air*, 'maiden flight', and extended to *baptême du feu*, 'baptism of fire', which has been used in literary texts in English, but would not fit into modern economic contexts. It appears that not only did lexical divergence occur, the connotation of baptism was slowly dropped in modern English texts and replaced by more neutral terms such as 'inauguration' or 'new start' as highlighted in the examples above. This model thus demonstrates a strong cultural bond between the two languages historically, but one which has weakened in English through time.

The same process appears to have occurred in the MARRIAGE = MERGER model. Apart from the religious partnership of two people, there has historically been a strong link with a core concept of marriage 'uniting intimately or joining closely or permanently' (*OED*). Figurative extensions of this kind are attested in English from the sixteenth century onwards: 'the natures of men are so moved, nay rather **married to novelties**' (attest. 1576 – *OED*). The idea of uniting human qualities or notions of perception is also attested in French during the seventeenth century with examples such as: *marier des couleurs qui s'harmonisent*, 'marry colours in harmony' (attest. 1672 – *GRL*). More specific conceptualisation processes took place in both languages with the idea of 'joining two entities'; in the nineteenth century it was used in nautical terminology in English (*OED*) with the sense of fastening two ropes end to end, 'to **marry two ropes**', and to moor a boat in French (*DHLF*). Despite the close cultural link, the marriage metaphors described above show that there has been considerable contextual divergence between the two languages in present-day business texts. For example, mergers between companies are not normally considered in terms of marriage in English today, suggesting that there is also a weakening in this metaphor model.

One variation on the previous two models is that the history of the divorce metaphor incorporates a basic difference in contextual use of metaphors right from the beginning. Although English and French have long shared the notion of splitting two entities, English has always used this figurative extension in relation to mental qualities and has not included the idea of dividing physical entities or groups. In the sixteenth century, the English model was used in the sense of 'divorcing doubts' (attest. 1592) or '**divorcing terror** from one's heart' (attest. 1593 – *OED*). This contextual use is mirrored by French: *il y a divorce entre la théorie et* *la pratique, entre les intentions et les résultats*, 'there is a divorce between theory and practice, between intentions and results' (*GRL*). The evidence suggests that both languages maintained this line of evolution for several centuries until the present day. However, French has also developed the sense of splitting two physical entities or institutions, very common in modern texts, which has not occurred in English: *il est en train de se produire entre le service postal et le public un divorce grave*, 'a serious split is taking place between the postal service and the public' (attest. 1969 – *GRL*).

The godfather metaphor is another example of a model which has close cultural ties between the two languages but has undergone considerable differences in the latter half of the model's history. Apart from the original link of a 'male sponsor considered in relation to his god-child' (*OED*), figurative extensions can be found in both languages, probably via cultural transfer, such as a 'godfather' being 'an attendant to a knight in tournament' in the Middle Ages. Likewise, the person conducting the baptism of a bell was also known as the godfather.

From the sixteenth century onwards, each language employed different usages of the term specific to their own language, but related conceptually to existing metaphors. Thus, in English, the term was used for attendants to persons condemned to death by the Inquisition and, in jocular use, it was employed by Shakespeare in the sense of jurymen whose verdict brings a person to the gallows: 'In christning thou shalt haue two godfathers, Had I been judge, thou shouldst haue ten more, To bring thee to the gallows, not to the font' (attest. 1596, *The Merchant of Venice* – *OED*). In French, the metaphor was used during the sixteenth century for a person who dedicated his name to a particular piece of work, and from the eighteenth century onwards, it was used to designate a person who introduced a new member into a scientific or literary circle, including the Académie Française (attest. 1866 – *DHLF, GRL*).

In more recent times, a 'godfather' came to be known in both languages as the head of a Mafia clan, but the French language also branched out into a number of related concepts with the sense of promoting an idea, an organisation, a company and so on. It appears that the term was originally introduced just before the Second World War to substitute the English lexical item for the new concept 'sponsor' from the United States. Although in free variation with the English loanword *sponsor* today, the French term *parrain* is firmly entrenched, with a number of syntactic variations such as *parrainage*, 'sponsorship', described above, and *parrainer*, 'to sponsor'. The cultural choice of the term 'sponsor' in English (from Latin *spondere*, 'to promise solemnly') is speculative. The particularly pejorative usage of 'godfather' for the American mafia may have blocked the continuation of this metaphor in the business world. French seems likely to use the two terms in free variation for some time to come because of the firmly entrenched godfather model on the one hand, and the strong influence of English on the other.

Synchronic cross-language equivalence is thus modelled on processes of diachronic fluctuation which demonstrate a number of trends. The major trend influencing this model is diachronic divergence. The 'conceptual building block' of the BAPTISM = START projection contains shared concepts which remain similar until the eighteenth century. From the nineteenth century on, English used the term 'maiden' to substitute French *baptême de l'air* and so on, and certain non-metaphoric concepts are probably more suitable in many modern business contexts. In the MARRIAGE = MERGER model, the shared paths of 'harmony or joining two entities' in the sixteenth and seventeenth centuries led to a split later on in business contexts in the twentieth century whereby business corporations in the English-speaking world tend not to use the term 'marry' as in French. Parallel to this trend, divergence took place in the DIVORCE = SPLIT model whereby the two languages shared the idea of divorcing concepts as in the field of mental faculties, according to sixteenth-century attestations. However, English does not employ the same divorce collocations as French in the case of modern institutions or companies. A major trend of divergence can also be found in the GODFATHER = SPONSOR model in which French has widely used the godfather metaphor for business corporations to substitute the English-speaking cultural innovation 'sponsor'.

The main hypothesis accounting for divergence appears to be that conceptual networking of these metaphors has had a stronger hold in French. The cultural reasons are speculative but there is always the logical deduction that societies with a stronger cultural influence in a particular area will also have more influence on the metaphoric aspects of the language. It may have been the case that France – as appears to be the case in other countries with Latin languages, such as Italy and Spain – has maintained a social system of more closely-knit families together with a stronger influence of Roman Catholicism which, in turn, has reinforced religious and family metaphors. Certainly, a perusal of present-day religious metaphors in dictionary attestations suggests that they are more predominant in Italian and Spanish than in English.

Different cultural reasons are also responsible for the opposite trend of convergence, which is much rarer in this model. Cultural contact is an obvious one and is likely in the example of the 'marrying of two ropes' in English and 'mooring a boat' in French in the nineteenth century.

It may be the case that similar social processes operate within the societies of different languages and reinforce the same patterns, either by increasing or decreasing metaphoric output and contributing to convergence. Similarly, historical changes can lead to obsolescence, and thus convergence, in languages, such as a godfather being represented as an attendant to a knight or an attendant at the gallows.

We can thus conclude that, although there is a shared underlying concept of the family, with its beginning and end in the form of birth and death, actual linguistic metaphors in the languages themselves vary. Usage of family metaphors not only differs between the languages concerned, equivalence in type and frequency varies through time. The dominant trend of cross-language divergence is responsible for this diachronic process, resulting in a pattern of lower distribution in English.

It would therefore seem that there are ongoing patterns of metaphor creation. Evidence for the linking up of different historical periods can be seen in a number of different features. These allow us to lay the foundations of diachronic networking theory in metaphor paths. Before looking at this aspect in more detail, we need to explore in more depth the role of polysemous structures in chaining processes which can give us an insight into how regular patterns emerge in metaphor evolution.

6
Metaphor and Semantic Networks

6.1 Semantic fields and polysemy in meaning change

A central issue involved in ongoing diachronic networking systems will be discussed here: the feature of regularity with regard to semantic fields and polysemy. Recent research into semantic change has shown that the implication of metaphorisation in diachronic conceptual and meaning changes tends to follow regular patterns. One aspect of this research suggests that recurrent meaning extension is a common feature in the history of languages. It is likely that certain kinds of meaning extension are more frequent, more typical and more natural than others (Taylor, 1989: 121). In Chapter 1 we have seen that metaphor extension in phraseological units is a common feature in modern English. If we go back into three different periods of English such as Old English, Middle English and Early Modern English, they all show examples of this feature (Naciscione, 2004).

The role of semantic fields and polysemy is important to our understanding of meaning change and forms a fundamental part of theories on diachronic semantics today. One of the first linguists to develop semantic field theory was Trier (1931) who made the important point that semantic change affects semantic fields. He introduced a crucial element into diachronic semantics but the main problem with his theories was that they were developed before the notion of fuzzy boundaries in semantic categories. He viewed boundaries as rigid phenomena with no overlapping or accounting for polysemy. One of his main examples was the concept of knowledge in Middle High German and its changes in semantic fields between 1200 and 1300 (Figure 6.1).

Trier showed that the term *Wîsheit* was a general term for knowledge around 1200, representing a superordinate category with two subordinate categories of *Kunst* (courtly knowledge) and *List* (knowledge of

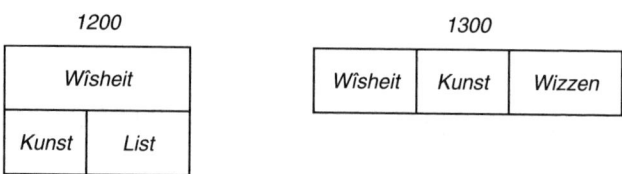

Figure 6.1 Trier's semantic field theory
Source: After Trier (1931).

technical skills). By 1300, the meaning of *Wîsheit* had narrowed to the sense of 'religious or mystical knowledge'. *Kunst* changed meaning to simply mundane skills and knowledge, replacing *List*, and the new lexical item *Wizzen* (knowledge of the artistic field) moved in. The result was three categories of knowledge of equal status.

It is often claimed, however, that semantic change cannot in fact be studied without drawing on a theory of polysemy because of the nature of the change. Where there is a synchronic sense relationship, there is usually a historical relationship (Traugott and Dasher, 2002: 11–13). As Ricoeur (1978: 122–3) puts it:

> despite every effort at partitioning description and history, the very description of polysemy makes reference to the possibility of semantic change. Polysemy as such, that is, regarded apart from consideration of its 'sources', refers to possibilities of a diachronistic character: polysemy is simply the possibility of adding a new meaning to the previous acceptations of the word without having these former meanings disappear. Thus the open structure of the word, its elasticity, its fluidity, already allude to the phenomenon of change of meaning.

Before looking further into the role of semantic fields in diachrony, it would therefore be useful to first look at some structural aspects of polysemy.

6.2 Vagueness and ambiguity

A basic definition of polysemy is given by Taylor (1989: 99): 'a monosemous lexical item has a single sense, while polysemy is the association of two or more related senses with a single linguistic form'. This is straightforward as a definition but other factors play a part which make the issue much more complex. Distinguishing between monosemy and polysemy is not always that easy. In line with prototype theory, some meanings can be more central than others and this implies that there can be fuzzy edges between semantic categories.

Furthermore, it is not always clear which meaning is the most central. To cite an example given by Taylor (1989: 100) with regard to the core concept MOTHER, an item we have discussed already with regard to radial chaining of literal and figurative meaning: can 'mother' have two or more core senses? One type of mother, for example, may be the natural, birth-mother of a child who has been adopted by someone else who, in turn, becomes the adoptive, nurturing mother. Are they both the child's mother? Is one 'more' the mother than the other?

Analyses of dictionary entries often show that there is a clear hierarchical ordering in polysemy. In an analysis of prototypical polysemy in the Dutch item *vers* (fresh) with regard to literal meaning, Geeraerts (1990: 195–210) suggests that up to twenty-one overlapping meanings may be ordered in a centralised to peripheral pattern, as attested in the *Woordenboek der Nederlandsche Taal* (*Dictionary of the Dutch Language*), the equivalent of the *Oxford English Dictionary*. Meanings roughly correspond to English definitions except for the sense of 'moderately cool' which is absent from Dutch *vers*. Meanings thus range from the first (centralised) dictionary entry: 'With regard to foodstuffs: recently produced and hence optimal for consumption as far as taste and nutritive value are concerned; recently harvested, caught, prepared, etc., and hence not yet subject to decay' to the peripheral, vaguer definition at the bottom of the hierarchy: 'Recently present or available in a particular context, in contrast with other things that are mentioned or implied in the context, though regardless of inherent newness.'

Vague, peripheral meanings such as these bring us to the problem of distinguishing between vagueness and ambiguity. A number of ambiguity tests have been devised to try and disambiguate polysemous structures but the problem remains that these tests can themselves involve ambiguity. A lot depends on individual contexts and it is difficult to give clear-cut definitions. Taylor (1989: 101–2) gives some examples of these ambiguity tests. The main feature of an ambiguous sentence is that it has more than one interpretation, for example, *there is a pig in the house* meaning either a 'farmyard animal' or the metaphoric 'gluttonous person'. Ambiguity can also arise in coordinated sentences such as: *Arthur and his driving licence expired last Thursday*. The verb *expire* must be ambiguous here, a driving licence cannot expire in the same way as a human being. A third test relates to anaphoric expressions using *do so*. Here the definition of meaning can be vague: *I saw a bird in the garden, and so did Jane.*

The exact meaning of the item *bird* is not clear because I could have seen a bird like a robin but Jane may have seen a completely different species like an ostrich.

Whatever theoretical examples may be devised to test ambiguity, it can be seen that there are examples which point to the fact that the boundary between monosemy and polysemy can be fuzzy, as can be the borderline between semantic fields. A more realistic distinction between different senses is one which resembles a continuum, rather than a distinct line (Cruse, 1986: 71).

Linguists writing before the arrival of cognitive linguistics were also well aware of this problem of vagueness as embodied by polysemy. In his discussions of Ullman's (1962) works on semantic change, Ricoeur points out the fact that a very general characteristic of language is the notion of *vagueness*, a term also used by Ullman to indicate the slight degree to which the lexical organisation of language is systematic. Ricoeur's view is that vagueness should not be understood in terms of a taxonomic order, but rather in a 'generic' sense which requires further definition on the basis of contextual features. The suggestion is therefore that vagueness, as an imprecise and indefinite notion, is not ordered. Most words in our ordinary language appear to correspond to this feature and to the idea that polysemy is a more ordered characteristic of a general phenomenon of lexical imprecision (Ricoeur, 1978: 113–14).

The feature of overlapping semantic fields may also be seen in what Ricoeur terms the opposite of polysemy: that is, synonymy. The former refers to several senses for one name and the latter to several names for one sense. Synonymy implies a partial semantic identity which results in the overlapping of semantic boundaries; the acceptation of one word is synonymous with the acceptation of another word: 'The image of paving tiles or of a mosaic is deceptive in this regard: words are not just distinct from one another, that is, defined only by their opposition to other words, as are phonemes in a phonological system; they also trespass on one another' (1978: 114).

The multiple facets of polysemy thus illustrate how meaning definitions cannot be confined to watertight compartments of clearly-defined semantic fields. The more recent approach of prototype gradation regarding centralised and peripheral meanings are also reflected in the different types of polysemes which are created in figurative networks. All polysemes of a network derive from a common conceptual source but tend to diverge in different but related directions. We shall now apply this model of prototype polysemy to the origin of networks.

6.3 Centralised meaning in metaphor networks

The idea of a central or core semantic origin in the mapping of polysemous metaphors can be seen in the metaphor network of the concept DRYNESS. This will be discussed in more detail below; suffice it to say that the large number of figurative polysemes found in this concept can be postulated as being traceable to a common denominator of DRYNESS = DEFICIENCY. In some cases, the more peripheral meanings in the network require a little more interpretative flexibility to match up with the core concept but it may be postulated that the polysemes were originally associated with this particular centralised concept. We shall see that the lack of a liquid is more centralised in a metaphor such as 'a dry area' = 'no alcohol sold' compared to another cluster involving 'a lack of interest' as in the metaphor 'a dry subject' = 'dull'.

Furthermore, polysemous items of metaphor networks cross the boundaries of language and culture. Comparisons of different languages reveal that many polysemes are shared from a common core concept. However, some may be different, and if they are used in another language, they may lead to misunderstanding or wrong interpretations. For example, if the expression 'he drives drily' was used in English from French *il conduit d'une manière sèche* (he drives in a fast and abrupt way), it may not be easily understood, even though the two languages ultimately share the base conceptual metaphor.

Prototype gradation in figurative polysemy thus shows there is a systematic ordering of attributes. These may be more or less central to the core mapping process, and may form secondary clusters, but all are linked to a central conceptual metaphor. At this stage, it should be pointed out that not all polysemy structures are systematic. There are areas in which polysemy reveals random features. Such is the case of homonymy.

6.4 Random polysemous features

It is clear that the origins of linguistic forms are complex and the combination of meanings attributed to them may vary considerably. We shall see below that polysemes are usually related in some form or other, especially when historical links are considered. Homonyms, however, represent features having unrelated meanings attached to the same linguistic (that is, phonological) form. According to Ricoeur, the case of homonymy has to be set apart from polysemy. Although homonymy and polysemy have the same principle regarding the combination, in Saussurean terms, of a single signifier with more than one signified, the former refers to the difference between two words and their entire semantic fields while the latter refers to a single word and its semantic variations. Although some homonyms may be relatively easy to trace from an etymological point of view, many semantic homonyms present a real problem in this respect. The divergent evolution of senses of words often reaches a point at which it is no longer possible to discern a correspondence of meaning (1978: 114).

Taylor (1989: 103) illustrates some homonymous differences with the following examples: the *neck* of a human being and the *neck* of a bottle are semantically related due to an original metaphoric extension. One could imagine intuitively that this would be the case. On the other hand, it would be difficult to imagine the link between the two meanings of 'die', which appear conceptually far apart. The meaning representing 'the end of one's life' comes, in fact, from Old English *diegan*, and the 'cube thrown in games of chance' is an original loanword from Old French *dé*. This is therefore a clear case of homonymy and should be distinguished from the contrasting example of the polyseme 'neck'.

The distinction between polysemy and homonymy, however, is not so clear in other pairs. Taylor raises this point with the items *eye* ('organ of sight' and 'aperture in a needle') and *ear* ('organ of hearing' and the 'grain-holding part of a cereal plant'). Research into the etymology of these two words reveals that the former is, in fact, a case of polysemy and the latter homonymy. The former involves metaphoric extension and the latter is derived from two distinct words in Old English. On the one hand, this observation may appear to be of no importance since the average speaker would not be aware of the historical background to these words. However, as Taylor points out, the distinction is important as far as motivated, polysemous categories are concerned. The distinction becomes clear in cross-language comparison. Homonymy tends to be accidental and therefore particularly language-specific. Polysemous categories are not accidental and point to trends in the formation of ongoing chained categories.

As Ricoeur (1978: 120) suggests, 'association is the guiding thread' in the study of metaphor and his ideas also reflect in many ways those of prototype polysemy:

> The innumerable borrowings that metaphor brings into play can indeed be assembled into broad classes that are themselves divided up according to which associations are the most typical, that is, the most usual; associations not only between senses, but between domains of sense, for example that of the human body and that of physical objects. Hence we again come upon the broad classes of Fontanier, where pride of

place is held by the transposition of the animate to the inanimate and, less frequently, of the inanimate to the animate. Transposition from the concrete to the abstract forms another large group.

The claim that polysemous categories contribute to the formation of ongoing chained categories is an important one as far as regularity in change is concerned. One polyseme sets the trend for the creation of subsequent polysemes. In certain rare situations which do not represent the norm, homonymy may not actually be random either. Traugott and Dasher (2002: 11–13) illustrate how convergent diachronic homonymy may pass through a stage of reinterpretation.

They give the example of the English homonym *lap* with regard to dictionary entries of two of its polysemes: 'to place or lay something so as to overlap another' and 'to take in a liquid with the tongue'. The first is from Old English *lapa* ('part of an outer garment which hangs down' – *OED*) and the second from OE *lapian*. In the nineteenth century, however, *lap* ('to take in a liquid with the tongue') was extended to mean 'to wash against with a slapping sound'. It could be construed here that some speakers felt them to be related since lapping waves not only involve water and slapping sounds but also visual overlap as in one wave flowing over another. In most cases, however, homonymy does not involve systematic change and should be clearly distinguished from systematic features of polysemy.

6.5 Chronological polysemy in diachronic change

Most words actually do have more than one meaning and semantic change usually passes through a transitional stage of polysemy which, in some cases, may last a very long time. If we take some traditional approaches to semantic change, such as Ullman's (1957) principles of semantic change by replacement, generalisation, narrowing, amelioration, pejoration and euphemisms, we can observe that polysemy is usually involved. Generalisation automatically involves polysemy in the same way as narrowing. Polysemy must also be involved in the other processes.

If the first example of semantic change involving replacement is taken into consideration, it can be seen from its etymology that the English word *bureau* went through the following chronological shifts: (a) a coarse, woollen cloth (twelfth century); (b) a cloth covering tables (thirteenth century); (c) a counting table (fourteenth century); (d) a writing table (fifteenth–sixteenth centuries); (e) a room containing a writing table (seventeenth–twentieth centuries); and (f) a department or agency, as in the Federal Bureau of Investigation (twentieth–twenty-first centuries). It is highly likely that these changes did not occur overnight and that both old and new meanings were used for some time before the new meanings entirely replaced the old ones. If we thus formulate a usual case of diachronic polysemy, item (a) first exists on its own, it is then joined by polyseme (b) for a certain period of time and then polyseme (a) is ousted by the new meaning. We can then have a chain reaction of shifts as follows: (a) > a + b > b > b + c > c, and so on.

We rarely know how long the period of polysemy lasts, but we can often see the historical links. For example, a case of pejoration would be the item 'awful' which originally meant 'magnificent'. The former sense was 'full of awe' and since today the word 'awe' by itself means 'wonder', we are able to comprehend the positive aspect of the former sense which subsequently became pejorative in the modern English sense of 'terrible'. Exercises in etymology can often discover the historical links in cases of pejoration. Thus, it is reported that King James II (ruled 1685–88) described the new St Paul's Cathedral in London as 'amusing, awful and artificial' (Culpeper, 1997: 38). In modern English, this would certainly not sound like a compliment to the architect. 'To amuse' formerly had the sense of 'capturing one's attention' and 'artificial' the sense of 'displaying art'. Explorations into semantic roots reveal that 'to amuse', linked to 'muse', signifies 'to be absorbed in thought', hence King James's meaning of 'capturing his attention'. 'Artificial', relating to the same roots as 'artefact', originates in the meaning of 'making art', and this again would explain the seventeenth-century sense.

These different meanings undoubtedly went through stages of polysemy of positive and negative values. The same can be seen in the meaning of modern French *terrible* which can have both the English meaning of 'terrible' or also the (more colloquial) meaning of 'marvellous', according to the context. Dictionary attestations reveal that this state of polysemy has lasted for at least four centuries. This is however, a different situation to irony, whereby an opposite value is used that does not constitute a standard attribute, for example, 'that's great!', used ironically to mean 'that's terrible!' Although irony could be used, the French item is an example of standard, non-ironical polysemy using positive and negative values.

Ullman's categories are useful if we wish to have an overview of what semantic changes are possible, but they are unable to hypothesise trends and why these take place. A new approach is to look at how regular changes actually operate in history due to the role of polysemy in the mapping of semantic fields. When a metaphor is created, polysemy comes into play. For example, a literal meaning A gives rise to a polysemous meaning B. There is an obvious link between the two which involves specific lines of direction in the mapping of the two meanings. This process is going on all the time and, if we look back at the past, the same chaining processes have always been in operation.

6.6 Regularity in change

It is clear from the evolution of polysemous structures in metaphoric mapping that there are regular patterns in their evolution. As Sweetser claims (1990: 9–19), the mass of metaphorically structured polysemy data and the systematic metaphorical connections between domains need to be analysed to understand the feature of regularity in diachronic semantics. If an intervening stage of polysemous relationships occurs in semantic change, the historical data involved in establishing polysemous patterns can provide an invaluable source of information on the cognitive structure of language. The historical order of sense-changes in polysemy can also provide information on the direction of change; for example, spatial vocabulary tends to acquire temporal meanings rather than the reverse.

With regard to the relationship between domains, Sweetser suggests, on the basis of historical mappings of metaphors, that a semantic field such as physical-domain verbs frequently become speech-act and/or mental-state meanings, and mental-state verbs come to have speech-act meanings, while the opposite directions of change do not occur. Second, the unidirectionality of these shifts (discussed in more detail below) might be explained by the inherent unidirectionality of metaphorical connections. Third, two overlapping but distinct systems of metaphors connect the vocabulary of physical action/motion/location with the domains of mental states and speech acts. The latter can be illustrated by the example 'I think I'm *getting somewhere* with that problem': the mental state/speech act 'I think' is linked to the domain of physical location.

In specific areas of lexis, it has been shown that there are strong links between the meanings of words in the case of languages which have a systematic use of the same vocabulary for root and epistemic modality. With regard to Indo-European, there are closely-linked classes of senses which follow non-arbitrary patterns of meaning extension. Such is the case of the verb *see* that can also mean 'know' or 'understand' as in the sentence 'I see what you're getting at' (Sweetser, 1990: 3–5). The argument is that the metaphor UNDERSTANDING = SEEING represents a logical semantic equation in the conceptualisation of our environment. The aspect of vision is an important one in our ability to operate successfully in our immediate surroundings. This 'logical' equation would explain why other verbs, such as *kick* or *sit*, or even other sensory verbs such as *smell*, are not used to express knowledge and understanding. Sight, perhaps even more so today in a society of television and computer screens, is a very important means of perceiving and acquiring knowledge in the human being – in contrast to other living creatures.

If we examine certain aspects of verbs of sensory perception such as seeing and hearing as discussed by Sweetser, their common evolution of meanings follows definite trends. Other sensory perception verbs – such as smell, taste and touch – are generally slightly less well-defined but do tend to follow a trend that indicates how a person feels: *it smells of a plot, it's not to my taste, it was very touching*, and so on. In the case of 'seeing', perception can be split up into sight and vision, while hearing develops towards heeding or obeying.

(1a) Physical sight ⇒ knowledge, intellection
(1b) Physical vision ⇒ mental 'vision'
(2) Hearing ⇒ listen, heed, obey

In (1a), physical sight stems from I-E **weid-* 'see' from which Greek *eîdon* and Latin *video*, 'see' have evolved. The metaphoric extension of knowledge or intellection can be seen in the English words *idea* and *wise*. A parallel in other I-E branches includes Celtic *fios* (Irish Gaelic), with the sense of knowledge. Buck (1949: 1041) suggests that the meaning 'know' is probably a secondary development which started in the perfective form of ancient languages such as Greek *oîda*, Gothic *wait* and Sanskrit *veda*, meaning to 'have seen'. This subsequently developed into the sense of 'know'.

Physical sight words in English have often evolved from Latin *spec-* and *vid-* roots. These include words in the physical domain such as *inspect, spectator, survey, view* and *vision*. Their etymologies have thus taken the following paths:

I-E * *spek'* > Lat. *specere, -spicere* 'look' > Eng. *inspect*
I-E * *weid-* > Lat. *videre* 'see' > Eng. *view*

In (1b), mental vision can be distinguished from the physical sight group in that metaphoric extension involves the focus on one stimulus among many others and the ability to monitor stimuli mentally and visually. This group has led to substantial lexical compounding with mental vision analogous to physical sight in its metaphorical origins. The future is understood as forward, *foresight*, the past as backward, *hindsight*

(Fillmore, 1982), up is the direction of authority while down is the symbol of subjection (Lakoff and Johnson, 1980). The latter can be seen in *to oversee* or *look down on*. The example of *overseer* in English has undergone parallel borrowing from Latin and Greek, the latter being seen in *episcopal* > Greek *epí-skopos* (= *supervisor* > government by bishops).

In (2), the *hearing* perception verb has adopted a trend in Indo-European languages of developing the sense of 'listen' or 'heed', whereby a further development has taken place with a semantic shift to 'obey'. Most hear/listen verbs are cognate, developing from I-E **kleu*- and attested in Greek *klúo* (Buck, 1949: 1036 ff.), and we thus have English *hear/hearken*, parallel with German *hören/horchen*. The 'obey' shift can subsequently be attested in such pairs as: English *hear/heed*, German *hören/gehorchen*, Russian *slušat'/slušat's'a*.

The trend in semantic change – which includes a distinct metaphorisation process as in the mental vision groups – tends to follow a one-way direction of concrete to abstract or physical to mental conceptualisation. There are, however, exceptions such as in the case of mental understanding becoming physical hearing. Latin *intendere* 'stretch out, direct one's attention to' came to mean 'understand, take heed of' in later Romance languages, for example, Old French *entendere* and Spanish *entender*, but in modern French the word *entendre* has come to mean 'hear' (Sweetser, 1990: 35).

Despite the exceptions, regular one-way trends are a focal point of Sweetser's hypothesis that there is a systematic pattern which has adopted a parallel form in independent branches of Indo-European. Multiple synchronic senses of a given word are normally related to each other and words do not randomly acquire new senses. Empirical research in this area has shown that 'certain semantic changes occur over and over again throughout the course of Indo-European and independently in different branches across an area of thousands of miles and a time depth of thousands of years' (Sweetser, 1990: 9). It is particularly this aspect of meaning change which suggests that metaphoric extension is the main cause and demonstrates a link between lexical development and human perception. It is for this reason that Sweetser claims that sense-changes in lexical items often follow set paths as a result of metaphoric extensions. If this is true, there could very well be diachronic universals of networking which are responsible for non-random paths of metaphor evolution. The metaphorical nature of semantic change in the Indo-European family provides some strong evidence to support this hypothesis.

It may therefore be postulated that there are specific paths in the change of concepts. Such would be the case of physical sight developing into the notion of knowledge and intellection, outlined by Sweetser, via the processes of metaphorisation or metonymisation. If semantic change in literal meaning is under consideration, it would mean that the status of metaphor in the lexeme undergoing change must at some stage disappear. A standard change would be LITERAL > FIGURATIVE > LITERAL. One major theory, which combines a number of specific features, has come out of this research in relation to regularity.

6.7 Unidirectional change

The theory of unidirectional change implies that trends become more directed to the speaker's viewpoint, in the same way as metaphorisation is linked to the speaker's conceptualisation of the environment. Traugott and Dasher (2002) outline the history of these theories as proposed in studies by Sweetser (1987, 1990, 1992) and Traugott (1989). A clear trend in the speaker's involvement of change is the case of subjectification whereby DEONTIC conceptual structures become EPISTEMIC, that is, there is a change from obligation to the verification of knowledge as in Traugott and Dasher (2002: 2):

(a) They *must* be married, I demand it: DEONTIC
(b) They *must* be married, I am sure of it: EPISTEMIC

This forms part of a grammaticalisation process in semantic change, defined originally by Meillet (1958) as the development of lexemes into grammatical items and described by Traugott and Dasher (2002) as a change from free to fixed word order. It is claimed to be unidirectional as in a chronological series of conceptual structures involving: SPATIAL > TEMPORAL > CONDITIONAL. This can be seen in the historical evolution of the expression *as long as* derived from Old English *swa lange swa*. The following three passages from different periods of English demonstrate the diachronic and unidirectional change of these conceptual structures (Traugott and Dasher, 2002: 36–7):

(a) Old English: SPATIAL
þa het Ælfred cyng timbran lang scipu ongen ða æscas
(then ordered Alfred king build -INF long ships against those warships)

þa wæron fulneah tu *swa lange swa* þa oðru
(they were nearly twice *as long as* the others (850–950 Chron A, p. 90))

(b) Early Modern English: TEMPORAL (+ CONDITIONAL)
They whose words doe most shew forth their wise vnderstanding, and whose lips doe vtter the purest knowledge, so *as long as* they vnderstand and speake as men, are they not faine sundry waies to excuse themselues? (1614 Hooker, p. 5)

(c) Modern English: CONDITIONAL
Galligan told the jury that it is proper for police to question a juvenile without a parent present *as long as* they made a 'reasonable effort' to notify the parent.

It can be seen that diachronic changes tend towards states of polysemy with the form in Early Modern English having the conceptual structures of both TEMPORAL and CONDITIONAL. Polysemy in diachronic semantics thus plays a part in both grammatical and lexical change.

In addition, there are a number of other features of meaning-change involving regularity. One claim, for example, is that the development of incremental meaning is largely regular, accounted for by Traugott and Dasher's model of invited inferencing whereby new meanings may arise in the individual and be affected by community acceptance of saliency (2002: 38–9). Innovation must be spread or propagated throughout a community as in the case of the coinage *millennium bug*. However, it is also assumed that meaning loss is unpredictable and irregular.

Research in diachronic semantics has thus come from a state of uncertainty about set patterns, when there was the search for semantic laws in Stern's day, to concrete formulations about how structures follow regular changes. The conception of regularity in semantic change today also claims that metaphor plays a major part in these diachronic conceptual structures. The change from SPATIAL to TEMPORAL also suggests that there is a unidirectional change from concrete to abstract: 'one of the clearest cases of regular direction in semantic change is the tendency for words to change from a more concrete to a more abstract meaning: for example, for words describing abstract domains such as time to be derived from words for more concrete spatial concepts' (Sweetser, 1987: 446). The reference here is that the timeline is metaphorically mapped onto a path stretching ahead of and behind the speaker, with the speaker situated at the present moment, another reference to the deontic trend.

Most of Sweetser's work has been in the Indo-European field, demonstrating that the same regular metaphorisation processes have been at work throughout a large number of European languages. These claims have been corroborated by other studies which suggest that the same diachronic processes operate in widely different language families (Haser, 2000). Sweetser's VISION > INTELLECT construct, for example, can be seen in languages including Korean, Indonesian, Yoruba and Quechua, HEAR > OBEY can be seen in, among others, Egyptian, Tamil, Japanese, Swahili, Zulu and Nahuatl (Haser, 2000: 176–7). These claims would certainly point to the case of diachronic universals.

At this point, however, it should be stressed that all these theories probably represent trends. Variations have sometimes been discussed in the relevant literature. Cotton and Sharp (1998: 217) argue that the concrete to abstract framework varies between metaphoric and metonymic creation in Spanish verbs in general. The claim that meaning always changes historically from concrete to abstract appears to be seldom true of metonymies but often true of metaphor creation in Spanish. Metonymy frequently involves concrete to concrete which can also apply to metaphor on a smaller scale.

The distinction between 'concrete' and 'abstract' should not be confused with the idea that the evolution of figurative language progresses from 'simple' to 'complex' structures through time. As Padel (1992: 37 ff.) puts it, ancient Greek works long before Homer expressed their ideas with complex abstract, metaphoric meanings. The notion that thought-processes developed from simple to complex forms, or from magical to scientific thinking, tended to be reinforced in psychology with Freud's distinction between 'primary' and 'secondary' thought-processes. The former were considered to be metaphoric, imaginative processes and the latter scientific or rational ones. In Freud's day, this trend was considered to be universal but it is rejected by most contemporary psychologists. In the same way, metaphorisation in earlier stages of language are not 'simpler' or representative of 'primary' forms. The same processes continue along the time scale.

Another regular feature in diachronic metaphor involves the chaining of items in specific semantic fields whereby whole series of related words are transferred figuratively from one field to the other.

6.8 Chaining in semantic fields

A number of different fields have been analysed in past studies with respect to their role in systematic chaining. A major theme is the relationship between humans and the animal/bird/insect category, as in Tourangeau and Sternberg's (1982) application of this combination in prototype metaphor theory described above (Chapter 1, Section 1.4).

Lehrer (1985) presents some interesting examples of this relationship in the history of English metaphors. This would support the idea that

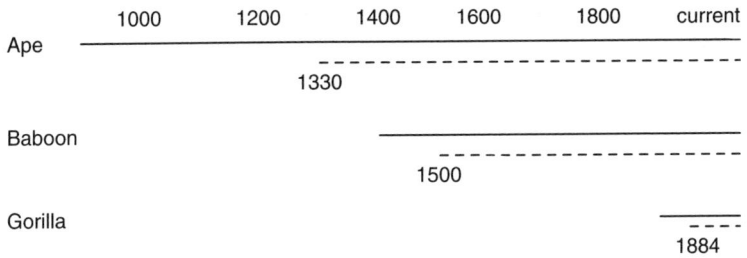

Figure 6.2 Diachronic chaining in the semantic field PRIMATES = BRUTISHNESS
Source: Adapted from Lehrer (1985).

semantic categories promote diachronic networking. Two examples will be illustrated here from the animal/bird categories. In Figure 6.2, it can be seen that the metaphorical meaning for *ape* (a fool) developed early on (1330) and attracted the items *baboon* (general term of abuse) around 1500 and the term *gorilla* (brutish person) attested in 1884 (*OED*). The terms indicate pejorative senses applied to humans with a general connotation of brutishness and infer that the earlier metaphoric senses have attracted similar concepts related to the primate group at later dates. As Lehrer points out, there appears to be a triggering mechanism: 'when a member of an animal word set acquires a metaphorical meaning, it facilitates a comparable change in other members of the set' (1985: 289). The continuous line indicates the existence of the lexical item in the English language, the dotted line its corresponding metaphoric meaning.

Another example of a triggering process is the bird category in English. Like the primate group, the bird set has had a history of generally pejorative metaphors when applied to humans. They usually imply the sense of 'foolishness'. The primate group illustrates long-term chaining, that is, triggering occurred at wide time intervals inferring that this connotation can stay for a long time in the conceptualisation of a language's speakers before the next change takes place. The bird category offers examples of rapid change. Three of the items, *goose, cuckoo* and *pigeon* followed in rapid succession, even though the linguistic forms of the concepts had been present for a long time before. This would suggest that the semantic field has facilitated the innovation (Figure 6.3).

Chaining takes place in relatively rapid succession in the first three metaphors in Figure 6.3: first attestations (*OED*) being dated to 1547, 1580 and 1593. The item *coot* tends to be used in proverbial expressions like *as bald (mad, stupid) as a coot* rather than as a single lexical item. Some of the metaphors, for example *pigeon*, appear archaic today and an earlier sense

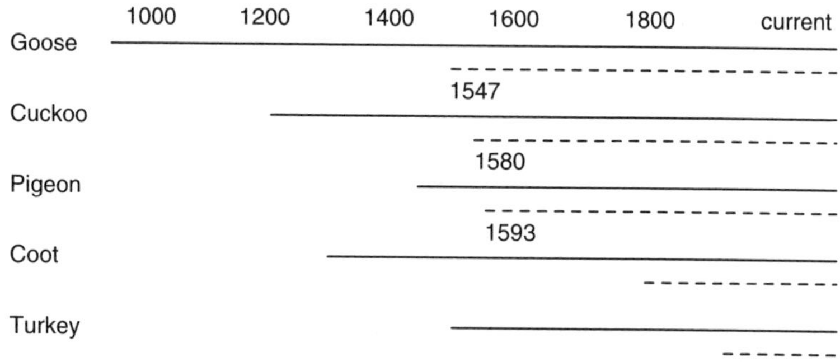

	1000	1200	1400	1600	1800	current
Goose				----	----	-------
Cuckoo			1547			
Pigeon				1580 ----	----	----
Coot				1593		
Turkey					----	-------

Figure 6.3 Networking in the semantic field BIRDS = FOOLISHNESS
Source: Adapted from Lehrer (1985).

of 'cowardly' in this item has become obsolete. First attestations of the last two in the list were not given but they were created at much later dates. Semantic fields thus have a role in the networking process and other chronological mammal/bird sets can be seen in the metaphors of SNAKES = TREACHERY, SCAVENGER BIRDS = GREED and MULE/DONKEY = OBSTINACY.

The vast majority of the mammal/bird semantic field appears to reflect pejorative senses. In a study by Allan (2003), 92 dictionary entries for animals out of a total of 99 actually signified stupidity compared to 7 which were used to portray cleverness. Even among these few, the notion of cleverness was identified with sharpness or shrewdness rather than other kinds of cleverness. She suggests that this overwhelming notion of stupidity may be associated with Lakoff and Turner's great chain metaphor (1989: 167 ff.): the application of an animal metaphor for a person (with rare positive exceptions) suggests that they are a 'lower' creature, or in some way sub-human.

This could imply that the whole semantic field of animals may attract new pejorative metaphors as time progresses. A selection of chronological entries of the ANIMALS = STUPIDITY metaphor can be seen in Table 6.1, showing items taken from Allan's list. Date entries (*OED*) have been selected as first attestations of metaphoric meanings.

A glance at the list of metaphoric creations in Table 6.1 would indeed suggest that the pejorative analogy of animals to humans is a central theme in the history of English and that this semantic field helps to trigger new entries as time passes. This chaining pattern is also apparent in other European languages, such as French, and therefore suggests that chaining in semantic fields is probably a universal diachronic feature. The interesting

Table 6.1: The diachronic model ANIMALS/BIRDS = STUPIDITY

Core concept	Entry	Date
Mammal	Ape	1330
Mammal	Sheepish	1380
Mammal	Mule	1470
Insect	Hoddypeak	1500
Bird	Daw pate/dawpaten	1529
Mammal	Ass-headed	1532
Fish	Cod's head	1566
Mammal	Calvish	1570
Bird	Cuckoo	1596
Mammal	Long-eared	1605
Mammal	Dunderwhelp	1621
Mammal	Buffle	1655
Bird	Dove	1771
Mammal	Tup-headed	1816
Mammal	Bovine	1855
Fish	Gubbins	1916
Fish	Like a stunned mullet	1953

Source: Allan (2003).

Table 6.2: The French model ANIMALS/BIRDS = STUPIDITY

Core concept	Entry	Date
Mammal	*Âne* (donkey)	1260
Bird	*Pigeon*	1490
Mammal	*Mouton* (sheep)	1566
Bird	*Linotte* (linnet)	1611
Bird	*Butor* (bittern)	1661
Bird	*Bécasse* (woodcock)	1696
Bird	*Dinde* (turkey)	1752
Bird	*Oie* (goose)	1835

point about a comparison between English and French is that, on the one hand, there are the same cultural patterns in conceptual metaphors such as BIRDS = FOOLISHNESS but, on the other hand, the items within the semantic field can actually vary considerably. This would in turn suggest that, despite the cultural overlap, chaining is also an internal process which may often be more common than borrowing between two languages. Table 6.2 gives a sample of some bird and animal species which have been equated historically with foolishness in French. It could be inferred that the base concept is foolishness or stupidity but that associated pejorative links may be included in this basic notion such as *being easily manipulated* in the sheep metaphor and the quality of *coarseness* or *rudeness* in the bittern metaphor. The dates are taken from the dictionary, *Trésor de la Langue Française,* and show how new items are added to the same semantic fields through the course of several centuries.

There are some matches between English and French, such as in the birds *goose, pigeon* and *turkey*. It is difficult to estimate when and if one language has borrowed from another, particularly since the dates are often far apart. A comparison of this kind may be seen in the first attestation of 1547 for the figurative meaning of *goose* in Lehrer's English data with that of 1835 in the French data. If the dates are close together, however, it might mean that an innovation in one language has spread to another rather than indicating a coincidental innovation in each language at approximately the same time. More significant evidence of internal chaining is the succession of French *linotte*, as in the expression *tête de linotte* (head of a linnet = unintelligent person), in addition to *butor* (bittern = coarse, stupid person) and *bécasse* (woodcock = stupid person) during the course of the seventeenth century. These are particular species of the bird family which are likely to be more entrenched in French vocabulary rather than more common bird species such as *goose* and *turkey* that may have a more general cross-language distribution.

How do these theories equate with major metaphor network systems? The notion of regularity and long-term chaining processes in semantic fields provides us with some vital information about how networks evolve through time. It leads us on to the theories of metaphor paths in language history which will be discussed in more detail in the next chapter.

7
Metaphor Paths in Base Concepts

7.1 Diachronic conceptual networking

If we wish to find out more about the origins of our family, the obvious way is to try and find the links between previous generations and set up a family tree. This is not always an easy task as it can be difficult to trace specific generations, but at least we know that a set pattern of descent exists and it is a question of finding the information which can fill in the missing links.

The discussion we have had in the previous chapter suggests that metaphor history also has set patterns and that, given the appropriate dictionary and encyclopaedic information, we should be able to trace language histories which fit into these patterns. With this in mind, we are now in a position to set up a number of hypothetical models of metaphor evolution. If we set out to trace individual metaphor histories involving such processes as regularity or semantic chaining features, we can see that there are specific trends in diachronic metaphor paths. Aitchison (1992) suggests that languages (and cultures) tend to select metaphorisation processes which follow specific grooves. For example, in English, in the field of emotions, fear is usually based on two mental models, the EMPTY CONTAINER image as in:

There was a hollow feeling in Bill's stomach

or the FREEZING COLD image as in:

Fear froze Angela to the ground

Ancient Greek *phobos* (fear) uses a FLIGHT model, with the notion of 'panic-stricken flight', suggesting that emotion may follow several possible physiological or behavioural routes according to the path a particular language might select. A number of reasons may underlie this selection, for example, cultural reasons might mean that in former times flight may have been a rational reaction to this type of emotion. At the same time, once the path has been selected, there may be a subconscious desire by speakers of a language to keep their mental models consistent, to preserve the empty container or freezing cold images for fear while other models such as heated liquid are kept separate for anger, passion and happiness (Aitchison, 1992: 37).

On the background to the different cultural or physiological reasons for set directions in metaphor evolution, the following discussion will analyse how metaphor paths are conceptually linked to what will be termed here 'metaphor building blocks'. These are core concepts which generate paths within the conceptual boundaries of the culture in which the language is located. The core concepts in question belong to Lakoff's category of basic-level properties such as *tall*, *short*, *hard*, *soft*, *heavy*, *light* and so on, and thus belong to the likely candidates for universals. A closer look at these basic-level concepts will reveal, however, a considerable degree of cross-language variation in secondary conceptual clusters.

The paths have the potential of passing through different activated and dormant phases. The notion of dormancy means that the metaphoric concept is not actually in use at a particular time in the history of a language but that it could be re-conceptualised and come into, or back into, common usage. An example of a dormant metaphor would be the notion of the colour *green* referring to *ecological* before the 1970s. We have noted earlier on that this metaphor came into existence with the arrival of the Green Party in Germany during the 1970s and was quickly loaned to other European languages. However, the potential of *green* being mapped with the concept of *ecology* pre-existed this, since there is a natural link between ecology and the greenness of nature. It was therefore conceptually dormant before this period. Likewise, the notion of *dry* meaning *withered* which existed in Middle English could easily reappear due to the visual aspect of *dry skin* appearing *withered*. The metaphor is therefore in a dormant state at the present time due to its potential for reconceptualisation in the future, even if this never occurs.

Ignoring, for the time being, the fuzzy area of low metaphoricity and the subsequent state of conventionalisation, this corresponds roughly to what Kittay (1987: 20) calls 'metaphor retrieval'. Past metaphors, which are now taken to be literal, can generally be retrieved as metaphors at a later stage. A dormant metaphor is thus a concept which, given the framework of a receptive culture, may come into usage at some point in time provided the language's speakers naturally conceptualise and activate the metaphor. For example, the flight model for fear could act as a dormant concept in modern English. On this basis we may postulate a *dormant networking hypothesis* which is responsible for a large proportion of metaphoric production.

There are a number of possible scenarios if we compare evolution in two or more languages. Figure 7.1 suggests three possible scenarios in the initial stages of comparative metaphor paths: (1) concept X is activated in both languages at an early stage of the existence of written texts; (2) concept Y lies dormant in one language but is conceptually receptive to its introduction either inter- or intralingually due to a shared metaphor-building block within a common cultural environment; and (3) concept Z lies dormant in both.

We can thus see that Figure 7.1 compares metaphor evolution in two different languages. The three scenarios incorporating metaphor paths in two languages A and B arise from three building blocks. The vertical continuous lines represent activated phases and the vertical dotted lines signify dormant periods. They are divided up into historical periods by the horizontal lines. In the first scenario, concept X is activated in both languages at an early stage of the existence of written texts but they

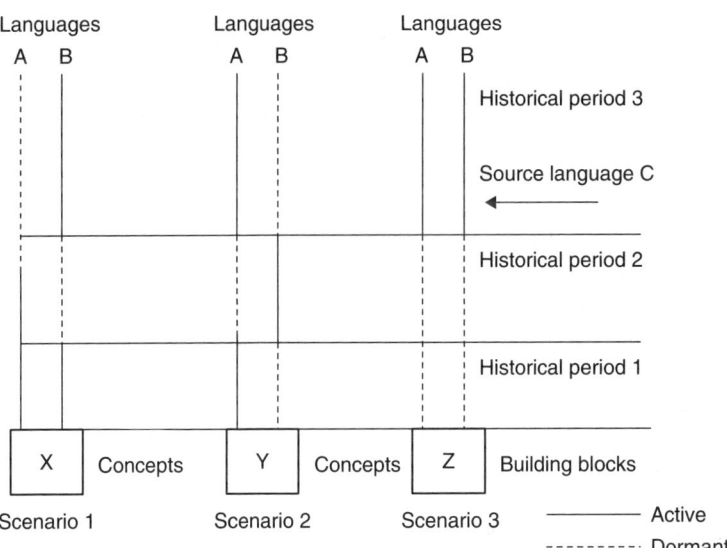

Figure 7.1 The comparative evolution of metaphor paths

diverge at the end of historical period 1. Language A continues until the end of historical period 2 during which B becomes obsolescent until historical period 3, at which time the metaphor in language A dies out. We thus have a synchronic situation today in which the metaphor exists in language B but not in A.

Another type of scenario can be found in the metaphor paths linked to concept Y. The concept is activated in A in historical period 1, at the end of which it dies out but is activated in B. In many cases, the question arises as to whether the concept is passed interlingually from A to B before its obsolescence or whether it is generated intralingually within B. In some situations, the process appears fairly obvious but this is not always the case. The reverse situation could occur at the end of historical period 2 with the result that today's synchronic situation would also be the reverse of scenario 1 with the metaphor existing in A but not in B.

A third example of dormant networking can be seen in scenario 3. Here cross-linguistic patterns are more uniform and straightforward with both languages activating the concept at the same time in historical period 3, either by language contact or intralingually. Language contact may, of course, involve a third language C as a source of the metaphor. The result is that both languages today would have the metaphor in their lexicon.

A primary reason for these paths developing specific directions is that, as we have seen, there is a tendency for metaphor clusters, which become predominant in the way of thinking of the language's speakers, to create subsequent metaphors along the same conceptual lines. With the help of this theoretical framework, the following analysis involves dictionary attestations and corpus data from general and literary texts collected throughout three historical periods, the first spanning a period from 1200 to 1500, the second from 1500 to 1900 and the third from 1900 to the present day. The dates indicated represent first attestations. The three time periods have been chosen to allow a comparative overview of metaphor paths in English and French from the Middle Ages on. A number of basic concepts (according to Lakoff's definition of the term) are included, and these reveal considerable cross-language variation, highlighting the random nature of activated periods in the regular network of metaphor paths.

7.2 The metaphor path of FLATNESS

The first concept, FLAT (*plat* in French), represents a pattern with a small number of paths and little cross-language variation in activation and dormancy (Figure 7.2). The core concept is a FLAT = UNINTERESTING

Metaphor Paths in Base Concepts 113

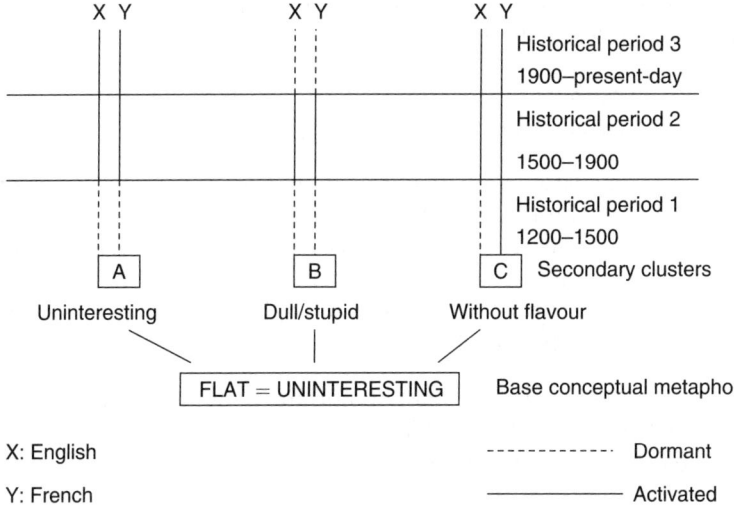

Figure 7.2 Diachronic networking in the FLATNESS concept

model. The notion of flatness is therefore linked to a particular pejorative quality lacking significant points of interest, as in a flat landscape which might appear more monotonous than rugged or mountainous terrain.

The central metaphor cluster appears to have followed similar diachronic paths in English and French, the metaphor being activated during historical periods 2 and 3, but with attestations not having been found prior to the sixteenth century. This would therefore represent a dormant phase in the metaphor's history:

> They are poor and flat in all other subjects (*OED*: 1656)
> *Les plus plattes raisons*/the flattest reasons (*Dictionnaire historique de la langue française – DHLF*: 1588)

Although the metaphor path may remain activated, collocations linked to the path are much less stable. Thus, the expression 'flat people' would not be used today but the collocation 'flat jokes' is used as in 'the jokes fell flat'. Likewise in French, *les plattes raisons* sounds archaic, but one is likely to say '*c'est un peu plat*' (it's a bit flat), with reference to an idea which is generally monotonous.

In contrast to the first metaphor path which is still alive today, cluster B in Figure 7.2, representing the connotation of 'dull' and 'stupid', is one which has become obsolete in both languages. According to dictionary attestations, the following example goes beyond the sense of 'uninteresting' and is definitely pejorative:

> I look for nothing from empty, dull, flat people (*OED*: 1878)
> *Un plat personnage*/a flat character (*DHLF*: 1798)

Cross-language patterns are identical, with an activated stage in historical period 2 and dormancy in periods 1 and 3. More variation appears in cluster C with the sense of FLAT = WITHOUT FLAVOUR. This path seems to have existed for a long time in French, covering all three historical periods, whereas the first attestations in English date back only to the beginning of the seventeenth century:

> Spirit of wine burned (. . .) tasteth nothing so hot in the mouth (. . .) but flat and dead (*OED*: 1626).
> *Un goût plat*/flat taste (*DHLF*)

The sense in French can be traced back to the fourteenth century in the expression *eau plate* ('flat water'), which meant pure water at that time but now represents ordinary tap water as opposed to sparkling (bottled) water. The English sense can be seen more commonly today in expressions such as 'flat beer' or 'the beer has gone flat'.

7.3 The metaphor path of SMOOTHNESS

In contrast, the SMOOTH concept represents substantial cross-language variation in English and French in its distribution of activated periods. There are four major paths generated from a base conceptual metaphor of SMOOTH = ATTRACTIVE/TRANQUIL (Figure 7.3). Cluster A, with the sense of friendly or polite, has identical activated periods in historical periods 2 and 3, although the sense in the French term *lisse* (smooth) seems to have been rare before the sixteenth century:

> With smothe smylyng
> (With smooth smiling (*OED*: fourteenth century))

However, sense B, which is related to the first cluster, 'smart or polished style', has continued in English from the Middle Ages until today, unlike in French which appears to be totally devoid of attestations:

> Whysperyng tounges . . . smothe folk . . . to shewe two facys in oon hood
> (Whispering tongues . . . smooth folk . . . to show two faces in one hood (*OED*: c. 1450))

Metaphor Paths in Base Concepts 115

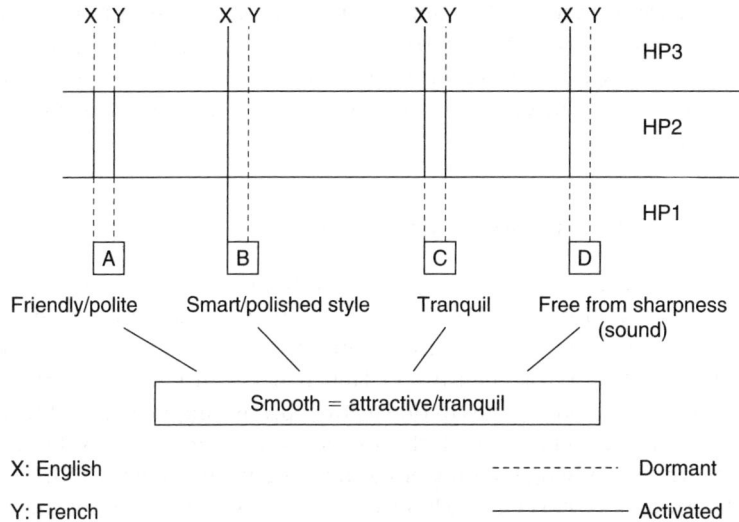

Figure 7.3 The diachronic network of SMOOTHNESS

This sense can often be heard in modern English in expressions such as 'he's a smooth talker'. A slightly different semantic track is found in cluster C with the connotation of 'free from excitement' or a 'tranquil state'. This sense appears to have entered English much later during period 2 and continues today with expressions such as 'things ran very smoothly'.

> That smooth and voluptuous satisfaction which the assured prospect of pleasure bestows (*OED*: 1756)

According to historical dictionaries, the French sense was only present during period 2 and was quite rare at the time (*DHLF*).

In cluster D, the metaphor based on the notion of 'free from sharpness' with reference to the perception of sound, taste and so on, is absent from French since other basic concepts, such as soft (*doux*), are used for this semantic field. First attestations are relatively late in the history of English; around the first half of the nineteenth century:

> It is not age, but constant use, that is the means of producing a smooth, clear tone (*OED*: 1836)

It can be imagined that a number of other scenarios are possible in this model and that more intricate patterns develop if additional categorisation features are introduced. One such pattern appears if we introduce the parameter of binary systems in basic concepts. Many such concepts have binary features, for example, dry/wet, rough/smooth, tight/loose and so on. The question arises as to which patterns arise from the same binary concept.

7.4 Binary concepts: TIGHT/LOOSE

Metaphoric concepts in a binary structure do not often follow the same pattern of opposites as their literal counterparts in semantic change. One such concept, the tight/loose binary feature, is a case in point. During the history of English and French it has displayed *metaphoric opposites* at different periods in one feature: precise/imprecise, but this is not the case generally with diachronic paths in binary basic-level properties. The underlying building block in the tight/loose item is TIGHT = CONSTRAINT/CONTROL and loose is the opposite with lack of constraint or control. The major paths which have been created are illustrated in Figure 7.4 and vary enormously in activated and dormant periods during their history. In both components there is considerable cross-language variation with certain paths never having existed in one of the languages.

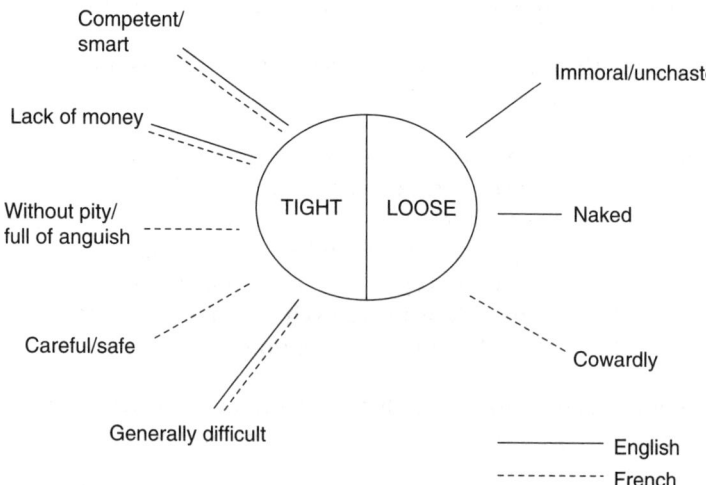

Figure 7.4 Metaphor paths in the TIGHT/LOOSE binary concept

In the *tight* metaphor, examples in the different clusters can be found in the *competent/smart* model such as:

That reverent, famous, most able, and tight writer (*OED*: 1655, obs.)

in which it could be construed that the subject has his writing well-organised and under control.

The notion of the need for constraint is found in the metaphor *lack of money* as in French *être serré* (to be tight) in the sense of having to have a tight control on expenses. The item has a long history and the equivalent is seen in English *tight-fisted* when it refers to a miserly person who does not want to open his hand to give money:

Oh! But he was a tight-fisted hand at the grind-stone, Scrooge! A squeezing, wrenching, grasping, scraping, clutching, covetous, old sinner . . .! (Charles Dickens, *A Christmas Carol*, 1843)

Two paths have only existed in French, as in expressions such as *avoir le coeur serré* (to have a tight heart = 'to have no pity'), extended to 'full of anguish or pain' in the twelfth century (*DHLF*). The original meaning is based on the idea of controlling or constraining someone in some way. The *careful/safe* path used in regional French in the seventeenth century is found in *être serré* (to be tight = in safety) with the idea of having a situation under control. Finally, a common use of *tight* today is in English *to be in a tight spot* with the notion of difficulty, or being constrained to make a huge effort. This is also found in French *le match de foot était très serré* (it was a close football match), meaning a game which was difficult for both sides.

These represent the major patterns in dictionary entries, although there are also exceptions, as can often occur in other models. The construal, for example, of English colloquial tight = drunk appears to be based on another kind of image. In some cases, more isolated examples such as these may be formed from another underlying concept.

The distribution pattern of *loose* (French *lâche*) is different in that metaphor paths have either existed in one language or the other but not in both. Conceptual links to an underlying conceptual metaphor of LOOSE = LACK OF CONSTRAINT would suggest that all items are in some way associated with each other. The image of immorality can be found in:

The loose encounters of lascivious men (Shakespeare, *The Two Gentlemen of Verona*)

The association of the cluster *naked* is probably an extension from the immorality group which took place in the sixteenth century (since nudity was frowned on) but is now obsolete:

> They are excedynge swyfte of foote by reason of theyr loose goinge from theyr chyldes age (*OED*: 1555)

The French sense of 'cowardly' or 'lack of courage' probably comes from the idea of not having a control of one's emotions and of being irresolute. It stems from Old French *soi eslachier* (*DHLF*: beginning of twelfth century) with the notion of becoming loose meaning being afraid. The metaphor does not seem to have appeared in the history of English. There is the expression in modern English, 'loose bowels', connected with the sense of fear, but the origin of this binary concept of 'tight' and 'loose' may depend on the notion of 'tight nerves'. Bracing up to problems may be analogical to the tightening of nerves.

In addition, it is difficult to draw definitive conclusions on the binary feature of basic-level properties in a comparative study since it is not always clear which lexical item in a given language corresponds best to an equivalent in another language. English *wet* has two counterparts in French: *mouillé* and *humide* but English *humid* does not correspond to French *humide*. This makes a comparative study of the binary concept *wet/dry* a difficult one. However, the component *dry* does match between the two languages and we shall conclude this analysis of diachronic networks with a comparative analysis of the DRYNESS concept since it reveals a different type of pattern to the concepts described so far.

7.5 Complex systems: DRYNESS

In the process of translation, an important exercise is always knowing which collocation patterns fit source and target languages. A selection of different collocations of 'dry' in English show that this word contains a large number of different metaphoric meanings (Baker, 1992: 53):

dry cow	dry sound	dry book
dry bread	dry voice	dry humour
dry wine	dry country	dry run

The dryness network represents in fact a vast pattern which goes back to Latin and Greek in Antiquity. An analysis of historical dictionaries in a number of different European languages shows that there are at least a hundred different metaphor entries for this item. In a discussion of these networks, the postulation of the base conceptual metaphor has to be interpreted with a certain amount of conceptual flexibility, as in the previous examples. Links tend to be more centralised or more peripheral as in polysemy structures and there are nearly always exceptions to the pattern. However, out of all the different metaphor types for dryness, the vast majority can be linked to an underlying base metaphor of DRYNESS = DEFICIENCY. This no doubt comes from the notion of a lack of water and, indeed, a considerable number of metaphors are associated with the idea of a lack of a liquid.

It may be assumed that a common image of dryness in European culture derived from the fact that water was a 'life-giving' substance and that, apart from areas in danger of flooding from the sea, or other climatic conditions, was a positive element in life. It could thus be suggested that this metaphor cluster is perhaps more prototypical of the DRYNESS = DEFICIENCY core concept than the other clusters. The symbol of lack of water, moisture or other basic liquid elements such as blood came to represent a deficiency in some human or physical characteristic. This is reflected in the medieval physiology of the humours discussed above, in which dryness represented one of the four fundamental qualities of our environment:

His blood grew dry and cold (*OED*: 1300)

Dry blood represented a lack of life in the same way as coldness, and the concept of dryness was correspondingly equated with a mental deficiency of some form or other in English up until the nineteenth century:

Madness, melancholy . . . and all diseases proceeding from a dry habit (*OED*: 1819)

Figure 7.5 gives an overview of the major secondary clusters in English and French.

Among the many expressions using the lack of a liquid metaphor are 'we have run dry' (out of petrol) and 'a dry area' (prohibition of alcohol). Cluster B can be found in 'he replied drily' or in French *d'un ton sec* (in a dry tone). Cluster C is now obsolete in English but still used in French today, for example, *il est très sec* (he is very dry = he is very thin). This is not always negative today but certainly used to be. In the Middle Ages, as we saw in Chapter 1, *he has dry arms* meant they were not only thin but old and withered. Cluster D represents the most interesting metaphor

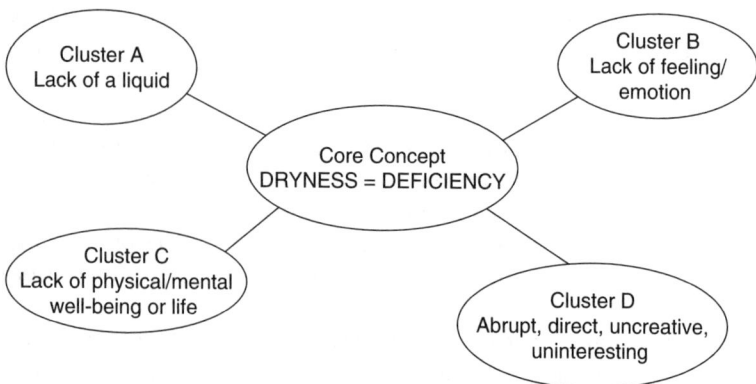

Figure 7.5 Secondary clusters in the DRYNESS model

path since it originated from a meaning of representing the bare essentials, shared by both English and French, and then diverged at a later date into two main groups: uninteresting/matter of fact in English and the notion of direct/quick/abrupt in French. The first group can be seen in the idea of 'dry humour' or a 'dry subject' in English, the latter in expressions such as *il a conduit très sec* in French (he drove very drily = he drove very quickly). English would not be able to use the dry metaphor here and conversely, French would have to use a term such as *ironique* (ironic) to convey the meaning of dry humour. Divergence in path clusters can therefore occur at any time in the history of a language in the same way as convergence can occur due to borrowing or parallel internal creation. The chronological development of this network is illustrated in Figure 7.6.

Thus, there appears to be a considerable amount of evidence to suggest that metaphors evolve along set conceptual paths. We cannot predict which way they are likely to turn but it can be seen that they follow logical conceptual directions which involve creations being built up on pre-existing models. Many basic concepts can be traced back to common underlying conceptual metaphors which start the chain going. In overlapping cultures as in European languages, many of these conceptual metaphors are shared but they may branch into secondary clusters and the linguistic forms themselves are subject to considerable variation.

The metaphor paths discussed so far trace the general directions involved. It can be seen in these basic models that the histories of metaphors do not all start off or come to an end at exactly the same time. In fact, there

Metaphor Paths in Base Concepts 121

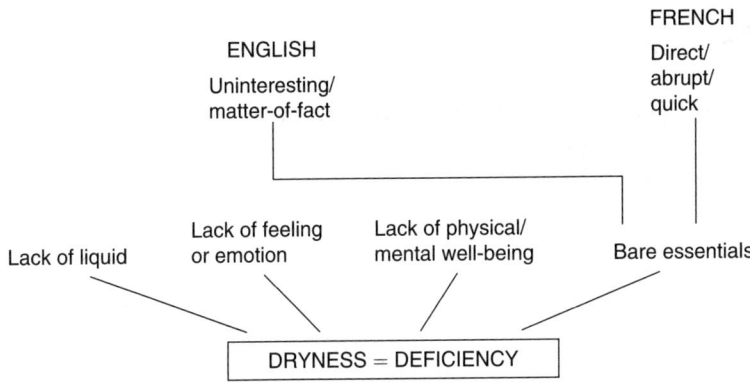

Figure 7.6 Cross-language divergence in the DRYNESS model

are quite a few variations which can occur throughout the lifetime of a metaphor. One of the major issues which arises, and which in many ways is linked to the duration of a metaphor, is its saliency at any point in time. How many speakers actually use, or still use, a particular metaphor? By looking at language over a large time-scale we are able to see more clearly how metaphor models can also change with time. The next chapter will therefore examine in more detail the issues of duration and saliency in long and short-term models.

8
Germanic Influences in Old English

8.1 Long-term metaphor

Metaphors can come one day and be gone the next. At the same time, we have seen that some metaphors may last for thousands of years such as the LIFE IS A JOURNEY model in Western society. Duration therefore varies enormously and it is difficult to categorise which metaphors are likely to last. At first sight, it may be assumed that long-lasting metaphors are similar to the types of universal features of basic concepts. This is very often true but it will be seen here that some do not necessarily last for ever, at least, not in their active stage.

A starting-point in this discussion would be to look at the history of the English language to find out how far back long-term models tend to go. By going as far back as Old English, we can clearly recognise which models have a long life. It will be seen, however, that the disappearance of conceptual metaphors in a particular metaphor path may not signify that they no longer exist elsewhere. They can live on in another form, perhaps transferred to another field of human experience. This process, which will be termed here *collocational switching* in diachrony, automatically involves a change of direction in metaphor paths. At the same time, some metaphors can sound 'more metaphoric' at one period of history than another or they may be used more often for various cultural or sociolinguistic reasons. The feature of saliency is an important one as it can throw doubt on the very existence of the metaphor itself. In this chapter, we shall therefore first look at the features of long- and short-term paths in relation to Old English.

As far as the overall aspect of long-term paths is concerned, Kay (2000: 273–85) defines them as covering *continuous and relexicalised metaphors* in his study of Old English dictionaries and thesauri. Employing the framework of Lakoff and Johnson's (1980) approach, he includes within the first group body metaphors such as *head*, as in the *head of a valley*. Kay's second group of relexicalisation would include a metaphor path which has remained but with an exchange of lexical items as in *neck of land* replacing Old English *sweora* (neck). The fire model that we have seen in the discussion on the physical effects of drugs metaphors would be an example in which both groups may be involved: the long-term path would be represented by the physiological counterpart within the body metaphor category, while the religious applications of fire discussed in Part III below concerning its use in Antiquity, and listed in the thesaurus under 'ardour, fervour and strong feeling' with terms such as *blæse* (firebrand), *bryne* (burning), *hæte* (heat), *lieg* (flame) and *wielm* (burning) would represent short-term paths.

Within the specific field of emotions, Fabiszak (1999: 133–46) has focused on the notions of joy, grief and anger. There are features within the semantic field of joy which reveal long-term trends and therefore possible universal trends along the lines of Lakoff's (1987) theories. Old English words for 'joy' can be represented by such terms as *bliss*, *gefea* and *wynsumnesse*. Some Old English terms for 'joy' are recognisable in modern English. In this small group, the lexical term *bliss* is similar to the related modern concept of 'bliss'. A major model in this group is represented by the UP = GOOD orientational image schema. Some of the expressions found by Fabiszak in the Old English Thesaurus are:

blisse astigan	'rise, ascend'
gefea astigan	'ascend'
wynsumnesse astigan	'ascend'

Related expressions in the *gefea* item are:

to gefea araran	'lift up'
to gefea aspringan	'ascend'
gefea him upahafan	'he was elated with . . .'

These expressions would therefore fit into the general principle that the direction upwards is metaphorically positive and, as a corollary, direction downwards may be assumed to be negative. If we compare Old English expressions with those of today, there are a number of contemporary conventional metaphors, such as 'his spirits lifted', which match the data conceptually.

Another physiological model found in the data on the 'joy' concept refers to the metaphor: BODY = CONTAINER FOR JOY. Thus Old English uses terms such as:

mid blisse gefyllan	'fill with joy'
mid gefea gefyllan	'fill with joy'
mid wynsumnesse gefyllan	'fill with joy'
blisse on breostum	'joy in heart'
blisse on mode	'joy in mind/heart'

Here again, a comparison with modern English reveals certain matches. Expressions which are often used today include: 'he was filled with joy' or 'his heart filled with joy'. Fabiszak claims that the concept of safety in a container is very close to the Anglo-Saxon mind and contributes to the positive quality of location inside a container regarding emotions. The aspect of belonging to a group is particularly important and there appears to be a link with the joy of being able to enter an Anglo-Saxon meadhall in which the company enjoys food and drink on festive occasions.

The poetry of this time also describes scenes in which there is light from the open fire of the meadhall and joy is often metaphorically associated with such light. The firelight is reflected in the company's faces and contributes to their joy, as in 'faces beaming with joy'. This would lead to a JOY = LIGHT model. Old English examples can be found in expressions such as *glade onsiene* or *glade anwlita* meaning 'joy in the face'. The 'beaming with joy' metaphor has also continued in other expressions today such as 'his face lit up' and so on. The notion of lightness and darkness have played a significant role in the history of European languages in the field of emotions. Light has always been a positive factor, as in proverbial expressions such as 'light at the end of the tunnel', whereas darkness is negative, being associated with the unknown and evil forces.

Another model in the emotion of joy during the Anglo-Saxon period, which appears to have continued until the present time, is the JOY = COMMODITY metaphor, for which Fabiszak lists numerous examples. She stresses the role of giving gifts at this time between the lord and his retainers in acknowledgement of their loyalty to him. One again, festive occasions in the meadhall, an important place in Anglo-Saxon custom, led to gift-giving and consequently a great deal of joy. The exchange of gifts is reflected in verbs of giving, getting, possessing, having, earning, rewarding, procuring and so on. Old English expressions have various collocations with these verbs and the different lexical items signifying joy:

blisse gifan	'give joy'
blisse begitan	'get joy'
dream agan	'possess joy'
gefea habban	'have joy'
gefea geearnian	'earn joy'
bliss leanan	'give joy as a reward'

The idea of giving or receiving can be found in present-day expressions such as 'it gives me great pleasure to . . .' and it therefore appears that the commodity model has also continued for a long time.

The long-term metaphor paths discussed here in relation to emotions reveal a number of significant findings. On the one hand, metaphors which appear to last indefinitely are indeed often linked to universal physiological models such as the LINK schema in LOVE = UNITY, basic taste perception in LOVE = FOOD, spatial orientation in UP = JOY, the body metaphor CONTAINER = JOY and basic visual perception in JOY = LIGHT. On the other hand, there appear to be just as many long-term metaphors which are associated with specific cultural features found in the history of the English language. The fact that joy is seen as a commodity would suggest that this is a social custom. A link can be seen in the models of love referring to gifts and treasure. Giving and taking appear to be strongly associated with emotions. Does this mean that the analogy with gifts and treasure is limited to one particular culture or could this human activity also be of a universal nature? A study of very different cultures may reveal that the analogy is common to mankind in general.

8.2 Short-term Germanic influences

We can therefore see that a lot of the types of conceptual metaphors that the Anglo-Saxons used in their speech so long ago are actually still used today. However, further research into the emotions in Old English also tend to reveal short-term patterns and metaphors that would sound strange today. The interesting point here is that some of the physiological models appear to have changed direction.

We have seen that some approaches to universal trends in emotions have been criticised due to the fact that they may be more culturally-oriented than previously imagined, as in the case of humoral theory influencing human temperament in the metaphoric lexis of Middle English from the fifteenth century on. Some arguments put forward by Gevaert (2001, 2002) will be examined here in relation to anger in Old English being more culturally-oriented, and therefore more time-specific, than proposed so far.

One of the major findings in Gevaert's work is that her models of anger in Old English, many of whose conceptualisations she considers to be metonymical or hyperonymical as well as metaphorical, can be divided up into three main periods: (i) prior to 850, (ii) 850–950 and (iii) 950–1050. Periods (i) and (iii) were influenced more by Germanic-based conceptualisation and period (ii) underwent considerable influence of Latinate origin. The influence in period (ii) was primarily due to translations into Old English from Latin by King Alfred and others, as well as influence from various biblical sources. Period (iii) was influenced heavily by English homilists such as Aelfric and Wulfstan who wrote in the vernacular. This contributed to the increase in Germanic metaphors at the expense of the Latinate base.

Some of the Germanic conceptualisations include the notion of strong emotions whereby the term *anda* can convey anger, zeal, annoyance, vexations and so on; bodily sensations correlating with the concepts of darkness, bitterness or heaviness as in *sweorcan* (to become dark, meaning angry) or *hefig* (heavy); bodily behaviour as in the terms *rēðe*, *wrāðe* and *gram* which all portray the conceptualisation of ANGER = FIERCENESS and the concept of swell as in the terms *ðrutian* (to swell with pride or anger) and *abelgan* (to swell with anger).

The heat model for anger seems to be a Latinate-based structure since the frequency of this model rose sharply during the period of heavy Latin influence from 850–950 and decreased thereafter. The types of heat expressions found in translations from Latin were in words such as *incendere* (kindle), *calere* (to be warm), *fervor* (heat) and *calor* (heat), all referring to anger. Gevaert (2002) notes that there is a substantial correspondence between the use of heat-conceptualisation in Latin and Old English in King Alfred's *Pastoral Care* with 70 per cent of the Old English heat expressions in her data showing a similar underlying Latin expression. With regard to the fire conceptualisation of anger, she feels that this is probably due more to biblical influence and refers to external fire rather than internal bodily heat. The notion of fire may, of course, also be associated with the wrath of hell linked to the image of burning flames.

Figure 8.1 illustrates the suggested replacement of the SWELL = ANGER concept in Old English by borrowing from Latin between 850–950. The HEAT = ANGER concept would, in fact, represent a long-term, or even indefinite model, in Western society but the suggestion is that it has

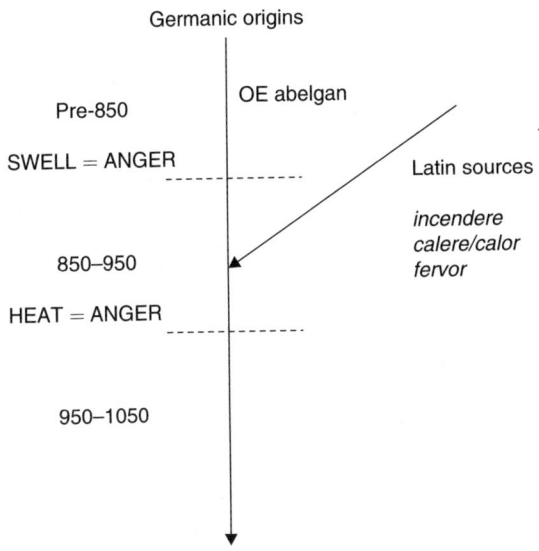

Figure 8.1 Replacement by borrowing of the SWELL = ANGER conceptualisation in Old English
Source: Based on Gevaert (2001, 2002).

crossed languages and that the English language has not always had this particular model.

This notion of a temporary period of Latinate influence introducing the heat metaphor into Old English raises the question as to whether present-day models of heat in the conceptualisation of anger are time-specific in the same way as suggested by Geeraerts and Grondelaers's (1995) theories on humoral theory. One thing which is clear is that certain Old English expressions would appear strange today. The idea of swelling is associated more with pride today than with anger, but swelling was a predominant model in Old English. Gevaert suggests that swelling is associated with the heaving of the chest of people who draw breath in anger.

It has been claimed, in fact, that there was a tendency in Old English literature to describe speech and other verbal functions in pectoral terms. Many contexts specify the chest as the centre of verbal activity rather than the mouth (Jager, 1990: 845–59). There was also an extension of this feature of pectorality from the physical to the psychological domain. It is possible that this development was aided by the fact that medieval psychology situated various mental and affective functions in the thoracic region (Le Goff, 1989: 13–26). If this is the case, it would explain the frequent representation of anger at that time in the form of the chest swelling. Jager points out that pectorality was often used by writers in the late Middle Ages such as Dante, Boccaccio and Chaucer. One of the main reasons for this would presumably be linked to the overriding religious themes in medieval works since Jager points out that the chest is not only 'the source of speech and the repository of God's word and inspiration but also (. . .) the location of knowledge, belief, love, the Holy Spirit, and the spirit or soul itself' (1990: 848).

The important role of the chest, with its various religious, psychological and emotional functions, as portrayed by this description, appears to have been displaced today to other parts of the body, such as the heart or mouth. Consequently, the feature of swelling in English has been reduced in its emotional representations, as in the characterisation of pride.

A few examples from the Old English epic *Beowulf* will be used here to examine not only the emotion of anger but also other emotions portrayed metaphorically. However, it should be noted that there have been a considerable number of translations of *Beowulf*, the latest standard work being by Heaney (1999), and a glance at the translations on the internet gives an idea of the enormous difference in styles of translation of this work. As implied in the problems of translation options discussed in Chapter 4, some internet versions of *Beowulf* offer a very literal translation and other versions rewrite the text in order to present a more readable, modern story. For the purpose of our study of metaphor, however, it is the more literal versions which tend to capture some of the symbols behind the original words. The following examples are taken from a translation of *Beowulf* by Chickering (1977), who tends to give a more literal rendering of the text to help students follow the original Old English version.

Here, the notion of swelling is indeed used with anger, in Chickering's translation of the part of the story in which the dragon (literally here 'barrow-snake') guards its underground treasure:

wæs ða gebolgen beorges hyrde (2304)
(By then the barrow-snake was swollen with rage)

The SWELL = ANGER metaphor thus appears to be linked specifically to the Old English period. The interesting point about the swelling symbol is that it also appears to be used with other emotions, such as sorrow or grief, hence the probable heritage of other collocations such as 'swelling with pride' in modern English. Even more interesting is the fact that the combination of swelling and grief is also associated with heat. As Aitchison (1992: 35) points out, 'the notion of "hot grief" nowadays seems fairly alien, with modern-day concepts of grief being somewhat cooler, as suggested by Swinburne's "grey grief" (*A Match*), and Robert Browning's claim that "hopeless grief is passionless" (Sonnets, *Grief*)'. The former HEAT = GRIEF metaphor can be seen in *Beowulf* – and also in Bach (with variations in the translation):

> gyf . . . Þa cearwylmas colran wurðaþ (*Beowulf, 282*)
> (If the waves/swellings/boilings of grief become cooler)
> Denk nicht in deiner Drangsals Hitze,
> Dass du von Gott veranlassen seist (Bach, Cantata 41)
> (Do not believe in the heat of your distress/grief that God has abandoned you)

Another example of this threefold combination taken from Chickering's translation is the following:

> Ic ðæs mod-ceare sorhe-wylmum seað (1992–3)
> (Cares of the heart, sorrow-surgings boiled within me)

At the same time, there appears to be variation between hot and cold in the grief concept so that the other end of the temperature scale was also employed by the Anglo-Saxons. The notion of 'cold grief' appears several times in *Beowulf*:

> Denum eallum wæs, winum Scyldinga, weorce on mode to geþolianne (1417–19)
> (To every Dane it was a wound mind-deep, cold grief for each of the Scylding nobles)
> gar-cwealm gumena – him bið grim [se]fa onginneð geð mor-mod geong[um] cempan (2043–5)
> (The spear-death of men – has a fierce heart – begins in cold sorrow to search out a youngster)

There therefore appears to be a mixture of images so that one may die out later on in the history of a language while the other one continues. It is clear that emotions, as well as images, can be mixed. It is often said that laughter and tears are very close together. Likewise, two emotions such as anger and grief can be close together or mixed. A certain event may cause a considerable amount of grief and then, if the cause of grief was unnecessary, anger may quickly ensue. The mixing of emotions can also be seen in *Beowulf* in this way and this may also lead to the mixing of images:

> þa se ðeoden mec ðine life healsode hreoh-mod þaet ic on holma geþ ring (2131–2)

(In his angry grief the king implored me by your life, Hygelac, to show my courage)

The process of diachronic metaphor shifts between emotional fields resulting in different sets of metaphoric collocations is a feature which occurs in a number of different passages taken from the *Beowulf* manuscript. An image which is well embodied in Old English is the concept of sharpness which Gevaert (2002) claims to be another metaphor for anger. The actual word 'anger', in fact, comes from Old Norse *angr* (affliction) and was loaned into Middle English in the thirteenth century. A basic metaphoric concept of anger in Old English is affliction which corresponds to the Old Norse term. Although, apparently, no new conceptualisations were linked to later incoming French loanwords for anger from the fourteenth century on, the new source domain of sharpness in Middle English was associated with the new lexical term of anger. This fits in with the Old English conceptualisation of anger as something which hurts.

The search for sharpness metaphors in the *Beowulf* text reveals that it was also used for other emotions such as hate:

ne wæs hit lenge þa gen þæt se [e]cg-hete aþum-swerian æfter wæl-niðe wæcnan scolde (83–5)
(it was still not the time for the sharp-edged hate of his sworn son-in-law to rise against Hrothgar in murderous rage)

Since the concepts of spears and swords are frequently used in this text and often combined in new compound nouns such as the example above of *spear-death*, or in other compounds such as *Spear-Danes*, there may be a correlation between these weapons and the concept of sharpness.

The conclusion may be that the sharpness model, which replaced the swelling image in the lexical item 'anger' during the Middle English period, may also be of Germanic origin. The search for the sharpness image in other former Germanic languages can come up with some interesting examples. One of these, a central concept based on a 'sharp fight', will be examined below.

8.3 Links to other Germanic languages

One of the earliest forms of poetry in the German language was the anonymous *Hildebrandslied* which was passed down in the oral tradition during the different migrations of peoples between the fifth and seventh centuries. It deals with the defeat of the Burgundians in 437 by the Goths and the death of Attila the Hun. The story was finally written down by two monks in the ninth century and was thereby Christianised. The language it was written in was Old High German (OHG). Chronologically earlier than *Beowulf*, it contained the same mix of pre-Christian and Christianised elements, as well as the traditional Germanic values of honour and revenge. A small part of the manuscript has been preserved which gives us a good idea of the structure of the language at that time.

Looking at the 'sharp' image, which may already have been conventionalised by then, it is used in the following OHG example:

do lettun se aerist asckim scritan
scarpen seurim*: dat in dem sciltim stont*
(then they broke their ash spears
in the **sharp (fierce) battle:** which stuck in the shields)

If we move forward in time in the Middle Ages, between *Beowulf* and *Chaucer*, we come to the corresponding Middle High German period and the famous epic of around 1200 of the *Nibelungenlied*, the poem of the Nibelung peoples. This is also very similar to *Beowulf* with heroic Germanic deeds of fighting dragons and so on and contains a mix of Germanic and Latinate influences. In Adventure I of the 'C' manuscript, the 'sharp' image also appears with 'fight':

Ellen in waren undertan ouch die besten rechen von den man hat gesaget
Starch un vil chuene in **scharpfen striten** *unverzaget*

which is translated by the Online Medieval and Classical Library (OMCL) in the following way:

To them owed allegiance the best of warriors, of whom tales were ever told, strong and brave, fearless **in sharp strife**

The OMCL translates medieval works in a style of English appropriate to capturing the atmosphere of the time. For example, an English translation of a passage from the same chapter in the *Nibelungenlied* is as follows:

Why speakest thou to me of men, dear brother mine? I would fain ever be without a warrior's love. So fair will I remain until my death, that I shall never gain woe from love of man.

In this almost Shakespearian style, the expression *in scharpfen striten* in the Old High German text has been translated by the OMCL as 'in sharp strife', but in modern English style it would probably be represented as 'in fierce battles'. In other words, there is a different collocation today with the words 'sharp' and 'battle' and 'sharp' would probably be replaced by 'fierce', or another etymologically-related word in the semantic sense of 'keen'. The word 'keen' not only literally means 'sharp', as in a 'keen sword' but also meant 'fierce' and 'brave' in Old English, as in Old High German. This sense is maintained in modern German 'kühn', and German has also continued with the collocation 'sharp battle', as in the modern German translation of Old High German:

Dann liessen sie zuerst die Eschenlanzen bersten
In scharfem Kampf*, dass sie in den Schilden steckten*

The result is that the metaphoric image of 'sharp' in English has died out in one particular sense, 'a sharp battle', or the medieval 'sharp anger', while it has continued in other Germanic languages. However, English has the metaphoric concept of sharpness in mental faculties such as *sharp wit*, *a sharp mind* and so on. The evolution of metaphor thus implies that, with the death of metaphor paths, there are changing patterns of collocations both within a language and from the cross-cultural perspective. This is illustrated theoretically in Figure 8.2.

In Figure 8.2, Image A is created from a base metaphor concept and continues on a long-term basis in language X. Collocation B in the same

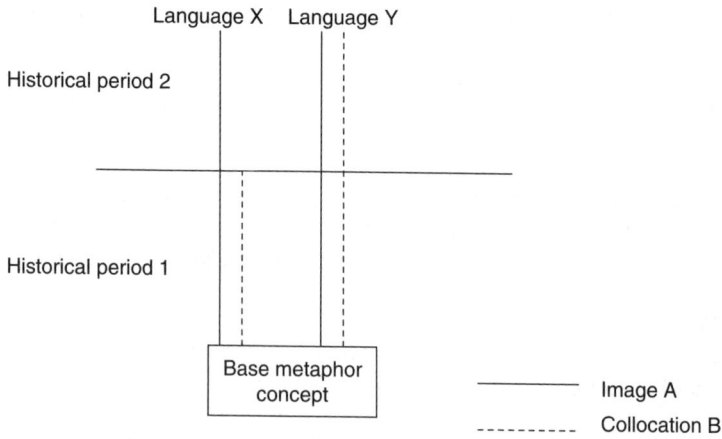

Figure 8.2 Changing evolution of cross-language metaphoric collocations

language, however, dies out at the end of historical period 1. Image A likewise continues in language Y but the same collocation also continues. The result is that there is a cross-language difference in collocations in historical period 2, even though the two languages may have had the same metaphoric associations originally. This could, in principle, be the situation of the sharpness metaphor between English and German except that, in this case, (a) more research would be needed on the sharpness collocations in Old English regarding SHARP + FIGHT and (b) the 'sharp' image has to a certain extent become conventionalised. The degree of metaphoricity tends also to vary with the type of collocation but many sharpness collocations are now conventionalised – a *sharp practice*, *a sharp appetite* and so on.

8.4 Collocational interchangeability in Germanic origins

The case of the SWELL metaphor in Old English is a case of collocational switches signalling the end of particular metaphoric mappings such as the SWELL = ANGER model changing to SWELL = PRIDE. This collocation switch is illustrated in Figure 8.3. The networking process thus involves a change of emotions in the swelling metaphor between the medieval and modern periods; swelling starts off with anger and finishes with pride in this particular model.

The SWELL metaphor in Old English was seen to be a predominant image at that time and was associated with a number of very different

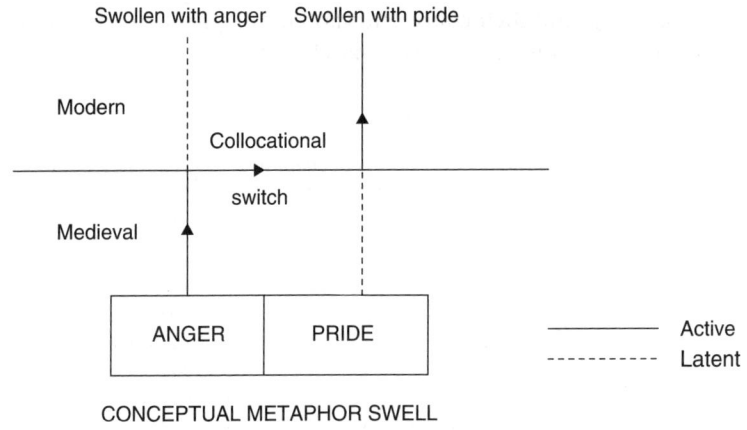

Figure 8.3 Collocational switching resulting in a change of metaphor paths

emotions, including grief. The swelling of the chest was perhaps seen to be a sign of frustration of all kinds. In addition, swelling was sometimes associated with heat. Collocational switching has therefore occurred in English with the changing of images associated with grief, rather than the changing of emotions associated with a particular image. Grief has taken on the notion of coolness, as opposed to heat, whereas anger has taken on the Latin image of heat. As is often the case, particularly in collocational switching within a relatively homogeneous culture, metaphoric images are close together, as in the swelling of the chest and the presumable consequence of physiological heat.

The closeness of images can also be seen in a cross-language approach to collocational switching. The Germanic sources of emotion metaphors indicate that different collocations may evolve in conventionalised metaphors such as *sharp* together with other synonyms such as *keen*. This type of lexis reveals a closely associated network of historical collocations with a mix of divergent patterns. A comparative view of the histories of these two words in English and German illustrates the point.

The modern German cognate of English *sharp* is *scharf* and English *keen* is represented by German *kühn*. The word *sharp* has a basic literal meaning of *having a keen edge or point*, according to the *OED*, hence the synonymy of the two words. It is cognate with other older Germanic languages such as OE *sc(e)arp*, OHG *scarf, scarpf* and ON *skarpr*, deriving from proto-Germanic **skarpaz*. *Keen* has other Germanic cognates such as OHG *kuoni*, and ON *koenn*, deriving from Proto-Germanic **konjaz* or **konia*. Both synonyms derive from the basic senses of *fierce* and *brave*, as attested in medieval literature. Some of the conventionalised metaphoric collocations of English *sharp*, and their equivalents and non-equivalents in German, can be seen in the present-day examples in Table 8.1.

Table 8.1: Present-day collocations of *sharp* in English and German

English	German
1. *Sharp mind*	*Scharfsinnig*
2. *Sharp tongue*	*Scharfe Zunge*
3. *Sharp wind*	*Scharfer Wind*
4. *Sharp frost*	*Scharfer Frost*
5. *Sharp cry*	*Schriller Schrei*
6. *Sharp pain*	*Heftiger Schmerzen*
7. *Sharp practice* (dishonest business)	*Gaunerei*
8. *Sharp edge* (hunger)/*sharp appetite*	*Grosser Hunger*

In Table 8.1, numbers 1 to 4 have equivalent sharpness metaphors, whereas translations of items 5 to 8 require other lexical and syntactic structures. Without undertaking the difficult task of calculating the percentages of equivalents between the two languages, a perusal of bilingual dictionaries reveals that there are a large number of matching equivalents of sharpness due to a common cultural heritage of metaphors.

However, there are also German metaphors of sharpness which are not used in English:

1. *Scharfer Kampf* (hard or fierce fight)
2. *Scharfes Essen* (spicy food)
3. *Scharfer Widerstand* (stiff opposition, strong resistance)

The first example has already been discussed in relation to the disappearance of this collocation since the Old and Middle English period. The word *fight* would probably require another word such as *hard* or *fierce*. There are also other examples including *spicy food* and *stiff opposition* which use the conventional metaphor *sharp* in German. In the second example, this would be the only option; in the third example, other synonyms are possible such as *hart* (hard).

The metaphor *sharp* thus has a mix of cross-language distribution. This is not the case of the synonym *keen* which has followed a widely divergent pattern of collocations compared to English. The cognates in English and German appear to have started with the same attributes of *fierce* and *brave*, although etymological dictionaries (*Oxford Dictionary of English Etymology* and *Duden Herkunftswörterbuch*) also record an earlier sense of *wise*. This might assume that the two lexical items had different semantic origins, literal senses of *a keen edge* for one and *wise* for the other. They then joined together in the same semantic cluster of *fierce* and *brave* at some time during the Middle Ages. However, if *keen* changed from *wise* to *fierce*, this may only be a case of semantic change rather than metaphoric extension and, according to the information supplied by etymological dictionaries, this seems to be the case. If so, *sharp* semantically joined *keen* in two developments: the former metaphoric and the second a literal semantic change.

Collocations can thus be mixtures of metaphoric and literal extensions which overlap and change patterns through time. For our purposes of establishing collocational change, we could take the hypothetical second stage of fierceness and braveness in their etymology as a starting-point for diachronic divergence. The following present-day conventional metaphors of *keen* display an obvious synchronic overlap of metaphoric senses in English due to their level of synonymy but differences do occur:

1. *Keen wind*
2. *Keen frost*
3. *Keen mind*
4. **Keen tongue*
5. **Keen cry*
6. **Keen practice* (dishonest)
7. **Keen edge* (hunger but possible for competition)
8. **Keen pain?*

Examples 1 to 3 are straightforward synonyms with *sharp* and have the same collocations. Examples 4 and 5 are not possible. Example 6 might be possible in another context such as sport while example 7 can definitely be used as a collocation in another context such as competition. Some examples, as in 8, may be more be more doubtful or less salient in the language community. It can thus be seen that this list substitutes *keen* for *sharp* in conventional metaphors and clearly demonstrates the variety of overlapping and differences in the collocations involved.

The German cognate of *kühn* can only be used today in the original sense of *brave, bold* or *daring* as in *kühner Entwurf* (bold plan, project).The extension of *keen* in English towards the synonymous sense of *sharp* has not occurred in German and therefore there appears to be no change in the semantic evolution of the German item. The English 'sharpness' network of collocations has thus become intertwined with a number of different parameters: (a) metaphoric extension along a number of paths from the medieval base concept of *fierce/brave*, (b) the mixture of collocations with the synonym *keen* which does not appear to be metaphoric in origin and (c) varying equivalents with other languages such as German which come from the same origin. The result is a variety of overlapping collocation scenarios in a comparative network (Figure 8.4).

Numbers 1 to 7 in Figure 8.4 represent the different types, for example, 1 would be a collocation with 'sharp' only, 2 with 'keen' only, 3 with German '*scharf*' only, 4 with both 'sharp' and 'keen' and so on.

The foregoing models thus show that a number of possible historical patterns of metaphor evolution may arise: models may be of long duration or time-specific. Time specificity can be dependent on collocational switching which terminates a particular mapping equation and therefore varies the duration of metaphor paths. Another major factor involves the issue

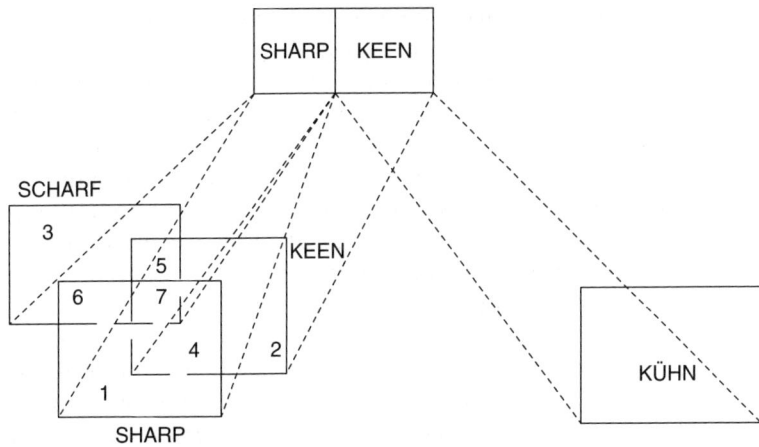

Figure 8.4 Diachronic network of comparative collocational metaphors in English and German

of saliency. This tends to be a very grey area since it is sometimes uncertain whether a metaphor path is actually continuing or not.

8.5 Cultural influence and saliency

Changing cultural features in history obviously greatly influence the duration of metaphors. In his study of memory metaphors, Draaisma (2000: 3) found that technology has played a major role in images throughout the history of language, ranging from Plato's wax tablet to modern-day computers. At the same time, the actual use and frequency of particular metaphor images tend to vary along the time scale. We have seen that different cultural domains may correlate with varying degrees of metaphoric activity through time (Smith et al., 1981). Their study found that there was a shift from social and religious life to nature and the environment as source domains in texts taken from American literature. These shifts occurred over a number of centuries but such shifts may be much shorter and a number of other patterns may be revealed. In a study of metaphor in British political party manifestos during the twentieth-century post-war period, Charteris-Black (2004: 80–4) suggests that there are two major types of change in diachronic metaphor shift: the first is a conceptual shift in the source domain, which he terms a macro-shift, and the second is a shift in particular metaphors within the same source domain, termed a micro-shift.

The study observed a macro-shift in the use of conflict metaphors, from 32 per cent in an early corpus (1945–70) to 43 per cent in a later corpus (1974–97). This change was seen to be due to the relative distance from the Second World War, so that as experience of war decreases, a conflict lexicon creates more semantic tension. On the other hand, there was an increase in the use of building as a source domain during the course of the early period; and in the later period the macro feature of building decreased. However, micro variations took place in that the notion of *framework* increased over that of *structure*. Explanations for these fluctuations in metaphor shift therefore depend on historical events. The presence of war can influence the use of conflict metaphors and, in the case of building metaphors, Charteris-Black suggests that the decline of structuralism and the growth of looser, post-structuralist theories in intellectual thought may very well account for the decline in the use of conceptual metaphors such as *structure*.

The types of images used in metaphor networks are therefore linked to historical events which influence how society thinks and conceptualises its environment. An important feature which emerges from this discussion is therefore the question of saliency. We have seen that metaphors can come and go, but it is evident from the discussions above that some never quite disappear although they are not always in mainstream usage. This would be the case of the political metaphors just described. It tends to be a more complex issue than simple creation and obsolescence since metaphor paths can represent fuzzy areas in their states of existence and continuation.

8.6 Diachronic saliency

In order to try and unravel some of the complexities, we shall explore the idea of setting up different models of diachronic saliency in which source domains fluctuate through time but may never die out. Different levels of saliency occur according to the historical period in question. Low levels of saliency may result in language users finding items which do not fit into conventional ways of thinking at the time hard to comprehend.

Figures 8.5a and 8.5b compare saliency curves in time-specific paths with long-term models having fluctuating saliency.

Figure 8.5a represents a standard time-specific metaphor which has a high level of saliency at its creation and gradually loses saliency until obsolescence. Figure 8.5b represents a long-term item which has time-specific characteristics due to fluctuating saliency. This could represent a relatively indefinite path so that points of birth and death have not been inserted.

Germanic Influences in Old English   139

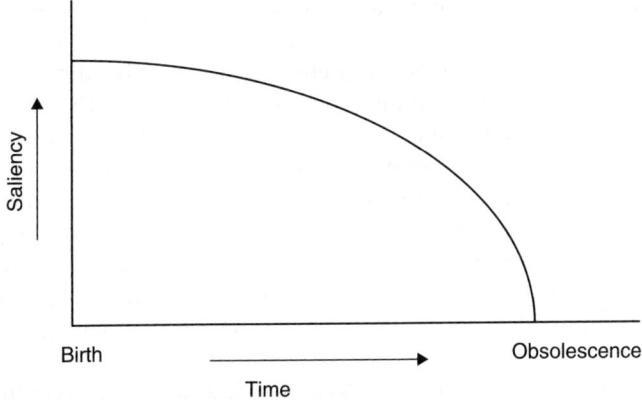

Figure 8.5a   Diachronic saliency in time-specific metaphors

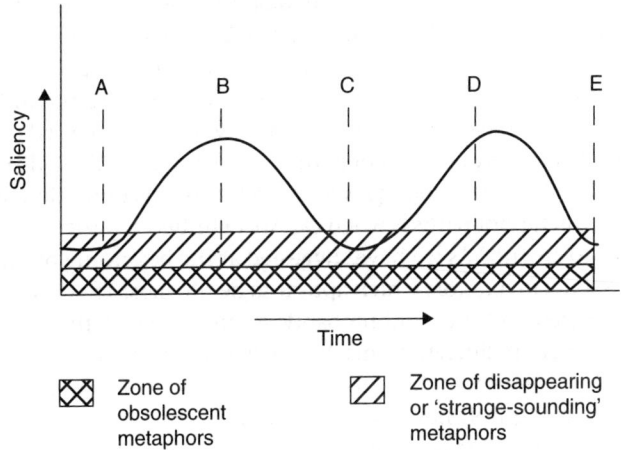

Figure 8.5b   Fluctuating saliency in long-term metaphors

At point A of the path, a given source domain of the metaphor is not very common in the language community and the item may sound a bit strange. It is very likely in this case that the metaphor was more salient at an earlier period and that this thus represents a zone of gradual disappearance. The level of saliency would otherwise probably have been much higher, with a gradual decrease in the case of fluctuation. However, over time, this particular path rises to a high point of saliency at B, falling off to a later historical period at C, but only entering the 'disappearing' and not the 'obsolescent' zone. Language users would therefore find the metaphor natural and easily comprehensible at point B but much less so at points A and C. The result is a long-term metaphor path, following a different scenario to metaphors which become obsolete over the course of time. Of course, the margin between the levels of saliency in the disappearing and obsolescent zones may be very slight or even debatable according to the metaphor in question. In a large number of metaphors, the scenario is therefore likely to be from points B to C unless a cyclic network is involved. In this case, the history of the metaphor would involve a repeated period of increasing saliency to D and then falling off again to point E.

Scenarios of saliency may refer to underlying base concepts or individual items or the network involved. On the basis of the debate on the Old English anger model, the SWELL = ANGER projection would be an obsolete base concept, and conflict metaphors in political discourse would represent fluctuating ones. The individual item 'loose' meaning 'naked' in the general LOOSE = LACK OF CONSTRAINT base concept (proposed in Chapter 4) is an obsolete one, whereas the differing items in the BIRD = FOOLISHNESS base concept, goose, cuckoo, pigeon and so on are arguably less salient today, although they may still be used.

Differing patterns of metaphor paths may be linked to these diachronic saliency models. The obvious question which arises in connection with the saliency of metaphor paths is when can we definitely say that a metaphor has come to an end? As we have suggested at the beginning of the book, there are some metaphors which appear to be timeless. They always seem to have existed and they will probably go on for ever. Others definitely disappear, often in different forms. We shall now look in more detail at the process of obsolescence which also reveals a number of complexities. The term 'dead metaphor' has often been used in the literature and this is frequently represented by a range of controversial variants.

9
Metaphor Death

9.1 Problems of definition

The issues involved in defining when the status of metaphor dies out have been a subject of considerable debate for many years. Formerly, a word was considered to be either a metaphor or to have a literal sense, regardless of whether it may have been a metaphor at one time or not. More recent studies have claimed that the question is much more complex than simply whether a word is metaphoric or non-metaphoric, even if only certain sub-categories are taken into account such as 'conventional' (a concept defined in more detail below under Lakoff and Turner's (1989) discussion of disappearing metaphors), 'dying', 'dead' and so on. We shall first take a look at the different views on the stages of disappearing or extinct metaphors and then examine how this fits into an ongoing theory of evolution in metaphor networks.

Charteris-Black (2004: 18–19) points out the problems of fixing a point in time when a metaphor dies out. He suggests that there is a distinction between a metaphorical process whereby metaphor changes the entries of individual words in the lexicon and the outcome of such a process. Polysemes, idioms and proverbs are derivatives of metaphor and this implies that there is a scale on which metaphors can be more or less conventional. He suggests that while it may be theoretically possible to distinguish between 'living' and 'dead' metaphors with reference to etymological data, fixing a cut-off point on the time scale would be practically impossible.

An overview of some of the main definitions reveals that there tend to be two opposing, if not extreme views, on what constitutes a dead metaphor. In between these two standpoints are a number of approaches which claim there is such a concept as a dead metaphor existent within our conventionalised vocabulary and, paradoxically, maintaining a metaphoric status. Thus, at one end of the scale, the claim is that dead metaphors are not metaphors at all, comprising two separate categories, and at the other end, it is claimed that metaphors never really die out or lose their metaphoric status. Radman (1997: 153) claims that ideally an intermediate position should be maintained since the former view 'tends to neglect some important characteristics of metaphoricity by making it an indistinguishable part of literal language' while the latter pays no attention to the different stages that metaphor passes through in its usage from the idea of 'novelty' to 'trivial convention'.

Goatly (1997: 31–40) suggests metaphoric labels to describe a number of different stages in metaphoricity. His proposal is that metaphors evolve from activity to inactivity with items in the latter stage moving from a 'tired' to a 'sleeping' phase and thus a decrease in metaphoricity. After this stage, metaphors become 'dead and buried' and then simply 'dead'. From the inactive stage on, the metaphors thus represent differing degrees of conventionality.

There is no clear-cut boundary between the 'tired' and 'sleeping' stages. A 'tired' metaphor would be more likely to evoke reference to the original metaphor, as in 'squeeze' referring to a financial borrowing restriction. A 'sleeping' metaphor, such as 'vice', meaning depravity, is less clear than a 'tired' metaphor but enables the language user to make certain metaphorical connections, even though there is no historical etymological connection between depravity and a gripping tool. However, the imagery involved has allowed the construction of certain folk etymologies in spite of the historical facts, such as *in the grip of a vice* meaning 'addicted to depravity'.

The 'dead and buried' category usually involves a change of form which hides a metaphoric relationship. An example can be seen in the English word 'inculcate', meaning 'to indoctrinate', whose origin can be found in Latin *inculcare*, meaning literally 'to stamp in'. Unless an English speaker is a Latin scholar, there is no way of making the connection and the meaning remains opaque. Goatly's example of a dead metaphor would be, for example, *a red herring*, whose figurative meaning, 'a distraction', arose from a literal meaning, 'a spiced fish', which escaped convicts would scatter to put off chasing bloodhounds. Today, the type of fish is no longer eaten and can no longer be construed as a decoy. The metaphor is therefore truly dead.

Logically, one aspect which plays a part in these discussions is whether the historical dimension is taken into account in attributing metaphoricity to a specific item at any given time. This question is raised in Searle's (1979) discussion of metaphor categorisation and subsequently analysed in Traugott's (1985) debate on conventional and dead metaphors. Searle points out that the original sentence meaning of a dead metaphor 'is bypassed and the new sentence acquires a new literal meaning identical with the former metaphorical utterance meaning' (Searle, 1979: 122). Traugott claims that this statement obviously has the historical dimension in mind, since the definition 'identical with the former metaphorical utterance meaning' does not lose sight of its former metaphorical status. However, from a synchronic point of view, the term 'literal meaning' conjures up the idea of a dead metaphor having no metaphoric status at all (Traugott, 1985: 21). The gap between the synchronic and diachronic dimensions can be filled by the process of *re-etymologisation*, that is, by establishing the link between the former metaphoric meaning and the current literal, or dead metaphor, meaning. Much depends on how aware a speaker is of etymologies, the particular problem of which will be discussed in more detail below. Searle makes a graphic distinction between literal utterance, a simple metaphorical utterance and a dead metaphor (Figure 9.1).

In pragmatic terms, Searle defines sentence meaning as literal, and utterance meaning as conveyed or the actual meaning a speaker intends to convey. In (a) in Figure 9.1, a literal utterance whereby the speaker says S represents the sentence meaning P, such as *Mary is tall* and also represents the conveyed meaning R. In (b), a metaphorical utterance, such as *Mary is a block of ice*, the speaker says S is P but means (or 'conveys') that S is R. In (c), a dead metaphor, such as *Mary is cold* (= cold-hearted),

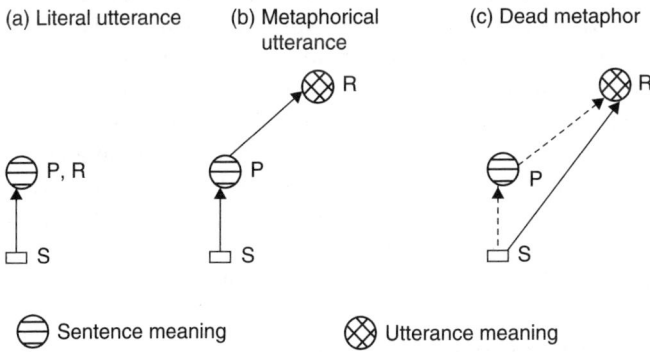

Figure 9.1 Relationship between literal and metaphorical meanings in dead metaphors
Source: After Searle (1979).

S bypasses P and conveys R which acquires a new literal meaning, although the former metaphoric sense could, in this particular case, be re-etymologised and thus identified as such.

It can thus be seen that the so-called dead metaphor of *cold* would still have a certain metaphoric status if this historical dimension is taken into account and that the re-etymologisation process is possible. If it is, Traugott claims, the 'dead or conventional metaphor', as opposed to literal status, is deducible. In the case of *cold*, the former link with 'cold-hearted' or 'distant, reserved' and so on can be made relatively easily according to context, but this is not always so. In many cases, a conceptual link requires a considerable amount of linguistic knowledge. Traugott cites a list of English items of Latin origin or derived from other ancient languages which conceptually have a metaphoric structure. A few examples of this list are given here:

(a) Assertives derived from vocalisation:
    advocate > Lat. *ad* + *vocare* 'to + call'
(b) Assertives from mental and psychological states:
    acknowledge > Old English *on* + *cnawen* 'on/in + know'
(c) Assertives from visual perception:
    declare > Lat. *declarare* 'make clear'
(d) Assertives from spatial perception:
    conjecture > Lat. *con* + *icere* 'throw together'

Unless an English speaker is particularly interested in etymologies or has a considerable knowledge of ancient languages, it is unlikely that the mental link would be made between the two historical periods. The result is that these items would not even be termed 'dead metaphors'. Furthermore, definitions of dead metaphors are hampered by other considerations such as metaphoricity being erased by clichés. In some cases, an expression could be perceived as metaphoric when it was not originally intended as metaphoric. In addition, individual perception may be influenced by whether an expression is from a foreign language or not. Although a native speaker of French will probably not perceive *coucher du soleil* (the sun lying down = sunset) as metaphoric, the newness of the concept for a learner of French may lead them to consider it a particularly colourful figurative expression (Radman, 1997: 153).

9.2 Patterns of metaphor death

It can therefore be deduced that the definition of whether a metaphor is alive or dead at a particular point in time is controversial and open to variation according to individual perceptions of the item concerned and to speakers of different languages. As Charteris-Black (2004: 19) points out:

> Just as the extent to which a metaphor is active may differ between individual speakers of a language, it is also likely to differ between speakers of different languages, since the metaphors that have become lexicalised in one language may not overlap with those which have become lexicalised in another. Therefore, a conventional metaphor in one language may appear highly innovative to a speaker of another language who is not particularly familiar with what has motivated the metaphor, or the extent to which it constrains literal readings. When it come to identifying conventional metaphor, our most effective approach is to refer to a corpus of language: it is frequency of occurrence within contemporary use which will provide evidence of the extent to which a linguistic metaphor has become conventional in a language.

Subject to these different criteria, it is clear that metaphors are created, exist for a certain period of time, and very often disappear as metaphors although they may become conventionalised and take on a more literal appearance. There must be some kind of ordering in patterns which determines whether metaphors quickly disappear or even reappear. A further analysis of Traugott's studies in literal and dead metaphor meanings reveals a number of relevant proposals.

The changing diachronic relationships between literal and figurative meanings appear to depend a lot on the overall concept of saliency and its different aspects. Traugott (1985) suggests three parameters in the literal/dead metaphor divide: (a) reference, (b) conceptualisation and (c) distance. These are discussed in reference to three categories of items with metaphoric links: (i) spatio-temporal terms such as *before*, *after*, *until*; (ii) performative verbs such as *inform*, *suggest*; and (iii) thematic structure in which the principal event, state and so on functions in a proposition as in *the horse belongs to Jenny*. Category (i) mainly refers to conventional metaphors, (ii) to dead metaphors and (iii) is only covertly metaphorical. 'Conventional' according to Traugott refers to expressions such as *I have him in my sight* where *have* and *in* literally refer to possession and inclusion but refer here to visual experience. This is in accordance with Lakoff and Johnson's (1980) conceptual metaphor VISUAL FIELDS ARE CONTAINERS. According to Traugott, the list of assertive verbs above would be dead metaphors.

The reference parameter (a) involves the notion of how strongly an expression is felt to be metaphorical. *Mary is a block of ice* has a high reference value in relation to its literal extension whereas the term *before* in *Mary left before Jane* does not. The conceptualisation parameter (b) defines how easy it is to understand certain metaphoric expressions; animate terms being easier to conceptualise than inanimate. *She is a worm* is easier to conceptualise than *She is a crumpled piece of print-out*. The distance parameter (c) refers to the degree of naturalness within a specific domain. Time, for example, is normally conceived along a front–back, up–down axis rather than in geometric ways so that the *path of time* would be less distant than a *corner in time*.

It can be seen that the parameters proposed all tend to reflect prototype theory (discussed earlier) in which certain concepts in a given domain are more prototypical than others. In the same way, the degree of metaphoricity in the three categories at a given point in time points to prototypicality and therefore to metaphoric saliency with regard to the perceiver. It appears that the degree of saliency in the two groups of three divisions proposed by Traugott reflects the degree to which a metaphor is perceived as conventional, dying or dead.

According to Traugott, conceptual organisation of this kind can also give us a clue as to *which types of metaphors* are likely to become conventionalised or simply die out. Large numbers of metaphors appear to group into coherent sets, each based on a schema, which are dependent on thematic relations such as prepositions and word order in grammar. These items are the ones which are more likely to become conventional or dead metaphors.

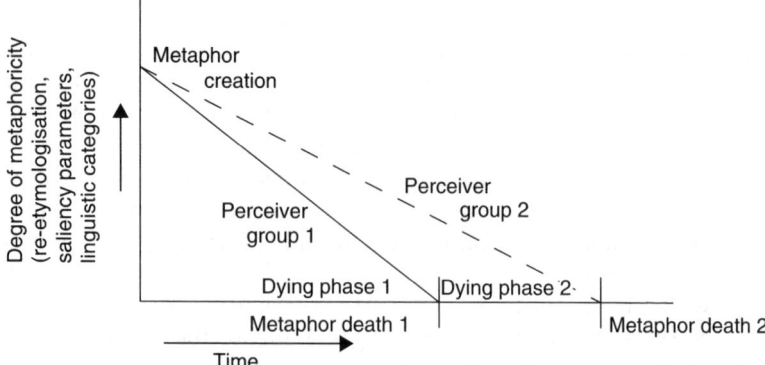

Figure 9.2 Variation in the perception of metaphor death
Source: Based on proposals by Traugott (1985) and Radman (1987).

The foregoing ideas are illustrated in Figure 9.2 in which saliency of metaphoricity depends on the perceiver group at any one point in time. It involves a standard item which undergoes a steady dying process between inception and death. The diagram involves linguistic features only, as opposed to other factors such as cultural influence and so on. The degree of metaphoricity, construed from Radman's (1987) and Traugott's (1985) proposals, thus depends on factors such as the possibility of re-etymologisation, saliency parameters of reference, conceptualisation, distance, and linguistic categories of spatio-temporal terms, performative verbs and thematic structures. Given the problems of defining exactly when a metaphor is dead, the dying process of a metaphor can vary according to the perceiver so that perceiver group 1 finds metaphoricity of an item less salient than group 2. Metaphor death would thus take place at a later time for group 2.

9.3 Regeneration of metaphors

Different factors thus influence the rate of metaphor death. However, dead metaphors can be regenerated at a later stage, either with the same linguistic item or, more frequently, with a different linguistic item but with the same idea generated from an identical conceptual base. We shall examine the question of regeneration in connection with Lakoff and Turner's views on the type of metaphors which die out (1989: 128–31).

Lakoff and Turner also view disappearing metaphors on different levels. A truly dead metaphor would be one which no longer exists at either the conceptual or the linguistic level. This would appear to be similar to Goatly's definition of a truly dead metaphor. If we take the word 'pedigree' in English, it was derived from Old French *pied de grue*, meaning the 'foot of a crane'. The explanation behind this is that the image of a crane's foot was mapped onto the image of a family tree diagram to represent genealogical origins (Figure 9.3).

The pedigree metaphor is therefore now dead both conceptually and linguistically. An example of another dead metaphor, which would still be alive conceptually but not linguistically, is 'comprehend', in the same way as 'grasp', meaning 'to understand'. The conceptual metaphor used formerly in Latin *comprehendere (com + prehendere* = grasp), UNDERSTANDING = GRASPING, is still alive today but not in this particular word. This would correspond, for example, to Traugott's list of dead metaphors in performative verbs originating from ancient languages. A third type, according to Lakoff and Turner, is the typical conventional metaphor

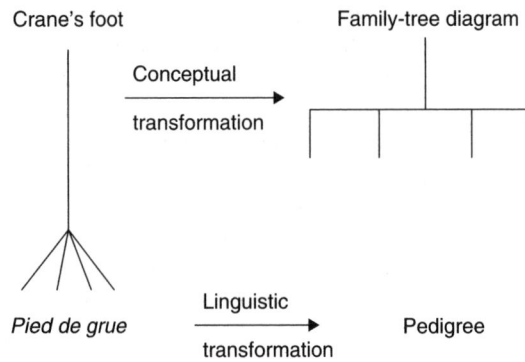

Figure 9.3 Death of the 'pedigree' metaphor

which forms part of our conceptual system. The expression, 'he's almost gone', used of a dying person, is not really metaphoric now, but is a part of language which conceptually is overwhelmingly metaphoric. According to this view, the conceptual levels of both dead and conventional metaphors would therefore be permanently active. The conceptual metaphors UNDERSTANDING = GRASPING and DYING = DEPARTING are an entrenched constituent of a conceptual system which can be regenerated at any time to form new metaphors on the same basis or give a new metaphoric input to an existing linguistic item.

If this view is accepted, additional features can be included in the model of networking theory proposed in Figure 7.1 on the comparative evolution of metaphor paths. Figure 7.1 suggests that metaphor paths originate from a base concept and either continue uninterruptedly throughout the lifetime of a language or enter phases of being active or dormant. The evolution of paths in this model is based on changing metaphoric attributes in the same linguistic item. For example, the long-term development of 'dry', even though it was spelt 'dri' in Middle English, would represent the same linguistic item. Metaphoric attributes of this item have come and gone throughout history or, in some cases, have remained.

The active and dormant phases suggest regeneration at the conceptual level. However, due to the problems of identifying metaphor death outlined above, the points of obsolescence in Figure 7.1 are unlikely to be clear-cut boundaries. They are more likely to represent fuzzy boundaries with a period of metaphors slowly dying off. In the same way as observed in Tourangeau and Sternberg's (1982) study of individual perceptual

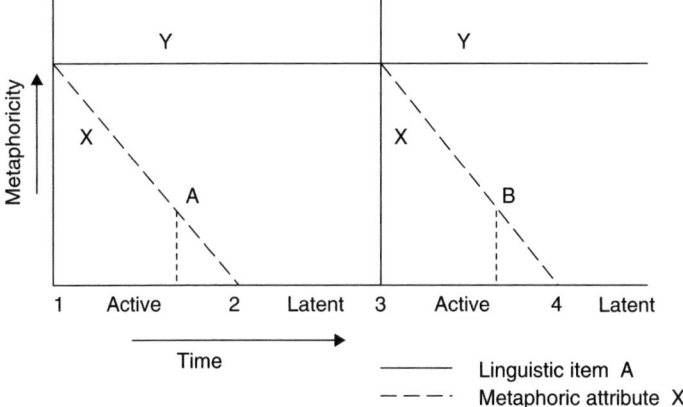

Figure 9.4 Regeneration in dead metaphors

variation regarding metaphoric mapping in the domains of world leaders and land mammals, there is likely to be perceptual variation in how metaphoric the dryness concept is: *dry wine, dry country* or *dry humour* probably have differing levels of metaphoricity.

In contrast, the inception of a metaphor is likely to be sudden, a new meaning is usually introduced at a point of time and quickly become widely known, particularly in the multi-media age. As the metaphoric element is new, the language user perceives it as being truly metaphoric, but this tends to decrease with time in conceptual metaphors. A standard item may therefore begin with a high degree of metaphoricity which slowly decreases in a straight line to its death. Although this may be the case for many metaphors, it is probably not necessarily so for every item since saliency may take on other progressional forms such as curves on diachronic scales. A diachronic view of saliency in metaphor regeneration is illustrated in Figure 9.4.

In Figure 9.4 metaphoric attribute X of linguistic item Y is innovated at point 1 on the time scale and decreases steadily to its death at point 2. This would represent its first phase of activity, after which it enters a phase of latency. Since the conceptual metaphor remains alive in the language, the same metaphoric attribute is regenerated with the same linguistic item at point 3. The cyclic pattern continues with a gradual decrease in metaphoricity to its second death at point 4. This represents an ideal scenario of a conventionalised metaphor but there are many other variations, such as related conceptual metaphor attributes being

150 *Metaphor Networks*

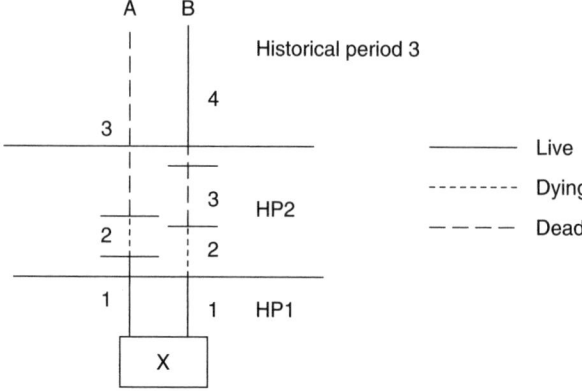

Figure 9.5 Diachronic phases of live, dying and dead metaphors
Source: Based on Figure 7.1, scenario 1.

regenerated with the same linguistic item or, in some cases, being associated with other linguistic items. At some point in time, for example, at A or B, the item would no longer be considered as a metaphor by a large section of the language community, and this would represent the fuzzy boundary in its existence.

If we take scenario 1 from Figure 7.1, a more likely development in metaphors which become sequentially active and latent through the course of time may be as illustrated in Figure 9.5.

Here, the metaphoric attribute in language A undergoes three phases of being live, dying and dead in the concept X network. Phases 1 and 2 would be regarded as active whereas phase 3 is latent, although representing metaphor death. Language B uses the latency in phase 3 to regenerate the metaphoric attribute which has remained alive until the present day.

The aspect of successive regeneration of metaphor may actually be more frequent than realised. With reference to metaphors of memory which often use different technologies as images, it appears that our conceptions of memory appear to change completely with each successive image. After a while, however, familiar features show through again and again and similarities may be identified on closer inspection (Draaisma, 2000: 232–3). On a longer time scale, this may produce cyclic networks in the history of language whereby similar attributes are successively regenerated.

It can be seen that the distinction between the conceptual and linguistic levels of metaphor, as emphasised in Chapter 2, are important features in analysing the birth and death of metaphors. The networking process depends on these two levels with regard to the ongoing evolution of metaphor. Although some metaphor creation represents isolated cases (this often happens in expressions such as proverbs or fixed figurative items which are related to specific events in the past) the vast majority form parts of networks. In the light of Lakoff and Turner's (1989) proposals, the different types of items involved in metaphor death would involve variations in the network at the linguistic and conceptual levels.

A final point should be mentioned about metaphor death with reference to the interpretation of conventionality. As Goatly (1997: 35–6) points out, this depends, to a certain extent, on the role of semantics or pragmatics. The comprehension of a strange-sounding metaphor may depend on the context in which it is used. A context-bound interpretation would be the field of pragmatics and would therefore be more related to a speaker's thought whereas an independent use of a metaphor would represent a semantic feature. The latter thus involves a decoded sense of a sentence in its own right rather than attempting to interpret a metaphor by examining the whole context. These two dimensions can influence the status of conventionality and whether a metaphor is dying or dead at a given point in time.

It is therefore not usual for metaphors suddenly to become obsolete. There are often different phases of obsolescence and the final outcome may be a conventionalised status from which there is no return, or a metaphor may enter a phase of latency. The latter signifies that it could be regenerated at a later stage due to its ongoing potential for reconceptualisation, even though it is not in common usage during the latency stage. Furthermore, we have seen that a metaphor concept may fluctuate in its saliency at different historical periods.

Another aspect in the ongoing fluctuation of conceptualisation involves our attitudes towards identical images and metaphoric concepts during the course of time. We may wonder whether particular conceptual metaphors actually meant the same to the Anglo-Saxons, for example, during the reign of King Alfred, as they do to the modern inhabitants of large cities in the twenty-first century. This is a valid point, since there could be all kinds of cultural influences which may change our perception of the environment, even though we use the same symbols many centuries later. We shall now explore how perception of imagery may change through the ages.

10
Historical Mindsets

10.1 Similarities between time-specific and culture-specific models

In the same way as perception of the environment differs around the world today in very diverse cultures, some linguists have suggested that this differentiation can also be felt across time. Take the case of spatial orientation. Let us consider an example discussed by Lakoff (1987: 310). If we focus on the notion of 'front' from the point of view of the observer (as opposed to the inherent front of objects that have one, such as a car) and ignoring certain complications concerning who is the observer, 'front' is normally construed in English to be the side facing the observer. In the case of the African language, Hausa, however, 'front' is the side facing in the same direction as the observer. Either choice is compatible with human experience but the difference illustrates the fact that these two languages have quite a different perception of spatial orientation.

Given the fact that this type of contrast exists between two cultures today and that language usually passes through different forms of culture along the time scale, it would be reasonable to assume that people in the past also conceptualised their environment in a different way. In other words, metaphoric images may have been created out of a different type of mindset. In this chapter, we shall look at how the evolution of metaphor also included the changing perception of images themselves.

In figurative terms, an attempt at fitting together the pieces of the evolutionary jigsaw puzzle of metaphor thus shows that the diachronic dimension resembles, in many ways, the synchronic, cross-cultural dimension. Metaphor paths evolving through time often follow the same patterns and directions but lose and gain figurative terms on the way. This accounts for the kind of time-specific variation we have seen. A glance at metaphors across different languages reveals such fluctuating trends: there are many similar metaphors which are created in different cultures, like the universally-oriented physiological models, but some metaphor groups may be more extensive in certain languages or be lacking completely in others. In both cases, cultural factors and internal clustering effects account for variation along these two specific dimensions.

By considering both the synchronic and diachronic dimensions, we are also able to see that time and culture-specific models sometimes match up, reinforcing their similarity. However, an analysis of both suggests that evolving models may progress at different speeds according to the language/culture involved. A number of examples have come to light in our study. We have seen that the centre of thought and feeling in modern Japanese is apparently the belly (*hara*). Padel (1992: 12–13) also implies that this part of the body was fundamental to the Ancient Greeks' understanding of thought and feeling: 'in ordinary fifth-century life, when people wondered what was going on inside someone, what mattered was that person's *splanchna*, "guts". It is easy to forget this and to fail to follow through the differences it makes. Psychology in tragedy's world has practically nothing to do with the head.' English translations of the Greek term *splanchna* (singular *splanchnon*) in poetry actually adopt words such as 'entrails' for divination and 'bowels' for emotion.

There is therefore a diachronic and cross-cultural match in the conceptual metaphor between Ancient Greek and modern Japanese. Does this mean that languages tend to use the belly as the centre for thought and feeling and then move on to other parts of the body such as the heart and head? This is very speculative. Certainly, there seems to have been a trend from the belly in Antiquity to pectorality in the Middle Ages, according to studies in European languages. We would first, however, have to work out equivalent metaphor models in early Japanese for comparison and then take the histories of a large number of cultures into account. What is more likely is that there are probably a far greater number of cross-cultural matches in general if the diachronic dimension is taken into consideration. This would reinforce the idea of diachronic universals.

Synchronic variation is often due to differences arising at *one* point in time, whereas there may have been more similar correspondences at an earlier period. Cross-cultural variation is thus due to diachronic merger or divergence. In the case of culturally-related languages such as English and Dutch, we have seen that, although the former has the GREEN = ENVY colour metaphor today, the colour used was originally yellow. We have also seen that Dutch uses both green and yellow today in the form of a fixed expression, *groen en geel van nijd worden* (become green and yellow with envy). The question here is whether English also used the two colours at a particular point in time, either as two separate expressions or fused into one idiomatic expression. This may very well have been the case before replacement took place.

The status of fusion is perhaps slightly different from separate expressions, since the latter may encourage replacement, but more detailed research would be needed to find out exactly why replacement took place in English. It may be that yellow with envy became lost in English because yellow was needed to occupy another part of the semantic space relating to cowardice. On a longer-term basis, therefore, conceptual metaphors such as colour in European languages and the belly metaphor in Ancient Greek and modern Japanese do not always match up because of the time difference. Cross-cultural metaphor paths are thus constantly corresponding, separating (or never meeting) at particular points on the time scale.

10.2 Attitudes towards imagery through time

This ongoing change along the diachronic scale raises the issue of what we shall therefore term here *historical mindsets*. Attitudes towards metaphoric imagery change through time. Not only isolated figurative items, but the whole image schema or cultural context in which they are situated, can change from one historical period to the next. Instead of symbols becoming obsolete as in metaphor death or conventionalisation, the same items used by a language community may be viewed in a very different way.

In order to demonstrate this more global aspect of metaphor evolution which encompasses the kinds of historical models we have proposed, we will use some of the findings outlined in Padel's (1992) study of symbolism in Ancient Greek. In the case of the history of figurative language in Western society, Padel's interesting work sheds further light on the origin of our metaphors and helps put their evolution over the last 7000 years into perspective.

One thought-provoking idea which comes out of Padel's study is that, although we may have the same metaphoric images today as the Greeks had in the 5th century BC, we may not actually *feel* the perceptions of these images in the same ways as the Greeks did. We perceive the effects involved in the mapping of an image onto a target domain but we do not necessarily experience the same physiological effect:

> later European writers . . . are affected, sometimes directly, by Greek poetry or philosophy and its strong shaping pressure on European thought. They are also influenced, partly invisibly, by Greek metaphors

that seep through in translation, and via Latin and medieval languages, into modern discourse. Their reading and their language endorse the imagery, though their physiological ideas, on the whole, do not.

(Padel, 1992: 85)

There is often a 'dissociation' between the way we speak about what we feel and what we believe happens inside us. Padel offers an analogy in the commercial field regarding the passion for spices in the early medieval period which, in many cases, slowly disappeared while leaving the commercial trade routes and networks in place. To a large extent, these trade routes paved the way for modern transportation in commerce and industry.

Another difference in the Ancient Greeks' perception of metaphor, according to Padel, is that 5th century BC Greeks did not distinguish literal from metaphorical meaning in the same way as we do. We are highly conscious of this division today while the Greeks expressed their ideas through the medium of metaphor without thinking that they were using metaphors. The Greek word *metaphora* did not actually come into existence until the 4th century BC (Padel, 1992: 9). It could be argued, however, that notwithstanding the definition of the phenomenon of figurative language, it remains probable that speakers today are still not always conscious of the figurative language they are using. Many speakers today, for example, would not automatically think that conduit expressions – his words *carry* little meaning, the idea is *buried* in terribly dense passages, your words seem *hollow* – are metaphoric in origin (Lakoff and Johnson, 1980: 11). If we take the wider sense of conceptual metaphor into account, as we have done in this book, by including items such as conventional metaphors or other figurative terms of low metaphoricity, it is certain that speakers use a large part of figurative language unconsciously. However, if the literal/figurative dimensions had never actually been defined, it is indeed likely that the unconscious element was more pronounced at that time.

Padel thus raises a number of issues about differences in the perception of metaphor between the Ancient Greeks and modern times. An example linked to the preceding point about consciousness or lack of it in metaphor usage is the Ancient Greeks' attitude towards personification. We have seen that it is a very effective tool today, as in the field of drugs metaphors. Padel gives the impression that it was all-pervasive in Ancient Greece and was probably very visual. Vase-painters depicted various Greek tragedies, representing characteristics through images such as a winged creature next to Aphrodite representing jealousy. Personification was a fundamental part of religious life in Ancient Greece. Not only in love, gods were symbolic of many emotions such as in Hesiod's *Theogony* (Birth of Gods). Fear and Terror are the children of Ares. Personal qualities such as Emulation, Victory, Strength and Force are the children of Styx. Zeus marries Themius (Right) and Metis (Cunning Thought), whom he later swallows (Padel, 1992: 157 ff.).

The point that Padel makes about the historical development of personification is that although the same process was used at later historical periods, such as the adoption of the image of a woman for the French Republic from 1789 to 1848 (and the same could presumably be said for the Statue of Liberty in the United States), the personifying mode was also used in a rather empty way. As soon as symbols became conventionalised, they became empty shells, as in so much Baroque allegory.

These arguments should be taken into consideration in discussing the overall development of metaphor from a historical perspective; it is likely that even our attitudes towards metaphor itself, as Padel also suggests, have changed through the centuries.

10.3 Changing attitudes in long-term models: Ancient Greece

We have seen that a lot of metaphors in modern English are conceptually networked back to former historical periods and often go back to the beginning of written records. It is clear that many images from Antiquity have lasted until the present day. Metaphors are often built up and networked to pre-existing ones. If we take some of Padel's Ancient Greek symbolism into consideration, we can see that there are a number of long-term correspondences with some of the examples we have discussed in modern European languages.

A starting-point in a discussion of changing attitudes to the same forms of symbolism is the container image, which Padel appears to claim to be fundamental to Ancient Greek thought. In the drugs metaphors network, an apparent universal trend, at least in European languages, is the inside/outside orientational schema. This may represent the base of a large number of long-term paths spanning many emotional fields. In the introduction to her book on Ancient Greek imagery, Padel starts with what she calls 'the divinity of inside and outside'. In line with the 'body as a metaphor' construct proposed by cognitive linguists such as Lakoff and Johnson (1980), she claims that the literature of Ancient Greek tragedies was often biological in that it was frequently based on what was considered inside or outside human beings (1992: 3).

She suggests further that everyone uses the outside world to speculate about an inner world, and vice versa. In classical Greek, outer and inner worlds explain and influence each other. This would fit in with the present-day notion of how the drugs world is regarded by conventional society; anything associated with drugs is definitely on the outside, or if not, on the perimeter, as in the expression 'being on the fringe of society'. Inside/outside orientation would thus be a long-term networking process throughout Western thought.

However, Padel also suggests that symbolism in the 5th century BC was dominated by the outer world in contrast to present-day thought being based on the inner world (the claim being that Freudian psychology, which is purported to be internally based, has had a major influence on contemporary Western thought). A theory put forward by Padel is that Ancient Greeks viewed changes in society as coming from the outside, the effects thereof subsequently being felt within the body.

The claim that contemporary thought is internally based may be construed in contemporary attitudes towards the drugs scene. The inner world is often viewed as someone's 'home ground', as an environment with which the perceiver is familiar. Anything outside the container image is considered to be alien. As we have seen, the use of inside or outside also depends on the perceiver's viewpoint: different sections of society use inside or outside orientation to describe their own particular world. 'Outside' represents the drugs world for conventional society and vice versa for drug addicts.

The first difference in attitudes diachronically would thus be that the starting point for viewing particular problems within the container dimension has changed: Ancient Greeks viewed social problems from the outside. A second major cultural difference is that emotions, as part of bodily functions were, according to Padel, inextricably linked to daemonic forces. Such forces helped to explain a large number of human activities and feelings and the idea of them is linked to one particular fluctuating dimension discussed below: the role of religion in the history of emotional symbolism.

A number of long-term metaphor models have been proposed in our discussion on universals. One example, found in the field of drugs, as well as existing in a large number of other fields of human experience, is that of disease. This feature is linked to the inside/outside orientational schema. Padel's findings about Ancient Greek disease are that:

> The prior cause of disease is outside. Doctors therefore record outside changes first. The itinerant author of *Epidemics* ('Stays Abroad') prefaces

his descriptions of diseases with 'situation', season, temperature, humidity, and prevailing wind:

> In Thasos, before and at the season of Arcturus, many violent rains, northerly winds . . . Winter northerly, droughts, cold periods, violent winds, snow. Spring northerly, droughts, slight rains, periods of cold . . . After the Dog Star, until Arcturus, hot summer. Great heat, not intermittent but continuous, severe. No rain . . . In winter paralyses began. They attacked many. A few quickly died . . . Early in spring burning fevers began . . . When autumn and the rains came the cases were dangerous.
> (Padel, 1992: 52)

The link between wind and disease continues today in proverbs such as 'it is an ill wind that does nobody any good'. Windstorms and snowstorms, as with hurricanes, tornados, cyclones and blizzards, were seen to be associated with the influx of large quantities of drugs and therefore disease, as in the example: *the crack hurricane: the new American plague.*

The origin therefore probably goes back to the Ancient Greeks' external view of bodily experience. In addition, disease, like pain, was not dissociated from daemonic influence. Ill people who 'found themselves in pain might have thought of daemonic sources, like the evil eye or an unpropitiated god. Something nonhuman had penetrated their innards . . . their underlying picture of innards in relation with the world and with the causes of disease is still propelled by divinatory arts and goes back to the *Iliad*' (Padel, 1992: 49).

The causes of disease and pain thus represented a different mindset at that time: it appears that they came from the outside and the gods had a role to play in their origins. This fits logically into the conception of gods at the time, as representative of different aspects of human experience, often with different names, in the same way as in Hinduism. They supplied an infinite number of explanations about life to the perceiver and therefore gave symbolic language a different aspect, even though semantically the symbols remained connected to the same fields in the diachronic networking process.

Also relevant here are the heat and swelling images of anger in the controversial debate about the origins of the heat metaphor in modern English. Padel does not appear to distinguish heat and swelling symbols as far as Ancient Greek is concerned. She rather groups them into what could be interpreted as a 'flux of feeling' image, to use her words. It is clear that both were used in Ancient Greek to denote anger and that the general 'flux of feeling' image was used to cover a considerable variety of emotions, including disease. To a large extent, this would be related to the origins of humoral theory in which the different types of fluids flowing around the body denote particular emotional states. This is also parallel to the frequent use of water, or other liquid symbols used for the emotions in Ancient Greek literature. This is particularly the case with the sea, which played an important part in Ancient Greek life.

As far as anger was concerned, 'boiling' was a frequently used symbol, which, fitting in partly with Lakoff's (1987) long-term hypothesis about the origins of anger metaphors in English, would refer not only to blood but also to other bodily liquids. There was an association with objects in the physical environment such as Mount Etna in Sicily where the volcano would erupt and boil over when angry. At the same time, the 'excessive flux' in the body can also cause swelling. Padel does not give any concrete examples of ANGER = SWELLING but her discussions suggest that the swelling symbol can be used for all kinds of emotions caused by an excess of liquid (1992: 82–3). Thus, boasting, likened to madness, is also swollen effects of the mind. This can be likened to modern English expressions such as 'a windbag' and other languages like the French *il est un peu gonflé* (literally, 'he is a bit swollen'), meaning he is boastful.

How would this affect the evolution of the anger metaphor in English? Without the relevant research on specific manuscripts, the question is difficult to answer, but there are a number of possible scenarios. Heat and swelling are obviously conceptually linked as far as the origins of our civilisation in Antiquity are concerned. One causes the other. If the swelling metaphor was a frequent one in Ancient Greek literature, it is possible that later manuscripts of Germanic languages opted for this feature rather than heat, thereby influencing early Anglo-Saxon manuscripts. Latinate languages may have preferred the heat symbol and thereby influenced later medieval scripts, particularly Middle English, according to our analysis of the Old and Middle English periods. This is a likely scenario since early Germanic literature must have been influenced by Antiquity. If, however, the swelling symbol did not exist for anger in Antiquity, its predominance in early Germanic texts may have been the result of the close conceptual association with heat and therefore represented an innovation or, on the other hand, it may have been a switch of collocational patterns from other 'swelling emotions'. This is obviously speculative but it can be seen that the two symbols do have similar conceptual origins in Antiquity.

Apart from swelling, heat was naturally linked to fire, and as we have seen in the love model, fire was linked to passion, as well as other emotions. As Padel puts it: 'Emotions burn . . . Madness, desire, sometimes fear or hope, and supremely anger, "boil" in, or burn, innards. Hearts are "set on fire" with important news, love heats Zeus's heart . . . Desire sets human beings on fire. "I saw inside his cloak and burst into flames", says Socrates, teasing the image. Flames flash from the eyes of those in love or mad with rage' (1992: 116–17).

There appears to be a long-term complex of symbolism associating the images of heat and fire, which are metaphorically used for a wide range of intense emotions. Heat and fire have often been used pejoratively and are frequently the cause of madness or delirium. The images themselves have pejorative connotations throughout history such as the flames of hell in medieval Christianity. It was seen in the present-day drugs scenario that heat is linked to the dangerous world of drugs, and the heat image is often employed for other dangerous areas such as the political 'hot spots' around the world. At the same time, our present-day notion of heat has undoubtedly changed. As Padel points out, in Ancient Greece fire was equally linked to daemonic forces: the Greek gods themselves would cast down their fiery rays on people as fever weapons, reflected in the name of the plague-bringing god *purphoros*, 'fire-bringing' (1992: 116).

The suggestion here is that while all these long-term images are still used – as we have seen in Kövecses's (1988) modern metaphors of love and the different examples illustrated by the drugs scenario – attitudes towards them have changed through time. Two of the main issues raised in this comparison with Ancient Greek philosophy are the perceiver's internal or external relation to his body and the role of daemonic forces. The latter raises another major aspect in the historical mindsets of Western thought: the influence of religion.

10.4 Religious mindsets

Religion is not the only major force in the formation of figurative language in a given culture and other aspects include the typical social forces of money, political power, social class and so on. In the history of Western thought, however, and certainly in a good number of other cultures, religion has played a major role in metaphor evolution. Religion still plays a large part in the creation of modern English metaphors, but its role continues to change and to influence time-specific items or the degree of saliency.

Charteris-Black (2004: 173 ff.) has studied the frequency of metaphor use in the Bible, making a comparison between the Old and New Testaments. The major lexical fields used for metaphoric symbols were found to be, in order of frequency: animals, conflict, plants, light, building/shelter, food and drink, body, journeys, weather, fishing and hunting and fire. Low frequency items included treasure/money, dirt and cleanliness, clothes and a mixture of miscellaneous items.

A second finding in the survey of the Bible was that frequency levels of different fields tended to vary between the Old and New Testaments, although this was probably influenced to some extent by the fact that, in the sample analysed, the Old Testament text is as much as four times as figurative as the New Testament. The results reveal that conflict metaphors are very salient in the Old Testament sample but are nonexistent in the New. Fire is of relatively low frequency in the Old Testament sample but nonexistent in the New.

This type of variability in metaphor usage is, first of all, a clear example of diachronic variability in saliency. The issue of saliency reflects the way in which we symbolise our environment and this changes with time. It contributes to changing conceptual mindsets. Second, and independently of the saliency feature, the type of use the symbol is put to also modifies the way we think. This can be illustrated by religion and there is an interesting link between the Christian and pre-Christian periods with regard to the role of the relevant gods of the two periods.

Charteris-Black (2004: 214–16) cites a number of examples of how the typical use of fire in a metaphoric context is as a form of punishment by God, indicating that fire is associated with divine anger (Old Testament):

> While he was yet speaking, there came also another, and said, The **fire** of God is fallen from heaven, and hath burned up the sheep, and the servants, and consumed them; and I only am escaped alone to tell thee
> (Job 1:16)

> But I will punish you according to the fruit of your doings, saith the LORD: and I will kindle a **fire** in the forest thereof, and it shall devour all things round about it
> (Jeremiah 21:14)

It was suggested that pre-Christian Ancient Greece reflected the role of gods and daemonic forces in attitudes towards metaphor. In the same way, the Bible uses the monotheistic Christian God to express dissatisfaction and to exact punishment. There is therefore a religious link – in the participation of a god – between the two historical periods, even though conceptual aspects are often different. The Bible, however, uses the symbol of fire in the same way as it is used today with regard to the emotions, particularly anger. Again, even if it expresses intense emotion, it is often used in biblical terms to express extreme rage, as in the following examples again from Charteris-Black (2004: 214):

> Therefore the LORD heard this, and was wroth: so a **fire** was **kindled** against Jacob, and *anger* also came up against Israel
>
> (Psalms 78:21)
>
> Behold, the name of the LORD cometh from far, **burning** with his anger, and the burden thereof is heavy: his lips are full of indignation, and his tongue as a devouring **fire**
>
> (Isaiah 30:27)

Divine punishment in the Bible is also used in a number of other prevalent metaphor models used extensively in Ancient Greek literature. Weather conditions, particularly extreme conditions, and war represent another two examples. Charteris-Black (2004: 210) points out:

> another dimension of the source domain that is available for metaphoric projection is the knowledge that strong winds can inflict damage and, therefore, very strong winds such as whirlwinds are associated with divine punishment . . . :
>
> For, behold, the LORD will come with fire, and with his chariots like a **whirlwind**, to render his anger with fury, and his rebuke with flames of fire
>
> (Isaiah 66:15)

We can link this context to the storms of the drugs scenario where, we have seen the same destructive effects with regard to societies buying and consuming the drugs. However, the different mindset of the *whirlwind* metaphor here is the addition of divine intervention. The same applies to aspects of the war metaphor, as described in the drugs scenario. It is termed by Charteris-Black as a conflict metaphor in the biblical context, including verbs such as 'fight', 'trumpet', 'defend', 'destroy', 'struggle', 'defeat' and 'conquer' and nouns such as 'shield', 'sword', 'bow', 'arrow' and so on (2004: 207–9):

> But thou, O LORD, art a **shield** for me; my glory, and the lifter up of mine head
>
> (Psalms 3:3)
>
> The wicked have drawn out the **sword**, and have bent their **bow**, to cast down the poor and needy, and to **slay** such as be of upright conversation
>
> (Psalms 37:14)

The *shield* metaphor in the first example refers to faith in God. The weapons metaphors in the second passage are used to denote the means by which evil men punish the virtuous. The religious content of these conflict metaphors is very apparent, much more so than in present-day war metaphors. However, as Charteris-Black (2004: 79, 103–5) points out, the religious aspect in the form of spiritual rebirth can often surface in politics, particularly in British party political manifestos and American presidential speeches:

> But a government can only ask these efforts from the men and women of this country if they can confidently see a **vision of a fair and just society**
>
> (New Labour)

> The brave Americans serving our nation today in the Persian Gulf, in Somalia, and wherever else they stand **are testament to our resolve**
> (Bill Clinton)

> An idea **ennobled by the faith** that our nation can summon from its myriad diversity the deepest measure of unity
>
> (Bill Clinton)

Another metaphor model which highlights the similarities and dissimilarities between pre-Christian, biblical and present-day creations is the basic binary concept of dark/light. There are some fundamental differences but, at the same time, deeper insight into the cultural layers also reveals threads of conceptual continuity. If we go back to Padel's findings in Ancient Greek metaphor of the innards symbol as the focal point of thought we find that this connects to darkness. The strength of this part of the body as the centre of thought and feeling is summed up in Padel's (1992: 75) words:

> Through multiple resonances of divination, Greek mentality associates the innards' darkness with their status both as the physical center of life and consciousness and as the source of potential knowledge. They are consulted, like gods and prophets. They 'speak', but not necessarily truthfully. Gods, too, often deceive. The first dream of Greek poetry is both god-sent and a lie. Innards command and advise, as gods do. Their power, their knowledge, may or may not derive from gods. They are the internal human center of divine attention and activity.

The somewhat ambiguous nature of this body part is reflected in good and bad interpretations of darkness. Much of its origin lies in the fact that darkness is equated with the losing of consciousness, falling asleep, dreaming and dying – not all of which are negative states. However, the unknown quality of darkness is also equated with danger and various negative features. According to Padel (1992: 68 ff.), the colour black, which can be equated with darkness, has definite negative qualities. Entities which become black signify danger, terror, madness and so on. The sea can become 'black', and therefore dangerous. In some cases, the colour may also be interpreted as evil. In line with humoral theory, madness darkens the innards. Black bile in Ancient Greek thought represented *melancholao*, the state of madness which was the forerunner of the emotion of melancholy in later European culture.

These negative effects arise from the basic concept that it is impossible to see what is in the immediate environment. This basic notion appears to have been transferred to Christianity with the dichotomy of light representing good and dark being equated with evil. Charteris-Black (2004: 185–90) cites a number of biblical sources which suggest that the good/evil model has been extended to the mapping: LIGHT = FAITH, DARK = SPIRITUAL IGNORANCE:

LIGHT = GOOD
When I looked for **good**, then **evil** came unto me: and when I waited for **light**, there came **darkness**
(Job 30:26)

Woe unto them that call **evil** good, and **good** evil; that put **darkness** for **light**, and **light** for **darkness**
(Isaiah 5:20)

LIGHT = FAITH
Then Jesus said unto them, Yet a little while is the **light** with you. Walk while ye have the **light**, lest **darkness** come upon you: for he that walketh in **darkness** knoweth not whither he goeth. While ye have **light**, believe in the **light**, that ye may be the children of **light**. These things spake Jesus, and departed, and did hide himself from them. I am come a **light** into the world, that whosoever believeth on me should not abide in **darkness**
(John 12: 35–6)

The ancient positive/negative aspect has therefore continued into Christianity but with different connotations. In our discussion of colour metaphors, we have also seen that black and white are often associated with darkness and lightness in modern English. In turn, they are also related to contrasts between positive and negative as in the negative effects of drugs:

> With higher doses and chronic use, the alertness and exhiliration so prized by coke's connoisseurs quickly turn into **darker** effects, ranging from insomnia to full-fledged cocaine psychosis (Chapter 3)

The positive/negative feature has therefore been networked through the ages as a long-term metaphor path. However, the role of religion shows how different cultural mindsets have shaped its direction. The connotation of gods playing a major role in the outside world, as in Ancient Greece, have been lost. An immediate association of light with Jesus may be made with certain religiously-minded people today, however, and this again raises the issue of saliency, or 'within domains' variation. Is there a dominant mindset at any given point in time existing alongside secondary or minority attitudes among the general population?

People today have varying beliefs; some may believe in a religion while others do not; some are ambiguous about the matter, believing in some form of spirituality but not in a particular god. This must influence the kind of speech which is used and the type of target audience, as can be seen in political speeches by leaders around the world today. We do not have this kind of information about the medieval and classical periods but literary texts do offer us an insight into changing attitudes. Factors such as the influence of religion are important in seeing how and why metaphor creation changes through the centuries.

So far, we have been discussing the different linguistic and cultural patterns which appear to form networking structures in the ongoing evolution of metaphor. These have involved the roles of cognition, universal and cultural aspects, cross-language equivalence, regularity in the evolution of semantic structures, metaphor paths, long- and short-term models and differing perception of imagery at a given historical period.

It is now time to pull these threads together to examine a concrete example of a historical network. In order to do so, we are naturally dependent on written texts. One of the major areas of written texts in our cultural history is, of course, the literary field. Which topics have been widely discussed in literature since the beginning of written literary texts? There are several possibilities but one which immediately springs to mind is the field of love. This does indeed offer very fertile ground for the exploration of metaphor and fits in well with our various discussions so far on the emotions. The emotion of love, being rich in metaphor both today and in the past, is able clearly to illustrate how metaphors are linked together through the ages. Finally, a large amount of research in this field has been carried out on modern English and this provides a useful background for comparison with historical metaphors in order to illustrate how figurative language has evolved.

Part III will therefore explore the historical network of love in European literature with the aim of applying the diachronic theories we have been discussing so far. Love metaphors will be traced back through time, starting with a comparison between medieval and modern English and thereafter establishing the links going back to Antiquity. We shall then evaluate the theories of diachronic conceptual networking within this particular semantic field.

Part III
Historical Networks

11
The Evolution of Love Metaphors: a Case Study

11.1 Exploring medieval metaphor

If we turn the clock back to the late Middle Ages, what kinds of metaphors were used in the discourse of love? First of all, as we have seen in the case of translating texts from different historical periods, a number of different factors would have played a part in the types of metaphor images used. These involve social class, regional variants, the type of medium (whether it was written or spoken language and what kinds of particular written medium were involved, such as personal letters or literary works) and so on. Obviously, we do not have access to spoken language of that time and the written medium is usually limited to more formal literary works. Our tools for investigating language in the past are therefore much more restricted than those we have today.

An exploration of literary works can, nevertheless, give us a good idea of a number of different varieties. One medieval poet who wrote about characters from very different walks of life was, of course, Chaucer. The types of attitudes portrayed by these different characters were often reflected in their language. We can see that these characters had a variety of different attitudes towards love in the same way as there are different attitudes today. The short answer to the question posed above is that, on the one hand, many of the metaphors used today were also used in Chaucer's time, displaying different variants. A lot of our figurative language does therefore stem from the medieval period. On the other hand, Chaucer also used a range of metaphors which would probably sound strange today, at least to a large section of the language community.

In this chapter, we will therefore first explore the way in which many modern love metaphors are linked to the medieval period through the common cultural heritage of English literature. Chaucer's work has been chosen for this investigation due to its rich variety of genres which can range from very aristocratic, courtly tales to the bawdy humour used by all kinds of social classes at the time. Metaphor models between the medieval and modern periods will be matched up with the help of recent findings relating to the modern period. In this way, we are able to establish links in metaphor paths.

A number of cognitive linguists, including Kövecses (1988) and Lakoff and Johnson (1980), have written widely on the subject of modern love metaphors, and their work will, in many cases, serve as a useful comparison to Chaucer. This comparative approach from a diachronic point of view can often illustrate the source of our metaphors, although it is limited is that many of our present-day models are culturally defined in the same way as those of the medieval period. We shall therefore subsequently explore time-specific medieval metaphors and attempt to see how these equate with ideas which are still current in modern Western societies. This field of research will be used at a later stage to construct historical networking models.

Before starting out on a historical analysis of love metaphors, it would be useful, within a cognitive approach, to try and situate the notion of love among the whole range of human emotions in order to identify causes. A number of cognitive scientists have contributed to global classifications on the subject.

11.2 The structure of emotions

One interesting analysis is by Ortony et al. (1988) who claim that emotions are valenced reactions to three particular phenomena: events, agents and objects. Their definitions of these phenomena are as follows:

> our conception of events is very straightforward – events are simply people's construals about things that happen, considered independently of any beliefs they may have about actual or possible causes. Our notion of focusing on objects is also quite simple. Objects are objects viewed *qua* objects. This leaves us with agents, which are things considered in light of their actual or presumed instrumentality or agency in causing or contributing to events.
>
> (Ortony et al., 1988: 18)

All emotions therefore presumably react to these phenomena. There are, however, a number of other aspects of human behaviour which tend to resemble emotions but are not necessarily reactions to a particular phenomenon. This is where the borderlines and definitions of particular emotions play an important role since some psychological *states* of human behaviour, or prolonged variations of typical emotions, may confuse the issue of classification. If we take, for example, the whole area of *depression* or *melancholy*, which should not be confused with the emotion of *sadness*, a medical book would define *melancholy* as a serious form of depression which is partly hereditary and occurs regularly in acute forms without any particular stimulus being implemented. In medical terms, *melancholy* would be a permanent *state* rather than a reaction to a particular stimulus causing a human emotion.

As far as defining an emotion is concerned, Ortony et al. suggest that a distinction should be made between emotions and *cognitive states*. In this light, the human reaction of *surprise*, for example, would not be included as an emotion (in contrast to Izard and Buechler's (1980) list of fundamental emotions we have seen earlier). As a cognitive state, *surprise* could be regarded as being concerned with aspects of knowing and believing rather than representing an emotion. The same would apply to *interest* or *a state of being interested*. Ortony et al.'s hypothesis for this argument is that, in an empirical study of isolating emotion from non-emotion terms, informants were asked to indicate how confident they were that 'feeling x' and 'being x' were emotions when x is a putative emotion term. They found that terms that were independently rated as good examples of emotions tended to be judged as referring to emotions comparably well in both of these linguistic contexts, whereas non-emotion terms show other patterns (1988: 174).

There are many other problem areas in the classification of emotions, such as the claim that some emotions are a mixture of two different types and that there are some emotions which are more representative than others. These approaches would be in line with prototype theory in cognitive psychology. However, given the limitations of definitions, where does the emotion of love stand with regard to reactions to the three phenomena outlined above? More details may be found in Ortony et al.'s classification (1988: 19), but a brief summary would divide their list of emotions into:

(1) *Consequences of events*. These split emotions into two dichotomies of pleased/displeased referring to implications for oneself or others. The resulting emotions are *happy for others, resentment, gloating, pity, joy, distress, satisfaction, fears-confirmed, relief, disappointment, gratification, remorse, gratitude* and *anger*.

(2) *Actions of agents.* The same pattern occurs with a split between approving/disapproving for self and others. This results in: *pride, shame, admiration* and *reproach*. In addition, there is an overlap with the first category in that *gratification, remorse, gratitude* and *anger* can also result from agents.
(3) *Aspects of objects.* It is in this category that the emotion of love appears. Objects cause a split into a general dichotomy of liking/disliking which results in *love* and *hate*.

The suggestion, therefore, is that a cognitive analysis of the origin of love would involve the reactions to a particular object which, presumably, could be either animate or inanimate. The latter categories would involve further differentiation of the forms of love.

Again, this type of analysis presumably refers to the modern Western world. Do people of all ethnic origins today have these kinds of feelings with relation to love? What about love in past centuries? We shall see below that classifications of love may not be that straightforward.

11.3 Concepts of love

The notion of 'different forms of love' cited above is a key point in this discussion. In the same way as defining categories of emotion, it is not easy, if not impossible, to define in scientific terms the notion of love and its different variants. As we have seen, Kövecses (1988) speaks of prototypical and non-prototypical love. He also suggests that the different types of cognitive models of love stem from three main sources: metaphors, metonymies and 'related concepts' (Kövecses, 2000: 122 ff.). To summarise some of the examples given by Kövecses, typical examples in the three categories would be:

Metaphor
LOVE IS A UNITY OF PARTS
They're **breaking up**
We're **inseparable**

Metonym
PHYSICAL WEAKNESS STANDS FOR LOVE
She makes me **weak in the knees**

Related concepts
Liking

Sexual desire
Intimacy
Longing
Affection
Caring
Respect
Friendship

The last category defines the range of attitudes towards the loved one and, once again, along the lines of prototype theory, they tend to be placed along a gradient relative to the central position of love. According to Kövecses (2000: 125), some are peripheral, such as friendship and respect, some are closer, such as caring, while very close concepts would be, for example, liking and affection. This categorisation appears to be somewhat subjective since a lot depends on individual love relationships. Respect may play a much more important role in one relationship than in another.

With regard to the other two categories, many other major models exist. It should be pointed out here that some of the expressions may have a regional element, such as in the LOVE IS A JOURNEY model, some of whose examples were discussed in Chapter 1. Studies carried out on American English demonstrated that some expressions were more prevalent in this particular variety in American English than in British English. 'We're just spinning our wheels' or 'it's been a long, bumpy road' in the LOVE IS A JOURNEY model may be more salient in the American variety.

Variations in the notion of love are reflected in the different types of figurative language which arise as a result. A study of historical patterns of love in different cultures around the world also reveals remarkable variation as to how civilisations conceptualise the subject. If we examine these different approaches as to what love means, or should mean, we are in a better position to understand how metaphors in this domain have originated.

Attitudes to love form part of ethnological or ethno-archaeological studies of cultures in different parts of the world, such as in the indigenous populations of South America or the South Pacific. These societies, such as the Incas during the peak of the Incan empire, had very specific views on the subject which are in many ways very different to those in modern Western society.

An analysis of some of the major religions in the world shows that they also play a major role in how we should view love and its function in society. In fact, a large part of our ideals stems from religious influences. With regard to the main religions which, to a greater or lesser extent, have either influenced Europe or have been studied widely by theological scholars, De Rougemont (1972: 71–7) divides the world's major religions into two groups: Western and Oriental. He claims that a fundamental difference between these two groups is the individual's relationship to God. The former group, which originated in the Middle East, does not embody a complete union with God during the lifetime of an individual except for communion in church, whereby the church acts as a link between the two. The latter, primarily located in Asia, embody complete union with God, or, in the case of a religion like Buddhism, a single Universal Being.

In the case of relationships between two people, de Rougemont also argues that there are fundamental differences in the notion of love between these groups. Christianity developed the idea of passion, which became predominant in twelfth-century Europe, while pre-Christian Greece did not hold this notion, hence the concept of Platonic love (derived from Plato's *Symposium*). Human love was generally conceived to be for pleasurable aims while passion, in its tragic or painful sense, tended to be despised. In Oriental religions, the Chinese traditionally regarded relationships as constituting 'fondness', rather than love.

Conversations with couples from India today who have had arranged marriages tend to confirm this situation. Even after many years, the relationship tends to be one of fondness rather than love. The lack of passion in African cultures has also been illustrated by Kövecses (1988). He points out the potential for these differences with an anecdote depicting the divide between Western and Bemba (Northern Rhodesia) cultures:

> Dr. Audrey Richards, an anthropologist, who lived among the Bemba of Northern Rhodesia in the 1930s, once related to a group of them [the Bemba] an English folk-fable about a young prince who climbed glass mountains, crossed chasms, and fought dragons, all to obtain the hand of the maiden he loved. The Bemba were plainly bewildered, but remained silent. Finally an old chief spoke up, voicing the feelings of all present in the simplest of questions: 'Why not take another girl?' he asked. (Quoted from Branden.)
>
> (Kövecses, 1988: 11)

Different cultural concepts of love are reflected in metaphor. These differences are often explained by a culture's history which, particularly in the case of English, is often linked to religion. The influence of Christianity on the English language will be an important part of the discussions to follow.

11.4 The historical networking of love metaphors

We have seen that a considerable amount of research has been carried out on present-day metaphors of love and that Kövecses (1988; 2000), for example, has developed ideal and typical scenarios in American English. We shall explore the idea that scenarios of this kind are linked to the notion of passion introduced into lyrical poetry of the late Middle Ages. Some of his examples would be a useful basis with which to compare metaphors from earlier periods of English. We shall therefore first look at items from literature of the Middle English period and compare them with some modern American examples to see how they have been networked diachronically. In order to give a full picture of the networking process, metaphors will be traced back chronologically to origins beyond the Middle English period. The major branch of conceptual metaphor in this domain is Latinate-based in the manuscripts available, and it is this path which will be examined in detail.

Kövecses's examples stem largely from spoken English. As we have pointed out above, analysis of data from the medieval period is logically dependent on written texts and it is therefore difficult to assess the extent to which literary ideas were reflected in the minds of the ordinary population. This is particularly the case if the majority did not read literary works. As de Rougemont (1972: 190 ff.) suggests, nobody can really demonstrate whether the influence of the arts in times past had a great impact on ordinary, daily life. Due to the continuous influence of television on people's daily lives today, however, many people claim that it must have a considerable impact on people's attitudes to love, which forms a large part of the content of soaps, Hollywood films and so on.

Although specific linguistic items will be analysed, the focus will also be on the conceptual level, that is on the different thought processes which have contributed to metaphor creation. The aim is not to present an exhaustive corpus of items but to give a few examples of how different types of models appear to be operating. In literary criticism, there has been a great deal of debate on how the imagery of love has contributed to literary metaphor, and this is an aspect which needs to be taken into consideration when understanding how metaphor paths have developed through time. Our starting-point would therefore be a comparison of some of Kövecses's models with medieval texts. We shall first look at some of the American English models and then compare them to Chaucer's metaphors of the medieval period.

11.5 Matches between Middle and modern English

Among of the major mappings Kövecses (1988) describes in modern English are the following:

LOVE =

1. FIRE: *she is his latest flame*
2. UNITY: *the perfect match*
3. TREASURE: *hello, my precious*
4. NUTRIENT/FOOD: *she's the cream in my coffee*
5. BLINDNESS: *he was blinded by love*
6. MADNESS: *she drives me out of my mind*

As would be expected, the first image of FIRE is also to be found in the medieval period. The fire symbols in Chaucer's case appear to be mostly associated with physiological features in which heat, as in Lakoff's examples, corresponds to intense emotion. The following examples are taken from *The Canterbury Tales* (ed. Hieatt and Hieatt, 1976), the first, from *The Franklin's Tale*, refers to *fyr* as passion:

> Ye knowen wel, lord, that right as hir **desyr**
> Is to be quiked and lighted of your **fyr** (310: ll. 321–2)
> (You know well, lord, that just as her desire
> Is to be quickened and lighted by your fire)

It should be pointed out that the dividing line between love and lust is not always that clear and the notion of fire can actually equally imply a number of different feelings. This will be discussed in more detail in the section on medieval Italian literature in the next chapter. Since *The Franklin's Tale* concerns primarily noble, courtly love, it appears that Chaucer's option for the fire image refers to this particular type of love. Although the concept of lust is usually portrayed by the LOVE = NUTRIENT/FOOD model described below in medieval literature, as well as in the modern period, fire can also be used for this purpose.

A very common notion of love in Middle English was also the symbol of unity, as in the second example in Kövecses's list, and this is often used by Chaucer. *The Merchant's Tale* has numerous examples of being united or bound together:

*Whan that the preest to yow my body **bond*** (285: l. 948)
(When the priest **bound** my body to you)

*They been so **knit**, ther may noon harm bityde* (248: l. 147)
(They are so firmly **knit** together that no harm may arise)

*And wher me best were to **allyen*** (248: l. 170)
(And where it would be best for me to **ally myself** = find a partner)

Unity is a very basic notion of matching partners and is likely to be a universal trend diachronically. A perusal of historical periods between Middle English and the modern period would probably reveal other such examples in literature. Kövecses (1988: 18) suggests that the unity metaphor goes back at least to Plato but since then has undergone many changes. The mythological version implies that unity of two human beings was the notion of originally being one. Later versions in history embody other kinds of unity in the form of complementary chemical or physical parts which fit together or in the form of biological parts living in symbiosis. This kind of unity is also used in recent expressions relating to how people work together, for example, in which terms such as 'physical chemistry' are used.

With regard to the unity issue, Chaucer was particularly interested in the whole question of marriage and we shall see that this was linked to the trends of courtly love at the time. Throughout the twentieth century, literary critics wrote about the 'marriage group' in Chaucer, a concept first identified as a dramatically integrated unit within *The Canterbury Tales* by Kittredge (1912: 435–67). It involves three tales, those of the Wife of Bath, the Merchant and the Franklin, which raise the issues of love, marriage and religion. In addition, *The Canterbury Tales* also dealt with the aspect of courtly love in the Knight's and the Franklin's tales. Other works by Chaucer, focusing on the theme of courtly love, included *Troilus and Criseyde*. The topic was a common one among writers of the Middle Ages but it has been suggested that Chaucer had a particular interest in the subject since he suffered an eight-year period of unrequited love for Joan, Duchess of Kent (Galway, 1938; 1945). During this period (1361–69), Chaucer was unproductive as a writer but his literary career revived subsequently, after the death of Joan of Kent, in a poem on his 'suffering in love' in the *Book of the Duchess* (cited by Galway, 1945: 433):

> *Myselven can not telle why*
> *The sothe; but trewly, as I gesse,*
> *I holde hit be a sicknesse*
> *That I have suffred this eight yeer*

This view has been contested by other critics who argue that the poet may simply have been making known his respect and esteem for the departed Duchess using common literary prose in the courtly style of the period (Stearns, 1942). Whatever personal reasons Chaucer may have had, this concept of love fits in perfectly with the courtly love model.

Following the basic-level symbols of fire and unity, a notion common to all periods might be the metaphor of *treasure*, the third item on the list taken from Kövecses's data above. The loved one is considered a precious entity and the following example is again taken from *The Merchant's Tale*:

Thanne is a wyf the fruit of his **tresor** *(242: l. 26)*
(Then a wife is the best part of his **treasure**)

Related to the idea of treasure is also the concept of gifts, which were considered to come from God:

A wyf is Goddes **yifte** *verraily (244: l. 67)*
(A wife is truly a **gift** of God)

The three models of fire, unity and treasure thus appear to be common notions of love in medieval literature.

The fourth correspondence is the case of the LOVE = NUTRIENT/FOOD metaphor. Some of the medieval correspondences are very clear in the following examples given by Kövecses (1988: 27–9) concerning the object of sexual desire as (appetising) food:

> She's quite a dish
> What a piece of meat!
> I hunger for your touch
> He's a real hunk
> Let's see some cheesecake
> Look at those buns!

Chaucer also used this kind of imagery in *The Merchant's Tale* when the main character, January, who was advanced in years, told his friends that he was seeking a wife who had to be very young:

> *But o thing warne I yow, my freendes dere;*
> *I wol non old wyf han in no manere;*
> *She shal nat passe twenty yeer, certayn;*
> *Old fish and yong flesh wolde I have ful fayn.*
> *Bet is, 'quod he, 'a pyk than a pikerel;*
> *And bet than old boef is the tendre veel:*
> *I wol no womman thritty yeer of age –*
> *It is but bene-straw and greet forage*

(248–50: ll. 171–8)

(But I warn you of one thing, dear friends; I won't have any kind of old wife; she shall not be over twenty, for certain; I would very willingly have old fish but fresh meat. A pike is better than a pickerel', he said, 'but tender veal is better than old beef. I don't want any woman thirty years of age; that's nothing but straw and coarse fodder)

The equation of love with food was therefore a clear image in Chaucer's mind. Many expressions also use the image of sweetness in *The Canterbury Tales*, for example, *mariage honey-swete* (*The Merchant's Tale*), in the same way as modern-day expressions, *honey, honey-pie, sugar* and so on.

It seems that eating may very well be a universal trend in metaphor creation since it is also used to symbolise sexual desire in very different cultures, such as the Bantu language of Chagga (Emanatian, 1995). This corresponds to a DESIRE = APPETITE metaphor in modern English discussed by Deignan (1997: 30–2). Hunger and desire represent two of our most basic desires and it is therefore not surprising that the two have been associated metaphorically. There are many equivalents in present-day fiction and journalism such as:

> A couple of girls, some drinks, all of which was very welcome at the time. Pleasant girls, too, not obvious tarts (fiction)

> Men know they fancy that bit of crumpet. They recognise boredom and seek variety (journalism)

The meat and fish symbols of Chaucer thus correspond to the tarts and crumpets consumed in modern Britain. Other matches are found in

Kövecses's (1998) discussion of intensity, in which he gives the example of *he was blinded by love* (item 5 on the list above) in the category of 'interference with accurate perception'. A LOVE = BLINDNESS model also occurs in *The Merchant's Tale*:

> *for Love is **blind** al day and may nat see* (258: l. 354)
> (for love is for ever blind and cannot see)

Similarly the present-day insanity metaphors, or LOVE = MADNESS (item 6), to denote lack of control in love, are found in Chaucer's Knight's tale:

> *But Palamon that love destreyneth so,*
> *That wood out **of his wit** he gooth for wo* (69: l. 598)
> (But love afflicted Palamon so much that he was completely **out of his mind**)

The examples of fire, unity, treasure, food, blindness and madness show that these images have probably remained in the conceptual systems of the English language for a long period of time. It could be argued that some of Kövecses's examples of love have thus been networked to former models which represent long-term metaphor paths.

11.6 Medieval courtly love

If we think of romance in the Middle Ages, a notion that immediately springs to mind is courtly love. Common today is the idea of true love. It may be recalled that a typical metaphor scenario, discussed earlier with regard to Kövecses's (1988) models, was the search for Mr or Mrs Right. This is also a commonplace notion today and is reflected in metaphors in other European languages, such as French *âme soeur* (sister soul). One of the problems with this attitude to love is that, as Kövecses (2000) points out, many people believe that there is only one true love in life and this experience cannot therefore be shared with more than one person. All other loves experienced are therefore not true.

It could be argued that a lot of present-day attitudes in Western society with regard to true (or romantic) love stem from medieval courtly love. Some aspects of courtly love are very conspicuous. As Burns (2001: 23) succinctly puts it: 'the legacy of courtly love . . . has been widely absorbed into American popular culture, attested variously in lovelorn laments of country-western song lyrics or in chivalrous valentines where beloved ladies are touted as having ultimate control over the male lover's delicate heartstrings'.

The romantic ideals of the two historical periods have a parallel to a certain degree but there are some fundamental differences which are apparent in medieval literature across Europe. One of these main differences is that true love requires suffering and is subject to very austere social and religious control. Love is almost legally binding and requires servility, patience, chastity and so on.

Medieval courtly love has been portrayed and described in a number of different ways, the two main approaches being traditional literary analysis and more recent feminist approaches. Schnell and Shields (1998: 785) consider feminist approaches from two viewpoints: while some critical analyses of courtly love have tended to be women-centred, other more recent approaches incorporate gender history in the form of a deconstructive feminism which takes both sexes into account. Whichever viewpoint is taken, a number of common features and divergences can be seen in the notions of love in the medieval and modern periods.

Medievalists often associate the appearance of courtly love in the Middle Ages with the earliest troubadour, William IX, at the end of the eleventh century. The term was coined by Paris (1883) to refer to the passionate love between Lancelot and Guenevere in Chrétien de Troye's twelfth-century romance *Lancelot or the Knight of the Cart*. Burns cites Paris's definition of courtly love as being an 'illicit, furtive, and extraconjugal liaison that placed the lover in the service of and at the mercy of a haughty and capricious lady, a state that inspired courageous feats and refined behaviour, and an art governed by highly codified rules of proper conduct, analogous to the tenets regulating chivalry' (2001: 28–9).

In his discussion on courtly language in Chaucer's *The Book of the Duchess*, Boardman (1997: 567–9) refers to the courtly lover as being 'rather proud of his melancholy and insomnia' and being 'a servant of love'. More negative comments have been made by Coffman (1945: 45) who raises the issue of these 'extraconjugal liaisons' described by Paris. He wrote that courtly love was 'abnormal' and like to the 'pseudoromantic films purporting to reflect the life of the modern aristocracy and the domestic scandals of the wealthy'. In many ways, the aspect of the media is still a relevant one at the beginning of the twenty-first century since a great deal of money is made out of reporting on the 'extraconjugal liaisons' of the rich and famous.

Burnley (1980: 131) suggests that a major difference in the notions of courtly love and that of today is that the former has a much broader semantic usage. It includes the affection between friends and the tie between the lord and his vassals, as well as its strong romantic connotations in the medieval period. These are reflected in some of Chaucer's terms: *love celestial, love par amour, love of kynde* and so on and can also be seen in French terms of the time *amor a desmesure, amor vilaine, bone amor* and so on. Although some of these terms could perhaps be used in the same semantic fields today, it is clear that the religious bond and the link between a lord and servants created a different social context at that time.

A feminist view of the differences or similarities in the role of women in love relationships between the two periods is offered by Burns (2001: 23–4). Similarity can be found in contemporary American self-help manuals for women trying to find the ideal man, such as *The Rules: Time-tested Secrets for Capturing the Heart of Mr. Right* (Fein and Schneider, 1995). This is marketed with a text offering a model of ideal feminine behaviour which imitates what 'twelfth-century male authors decry as the haughty and unresponsive ladylove'. The modern female reader is advised to withhold her affection, drive her suitor mad and thereby hold him captive. Although the implication is that the female role in this courtship is the dominant one, Burns suggests that it is in fact the man's desires and needs that govern this kind of modern courtship. Readers of *The Rules* are told that the man should take the lead and that the woman should pose as an exquisite 'beautiful creature'. It thus follows the medieval tradition in advancing an ideology of femininity that disempowers women in love while claiming to empower them. *The Rules* diverge, however, from the medieval paradigm in that they promise the reader a sweet love which is easy and comfortable. This differs from the medieval scenario which often involved 'adulterous liaisons and unsuccessful love trysts' (Burns, 2001: 24).

We can probably assume, therefore, that some notions of courtly love remain in the minds of people today while other aspects have clearly disappeared within our very different social context. The tales of courtly love in the Middle Ages involved primarily the aristocracy. Furthermore, literary critics of this period agree that it was only to be found in texts, not in real life. This is the view of Schultz (2002: 342–64) in a discussion of 'love service' in Wolfram von Eschenbach's medieval German epic, *Parzival*. Schultz also argues that, as a contrast to recent feminist approaches regarding the fate of women in the courtly love of today's world, the position of men in the courtly love of the medieval world was not to be envied either. He claims that there was a historical shift in noble masculinity in the late Middle Ages, which implied considerable constraints on the social behaviour of males aspiring to the love of an unattainable woman. The church had a considerable role to play in this development within the context of jurisdiction over marriage, particularly with regard to its indissoluble and monogamous status. 'As this shift takes place, noble men were expected to modify or abandon behaviours that previously defined them as men and to adopt a new, more civilised class and gender ideal' (Schultz, 2002: 350). If we accept these two interpretations of the ideal of courtly love, it would be possible to argue that women are handicapped by this notion in the modern world and that it led to a similar kind of subordination in men during the medieval period. It could be inferred that the same model has different social consequences according to the historical period in question.

It should also be added that the LOVE = UNITY model has varied between historical periods in regard to marriage and 'oneness'. During the 1960s, for example, the 'free love' movement rejected the traditional idea of marriage, chastity and fidelity for the rest of one's life, fundamental Christian principles which constituted the traditional UNITY concept. Hence the traditional metaphor, 'I'll have to ask my better half', is based on the understanding that there are only two components in this UNITY model and not a number of additional external links, either physically or psychologically, as in the 'free love' model.

In a different way, the Cathar 'heretics' of late medieval France also rejected aspects of the Catholic notion of marriage. Catholics considered marriage to be a religious sacrament and viewed adultery as being contrary to the order of nature and society. The Cathars did not support adultery, since they advocated chastity, but they felt there was a contradiction between passion and the concept of marriage which at the time was normally arranged. This contradiction could be seen in the courtly love literature which presented two types of relationship in love lyrics: passionate (or spiritual love) for one partner and the physical relationship (embodied in marriage) for another partner. The two kinds of love could not be given to one individual (de Rougemont, 1972: 297 ff.).

As de Rougemont points out, modern-day 'free love' and medieval heretical orthodoxy are not linked since the latter is no longer present or necessary in modern thinking, but they both represent alternative approaches to mainstream ideas. He also feels that there is conflict between traditional social values and those represented by the arts and literature. In the latter case, television presumably plays a major role. Undoubtedly there is potential for the existence of different ways of thinking about love which can vary at any one given point in time. Some ideas tend to be predominant and others represent a minor section of the language community. This results in synchronic and diachronic saliency in metaphor-producing concepts.

Synchronically, differing views about a concept could make a metaphor sound stranger to one person than to another. Diachronically, traditional values may seem more normal to some and stranger to others. With this in mind, some images may never disappear completely. While some people today consider that marriage or a love relationship is sacrosanct with very rigid laws, others may feel it to be a very free institution. Views on this changed quickly during the course of the twentieth century. There may still, however, be a common denominator between the two models for the vast majority of the population so that metaphors may generally be interpreted, whatever view one has.

The differences in the ways in which emotions are conceptualised within a society correspond to what Kövecses (2000: 172–6) calls 'within-culture variation'. He states that: 'we know from research outside linguistics that the conceptualisation of emotion is not the same, not homogeneous within a culture or society. Individuals vary, and there is variation according to social factors and through time.' He observes that within-culture variation is much more difficult to define than cross-cultural variation since very little empirical research has been carried out on the question so far.

We have already noted Kövecses's observation that there are two models of love in contemporary American society: an ideal and a more typical one. The difference between the romantic model and a more down-to-earth model perceived by many people is one of intensity. The whole notion of love may, however, be far more complex if other parameters, such as the sacrosanct nature of marriage, are taken into account. For many couples today, marriage is a necessity, for others it serves little purpose. As Kövecses suggests, 'there is not just one kind of anger, fear or love, but literally dozens'.

From a diachronic point of view, this implies that there is a constantly changing pattern of attitudes towards emotions, some of which may therefore appear strange to some and not to others at any given point in time. Half the population may find one metaphor obsolete and the other half would find it quite appropriate. Changing attitudes may also be reflected in relation to controlling anger.

One non-prototypical form of anger would be *channelling your anger into something constructive*. This may have constituted an ideal model of anger during the Victorian period when people were taught to control their emotions (Kövecses, 2000: 174), and although models may now have changed, many people might feel that such a former model should be retained, producing within-culture variation.

A further point on the use of particular models involves the actual medium in which the term is used. A subject like love is discussed in very different types of contexts and is very often, of course, dramatised in film and theatre. It may appear differently in the media, magazines, popular songs or poetry, all of which give this particular theme enormous scope for varied usages. These may also retain images of former times that are not normally used in everyday contemporary speech. It may be concluded that many of the different models used by Chaucer are probably still used in one form or another today but there are particular models which appear more salient at his time than at later periods.

11.7 Time-specific saliency in English medieval metaphor

The following analysis looks at data taken from Chaucer whose models appear to be more salient during the medieval period than the fire and unity models discussed above. The examples are taken from *The Canterbury Tales* (the Knight's, the Franklin's, the Merchant's and the Wife of Bath's tales). The plots in Chaucer's stories follow typical love scenarios. In the Merchant's and Franklin's tales, for example, the first stage of the scenario is a love triangle consisting of a husband-knight, his wife and a would-be lover. In the second stage, the lover makes his desires known to the lady in question. In the third stage, the wife is restored to the husband. The institution of marriage therefore triumphs in the end but, in contrast to the idealised model of love today, Holman (1951: 241–52) observes that a man cannot love his own wife in medieval romances, the courtly lover has to love the wife of someone else. The love triangle is typical in Chaucer's works: in the *Knight's Tale* it is between the main protagonists, Palamon, Arcite and Emily. This is not a case of marital infidelity, but the fight between two cousins for the same lady.

These scenarios give rise to the same kinds of emotions – pain, jealousy, and so on – which occur in the scenarios of today, but it can be seen that the ideals were often very different. Consequently, some of these ideals led to more salient metaphors at that time. We shall concentrate here on the comparison of actual models between the two historical periods rather than the structure and order of models in a given scenario.

The following examples from Chaucer (all cited from Hieatt and Hieatt, 1976) are perhaps typical of low saliency today. The images were vital features of the love relationship during the medieval period.

The following passage from the *Franklin's Tale* is one of the major representative aspects of medieval courtly love in the metaphors:

LOVE = SUBSERVIENCE and LOVE = LAW

> *Heer may men seen an humble wys accord:*
> *Thus hath she take hir servant and hir lord,*
> ***Servant in love** and lord in mariage;*
> *Thanne was he bothe in lordship and servage.*
> *Servage? Nay, but in lordshipe above,*
> *Sith he hath bothe his lady and his love;*
> *His lady, certes, and his wyf also,*
> *The which that **lawe of love** acordeth to*

(298: ll. 63–70)

(Here one may see a humble, wise agreement: she has thus accepted her servant and her lord, **servant in love** and lord in marriage; he was, then, both in lordship and in servitude. Servitude? No, but in the higher state of lordship, since he had both his lady and his love; his lady, certainly, and his wife too, which is in accordance with **the law of love**)

This is a passage on the strict rules of love and marriage in the courtly fashion with the use of conceptual metaphors such as *servant in love* and the *law of love*, representing ideals to be attained. Law implies duty, as in physical love, in the *Wife of Bath's Tale*, in which the term 'statute' is used. In this case, three former husbands were unable to fulfil their duties regarding physical love:

> *Unnethe mighte they the **statut** holde*
> *In which that they were bounden unto me*

(190: l. 198)

(They were scarcely able to keep the **statute** by which they were bound to me)

This is a more humorous, different view of love, narrated by the Wife of Bath, compared to the more chivalrous nature of the *Knight's Tale*, but still using the same kind of conceptual framework of duty and law. The metaphor 'statute' could more or less be regarded as a dead metaphor, not in the conventionalised sense, but having entered a phase of latency as described in Figure 7.1. This implies that, given the presence of relevant social customs at the time, the metaphor could be regenerated.

This framework is also seen in the *Merchant's Tale*. Here, the idea of physical love being a duty in marriage is apparent in the metaphor LOVE = PAYMENT/DEBT, within, however, the framework of 'lawful procreation' and 'being to the honour of God'. The following passage puts the medieval notion of love, sexual desire and duty into the perspective of the time:

> *If he ne may nat liven chast his lyf,*
> *Take him a wyf with greet devocioun*
> *By cause of leveful procreacioun*
> *Of children, to th' onour of God above,*
> *And nat only for paramour or love:*
> *And for they sholde lecherye eschue,*
> *And **yelde hir dette** whan that it is due*

(250: ll. 202–8)

(If a man cannot live his life chastely, let himself take a wife with great devoutness for the sake of lawful procreation of children to the honour of God above, and not simply for sexual pleasure or love; and let him do this because, also, they should eschew lechery and **pay their debt** to each other when it is due)

Religion is an overriding aspect of the metaphors of literary texts in the Middle Ages. As we have seen, the Christian religion considers marriage, in general, to be a sacrament: *mariage is a ful gret sacrement* (*Merchant's Tale*). Religion underlies the idea that lovers should suffer pain. Although the notion of pain is frequently used today, and particularly in contexts such as contemporary love songs, it is considered as an unfortunate experience in the course of love, rather than an objective, as in medieval courtly love. Pain is often associated with Cupid's arrows being shot down from heaven. The following examples come from the *Knight's Tale*. Palamon, at the sight of his loved one, Emily felt as if he had been 'stung to the heart':

> . . . *and cryde 'A!' as though he **stongen** were unto the herte* (52: l. 221)

He also feels as if he had been 'slain' by her eyes:

> *Ye **sleen** me with your eyen, Emilye* (74: l. 709)

Love is associated with the pain of Cupid's arrows:

> Love hath his fyry **dart** so brenningly
> Y-striked thurgh my trewe careful herte
>
> (74: ll. 706–7)

(Love has so ardently thrust his fiery dart through my faithful, troubled heart)

It can be seen from the last example that, although Palamon does actually marry Emily in the end, these images represent a lot of distress for him at the time since he is in fierce competition with his brother, Arcite.

The idea of pain is conceived as a heroic ideal and would not be listed under modern non-prototypical cases in Kövecses's examples. It could be argued that the Cupid symbol today is an example of being, or being struck, by love as a pleasurable event rather than following the ideal of pain. This can be seen in Valentine cards and country songs, as noted by Burns. The following two verses are from a country-rock song recorded by singer/songwriter Neil Young. The title is 'Field of Opportunity', a metaphor employed throughout the song to depict the procedure of hunting for yet another new love:

> I've been wrong before and I'll be there again
> I don't have any answers my friend
> Just this pile of old questions my memory left me here
> In the field of opportunity it's ploughing time again
>
> When I'm all done cultivating I'll be rocking on the porch
> Trying to picture you and where you are
> And there'll be no hesitating when Cupid lights the torch
> With those headlights coming down between the stars.

The intensity of Cupid's arrows are likened to the modern symbol of 'headlights'. The song is open to interpretation but the context seems to imply that Cupid's arrows signal another new and intensive love. It would therefore be a pleasurable moment rather than the medieval chivalrous image of pain.

Another concept which does not seem to be predominant in Kövecses's lists is the very salient medieval LOVE = PROPERTY/POSSESSION. Although modern songs again tend to idealise this notion today as in expressions such as 'I'm going to make her mine', the idea of property in marriage is not a major discussion point in general conversation today, even though it could perhaps come under the general unity metaphor. Marriage definitely represented this notion in the Middle Ages, as can be seen in this example from the *Merchant's Tale* which does not represent true metaphors but ideas which lead to metaphors:

And thanked God that he mighte han hire **al**
That no wight his blisse **parten** *shal* (258: ll. 385–6)
(And thanked God that he might have her **completely** so that no man might **share** in his bliss)

The notion of love at that time thus had the connotation of lack of freedom. The idea of property is propagated in the fact that if you are married, you are not free: *in libertee and eek in mariage* (in liberty and also in marriage: the *Merchant's Tale*).

In discussing time-specificity of love metaphors in Middle English, we therefore appear to have two kinds of groups: metaphor models such as those of subservience and law, which are highly salient in the former historic period but far less common today, and those such as pain which are a common feature today but represent different social ideals. The conceptual form of the metaphors are probably not totally obsolete but certain lexicalised forms, such as *statute*, would be.

The above analysis points to the fact that, besides the more time-specific metaphors we have just described and which may nevertheless linger on in the minds of some sections of the population today, a large number of models have been inherited from the medieval period. Where did Middle English metaphors of love come from? The next chapter will explore some of the answers.

12
Latinate-based Origins in English Medieval Metaphor

12.1 Literature as a record of metaphor evolution

An argument we shall pursue here is that literary texts in the past can demonstrate how each period of history networks its metaphor heritage to preceding time zones. Poetry or narrative expressed through the medium of metaphor draws on other contemporary or preceding works of literature. The metaphors of love we have seen in Chaucer are a clear example of drawing on contemporary sources which have, in turn, drawn on other sources at an earlier period. Of course, Chaucer was not the first author to convey courtly ideals in England. They were sung and talked about by troubadours in many different European countries, such as Spain, Portugal, Germany and Italy, as well as in England from the twelfth century on (de Rougemont, 1972: 78). Chaucer was, however, one of the main poets in Middle English and represents a major landmark in the history of English. He is therefore an important starting-point in researching into the sources of medieval English metaphor. We also have considerable knowledge of his contacts at the time and it is possible to trace back his ideas and forms of language to other sources: thus we shall trace the metaphors chronologically to their sources around Europe.

In this chapter, we shall be arguing that, due to Chaucer's contacts with France and Italy at the time, a large amount of English metaphoric imagery in the Middle Ages derived from Latinate-based sources. We shall therefore explore the literary history and contacts of the authors concerned to examine how figurative language was transmitted from one culture to another. A very high proportion of the love metaphor network extending to the modern period would appear to be due to poets like Chaucer who acted as vehicles for cultural transmission. Further research into medieval French and Italian literature reveals that conceptualisation ultimately stemmed from Antiquity and the Latin/Greek tradition. Although this may not apply to all semantic fields – we have already noted the influences of Germanic imagery on early forms of the English language – the particular area of love does seem to be dominated ultimately by Latinate paths. Again, both long-term and more time-specific models appear to be influenced by these paths. We shall therefore attempt to assemble the historical circumstances and literary examples leading to the section of the network in operation prior to Middle English.

Standard works on translations of the *Canterbury Tales* all mention the influence of French and Italian writers and works of the late medieval period, such as Jean de Meun's *Roman de la Rose* and Boccaccio's *Decameron* (for example, Hieatt and Hieatt, 1976: ix–xxiv). Chaucer's sources have been much discussed in relevant literary criticism. At the same time, however, Chaucer's originality of style in the *Canterbury Tales* has been widely acknowledged and has made the work a unique piece of medieval literature in its own right.

12.2   Medieval French sources

The influence of the *Roman de la Rose* has been of particular importance and it has been suggested that Chaucer even translated the medieval French novel into English (Hieatt and Hieatt, 1976). Economou (1965: 252) claims that the influence of the French poem is so great that it is essential to the understanding of the *Merchant's Tale*. The *Roman* constituted an allegory of courtly love, and the whole poem represents a huge network of symbols and metaphors.

The attitude toward love and marriage of January, the main character in the *Merchant's Tale*, is directly related to the confession of love by the character, Nature, in the *Roman*. It is outside the scope of this book to discuss in detail the scenarios of individual literary works, but there is no doubt that there are considerable resemblances between the types of love metaphors appearing in both poems. Among the long-term metaphor paths, for example, we can find the models of *fire* and *treasure* in the Old French texts of the *Roman*:

FIRE = PASSION

> *Et tout adés en regardant*
> *Recouverras le feu ardant.*
> *Qui ce qu'il aime plus regarde*
> *Plus alume son cuer et larde.*

> (And while you look at her,
> you will rekindle the burning fires.
> The more you look at the object of your love,
> the more you open up and set your heart afire)
>
> (2343–6)

Again, in reference to the object of love:

LOVE = TREASURE

> *Je mens: trop y a chier cheté!*
> (I am telling a lie: it is such a valuable treasure to have!)
>
> (2468)

These models would correspond conceptually to Kövecses's examples in modern English:

FIRE: she is his latest flame
TREASURE: hello, my precious

Among the more time-specific models, we can find, for example, subservience, law and property models. Love is personified in the following quotation of subservience:

LOVE = SUBSERVIENCE

> *Qu'Amors qui toutes choses passe,*
> *Me donnoit cuer et hardement*
> *De faire son commandement.*
> (Since Love, which is stronger than everything
> gave me the heart and courage
> to obey its command)
>
> (1790–2)

The Cupid symbol is also present:

> *Mes li archers, qui mout s'efforce*
> *De moi grever et mout se pene,*
> *Ne m'i lest pas aler sans pene*
> (But the archer, who doubled his efforts
> to injure me,
> did not let me get away without suffering)
>
> (1762–3)

The law model likewise:

LOVE = LAW

> *Se je les puis a mon droit prendre*
> *Je lor vodré chierement vendre*
> (If I can submit them to my law
> I will make them pay dearly)

(1967–8)

The symbol of love in the *Roman* is a rose, hence the title of the work, and the attempt to pick the rose in the garden in which the poem takes place represents the attainment of true love:

LOVE = PROPERTY

> *Mes vers le bouton se traioit*
> *Mon cuer, qui avoir le vouloit*
> (But my heart was attracted by the rose-bud,
> it wanted to possess it).

(1727–8)

These models match with the more time-specific models used by Chaucer:

SUBSERVIENCE:	*Servant in love and lord in mariage*
PAIN:	*Love hath his fyry dart so brenningly*
	Y-striked thurgh my trewe careful herte
LAW:	*Unnethe mighte they the statut holde*
	In which that they were bounden unto me
PROPERTY:	*And thanked God that he mighte ha hire al*
	That no wight his blisse parten shal

It is therefore likely that the underlying conceptual metaphors which Chaucer employed in his depiction of courtly love, at least to a certain extent, were drawn from French writers. In addition to these French sources, Chaucer was undoubtedly influenced by contemporary Italian writers.

12.3 Medieval Italian sources

A major source of Latinate-based metaphors into Middle English was what we shall term here the Chaucer-Boccaccio-Petrarch triangle. The three poets knew each other personally, partly because of Chaucer's extensive travels to Italy, and partly through the contacts made between Boccaccio and Petrarch. A number of scholars have tried to provide conclusive evidence not only for such personal contacts between Chaucer and his Italian contemporaries but also for the ways in which they influenced his writing. Opinions vary, but the overall conclusions point to a considerable amount of Italian influence on Chaucer, particularly as he also translated Italian works as well as French literature such as the *Roman*.

12.4 Chaucer and Boccaccio

Various links have been established between Chaucer and Boccaccio. For example, Boccaccio's *Filocolo* has been demonstrated to be the source of the *Franklin's Tale*. Edwards (1996: 141–62) claims that the source is specifically the section of *Filocolo* known as the 'Love Questions', not the entire text. He views the *Franklin's Tale* as a form of cultural translation of the *Filocolo* and the result is that social customs of love are thereby transferred.

Similarly, links have been made between the *Merchant's Tale* and Boccaccio's *Decameron*. Although scholars have often refuted such a correspondence, Beidler (1973: 266–84) claims that the plots of specific parts of both stories are almost identical, particularly the tale of a blind husband whose wife is unfaithful to him with a lover she meets in a pear tree while they take a walk in a garden.

We can particularly see a parallel between Chaucer and Boccaccio in the large range of love categories which they incorporate into their works. This differentiates them from Petrarch whose works focus on the traditional aspects of courtly love. In the *Decameron* there is, in fact, a gradation of love stories ranging from the extremely bawdy to highly noble plots, implying that the boundaries of love are extremely wide in the mind of this particular author (Clubb, 1960: 188–96). Clubb discerns four major types within these boundaries, although the internal boundaries of the four individual types appear somewhat vague: (a) the bawdy story referring purely to lust; (b) a total lack of affection in a love relation; (c) courteous banter and elegant lyrics; and (d) the highest level of noble love which obviously refers to the courtly version. We thus have different synchronic models which reflect the type of diversity seen in 'free love' and traditional values raised in the last chapter. This would also correspond to the fine line drawn between love and lust in metaphor models such as FIRE, which was also raised in the preceding chapter with regard to such models in Chaucer's works.

Categories (a) and (d) are distinct, but those in between probably refer to a variety of more ambiguous behavioural attitudes in love, such as the LOVE = GAME model in Kövecses's list. The 'false-hearted lover' is a familiar concept in poetry and song throughout the ages and the ambiguities of love were a popular topic in the Middle Ages. Butturff and Butturff (1971: 52–8) emphasises the important role of sophistry in the *Roman de la Rose*. There are two groups of speakers in the allegorical structure of the *Roman*: those who use sophistry and lead the lover to disaster and those who pursue wisdom through their proper use of rhetoric. We can therefore see another duality in the overall love paradigm: false and true love, common to all ages.

Discussions of love in the Middle Ages are therefore not limited to courtly love, which springs to mind as typical of medieval literature, and Chaucer reflects this in the *Canterbury Tales*, from the bawdiness of the *Miller's Tale* to the highly chivalrous *Knight's Tale*. It would appear that Chaucer wished to emphasise the contrast by placing the *Miller's Tale* immediately after the *Knight's Tale*.

Many of the conceptual metaphors used in the range of love categories nevertheless appear to be the same. The aims of the lover may vary, but since a false/true attitude may come into play, a bawdy story may use the same metaphor models as one about a chivalrous knight. In the *Miller's Tale*, the story of lust between the student, Nicholas, and his landlord's wife, Alison, uses the same types of metaphors that would be used in courtly love: UNREQUITED LOVE = DEATH (*to die for suppressed love*), LOVE = SUBSERVIENCE (*to be his to command*). Nicholas expresses his wishes as:

> *And seyde, 'y-wis, but if ich have my wille*
> *For deerne love of thee, lemman, I spille . . .*
> (and said: 'Unless I have my will of you,
> sweetheart, I'm sure to die for suppressed love . . .)

Alison's reaction to his conquest of her is to say:

> *And swoor hir ooth, by Seint Thomas of Kent,*
> *That she wol been at his commandement*
> (and made her oath, by Saint Thomas à Becket
> that she would be his to command).

Like the *Canterbury Tales*, the *Decameron* also has stories of meetings between lovers while the husband is absent. Although the theme may be similar to the courtly love triangle, some of Boccaccio's stories also represent comic bawdy situations as in Chaucer.

Another contrast to courtly ideals is that certain metaphor models, such as LOVE = PAIN, refer to some of the natural consequences of love, rather than reinforcing the notion that suffering is required in order to experience love. The pains of jealousy, or bereavement and lost love are found in Boccaccio's metaphors. For example, Bernabo is intensely jealous (*Decameron*, Second Day, Novel IX), when, for the purposes of a bet, Ambrogiuolo has to prove to Bernabo that he has taken certain articles from the room in which Bernabo's wife, Zinevra, was sleeping. In order to prove that he had been in her room, he noted the fact that she had a mole under her left breast.

> *Quando Bernabo udi questo, parve che gli fosse dato d'un coltello al cuore, si fatto dolore senti* (*Decameron*, Second Day, Novel IX)
> (When Bernabo heard this, it was as if a knife pierced his heart, so great was the pain he felt)

The FIRE = JEALOUSY model is also found in Chaucer as in *'the fyr of jealousy'* (*Knight's Tale*). This tale also describes the numerous characteristics of the 'fiery strokes of desire which the servants of Love endure': as well as the rather negative aspect of jealousy, they include anxious labour, extravagance, flattery and foolhardiness, while the more positive aspects involve pleasure, hope, desire, beauty, youth, riches and enchantment.

In the case of bereavement, two lovers in a story of the *Decameron* (Fourth Day, Novel VI), Gabriotto and Andreuola, tell each other about similar dreams in which Gabriotto suddenly died in unforeseen circumstances. When Gabriotto dies later that day, Andreuola naturally suffers a great deal of emotional pain:

> *Cosi lagrimosa come era e piena d'angoscia ando la sua fante a chiamare, la quale di questo amor consapevole era, e la sua miseria e il suo dolore le dimostro.*
> (She went tearfully and sadly to call the maid to whom she had confided her love and showed her the distress and pain she suffered)

The LOVE = PAIN models are therefore more varied than the UN-REQUITED LOVE = PAIN MODEL we shall be discussing in Petrarch below. Boccaccio's writings also bring out a clear distinction in the FIRE model when relating to the flames of passionate love or the flames of hell. An example of the passion model can be seen in:

Come colui che tutto ardeva in amoroso fuoco (Third Day, Novel II)
(And being all aflame with passion).

This contrasts with the hell reference:

Io n'andrei in bocca del diavolo nel profondo del Ninferno e sarei messa ne fuoco pennace (Third Day, Novel VII)
(I should fall into the jaws of the Devil in the abyss of hell and be cast into the avenging fire).

We can therefore conclude that a single model such as LOVE = PAIN can have variations in its connotations while a source concept such as FIRE may also lead to different interpretations. This introduces variations to the courtly love ideal where fire may not always be linked to intense feeling but also have religious connotations.

12.5 Petrarch

The Boccaccio-Petrarch dimension of the 'poet-triangle' has been the subject of considerable controversy due to the unreliability of the evidence available on the possible encounters between the two poets. Petrarch was a somewhat older contemporary of Boccaccio and the latter had already praised the works of Petrarch on three different occasions prior to their first meeting in 1350 (Wilkins, 1963: 79). Retracing meetings is a complex matter since Petrarch only spent the early days of his life in Italy and his family then moved to Avignon in the south of France. It was here that he established friendships with popes, especially Benedict XII, and cardinals such as Cardinal Pietro. Later on, Petrarch found a place of seclusion at Fontaine de Vaucluse, not far from Avignon, from where he used papal emissaries in his connections with literary writers in Italy. An important person in this respect was an intimate friend, 'Laelius', whose name has taken on different spellings according to the different international literary works in which he appeared. Laelius was also known to Chaucer.

According to Wilkins, it is likely that Boccaccio's initial readings of Petrarch's works followed his meeting the emissary Laelius in Italy. Boccaccio apparently had permission to make copies of Petrarch's works at that time. When he met Petrarch several years later, he was allowed to read *De Vita*, which he subsequently reworked. Clearly aspects of Petrarch's poetic style were passed down to Boccaccio.

The link between Chaucer and Petrarch has also been established and further reading into the connections of the poetic triangle reveals a pattern of interwoven meetings in Italy. Petrarch's emissary, Laelius, could very well be the same character as Chaucer's *Lollius* who appears, among other texts, in *Troilus and Criseyde*: 'as writ myn auctor called Lollius' (Canto 1, line 394) and *The which cote, as telleth Lollius* (Canto V, line 1653) (Hornstein, 1948: 64). Since he had strong literary interests and emerged as an important figure on the political scene, Petrarch's Laelius was no doubt a go-between for the literary circle of Italian writers and political leaders whom Chaucer was to meet later on in France and Italy.

Laelius may represent the initial piece of evidence of a link between Chaucer and Petrarch, but more importantly Chaucer was the first English poet to translate Petrarch's poetry. His use of Petrarch's sonnet (no. 132) in *Troilus and Criseyde*, in the words of Thomson (1959: 313) is a 'landmark in literary history' and thereby 'marks the beginning of English Petrarchan love poetry'. It may thus be assumed that the influence of Petrarch on Chaucer was considerable.

It appears, however, that Chaucer's translations were not always exact. Whether this was due to error or, more likely, to personal modifications of source texts, is debatable. Metaphor models were also modified in translation, an example being a hot/cold metaphor in sonnet 132. It appears that the notion of binary concepts in metaphors is a recurring one. We saw above that the idea of true/false love is probably a timeless model. Another long-term feature is a binary concept such as bitter/sweet love. Likewise, the notion of hot/cold love, which we shall see later, is an image that has been used in literary works for a considerable length of time.

The 'mistranslation' of a hot/cold metaphor in sonnet 132 is an interesting one since Chaucer has transferred the Petrarchan external heat metaphor of love to one which could be interpreted as internal physiological heat. Chaucer's translation is restricted to the following two lines:

> *Allas! What is this wondre maladie?*
> *For hete of cold, for cold of hete, I dye*

Petrarch adds a final line with a reference to the heat of summer seasons and the cold of winter. By omitting this line, Chaucer wishes to imply that love is due to bodily heat. Although Thomson (1959: 321) claims that the isolation of a final couplet by metaphor, as well as by rhyme, was a later Shakespearean procedure, the heat metaphor in this case represents an interesting example of how the importation of such a metaphor from another language has given rise to a different mapping procedure.

If we now look at the first few sonnets of Petrarch's *The Canzoniere*, there are some remarkable matches with some of Kövecses's examples in modern American English. Petrarch's poetry relates to his life-long experience of unrequited love with a woman called Laura whom he briefly met in papal circles at Avignon. In Petrarch's sonnets 1–30, the following metaphor models match up: LOVE = A JOURNEY, TREASURE, AN OPPONENT/WAR, CAPTURE, MADNESS/INSANITY, FIRE, COLDNESS.

LOVE = A JOURNEY

> *Et se tornando a l'amorosa vita*
> (And if in returning to the loving path) (Petrarch: sonnet 25)

Compared with: 'The road covered is the progress of the love relationship'

(Kövecses, 1988: 16)

LOVE = TREASURE

> *Quando il sol gira, Amor piu caro pegno,*
> *Donna, di voi non ave*
> (Lady, beneath the sun's circle, Love has
> No greater treasure than you) (sonnet 29)

Compared with: 'You're my treasure!'

(Kövecses: 34)

LOVE = OPPONENT/WAR

> *Trovammi Amor del tutto disarmato*
> (Love discovered me all weaponless) (sonnet 3)

Compared with: 'She was overcome by love'

(Kövecses: 61)

LOVE = CAPTURE

> *Quando I'fui preso, et non me ne guradai,*
> *Ché I be' vostr'occhi, donna, mi legaro*
> (That I was captured, and did not defend myself
> Because your lovely eyes, my Lady, had bound me) (sonnet 3)

Compared with: 'She captured my heart'

(Kövecses: 72)

LOVE = MADNESS/INSANITY

> *Si trav è 'l folle mi' desio*
> (My passion's folly is so led astray) (sonnet 6)

Compared with: 'She drives me out of my mind'

(Kövecses: 52)

LOVE = FIRE

> *Canzon, I' non fu' mai quel nuvol d'oro*
> *Che poi discese in pret pioggia*
> *Si che 'l foco di Giove in parte spense*
> *Ma fui ben fiamma ch'un bel guardo accense*
> (O song, I was never that golden cloud
> That once fell as a precious shower,
> So that Jove's flame was quenched a little
> But I have been the fire that a lovely look kindled) (sonnet 23)

Compared with: 'She set my heart on fire'

(Kövecses: 44)

LOVE = COLDNESS

> *Ma gli spiriti miei s'aghiaccian poi*
> *Ch'I' veggio al departir gli atti soavi*
> *Torcer da me le mie fatali stelle*
> (But then my spirits are chilled when I see
> At your departure, my fatal stars
> Turn their sweet aspect from me) (sonnet 17)

Compared with: 'Their relationship is getting lukewarm'

(Kövecses: 65)

Some of Kövecses's list can therefore be retraced to Petrarch's poetry and an examination of Chaucer's metaphors show similar patterns to some of the models we have seen, such as the treasure and fire models. A variation on Petrarch's fire model is that it also implies suffering, 'the fire of suffering' or 'the fire of martyrs' (*foco de' martiri*). This is probably linked to the image of the fires of hell. The metaphor of coldness is likewise reflected in the sense of lack of passion due to unrequited love in the *Franklin's Tale*:

> *Him semed that he felt his herte colde*

The implication here is not that Chaucer has directly copied Petrarch's models but that there was a common framework of conceptualisation at the time. This was transmitted via poetry and between the poets themselves. The models were then passed down the generations to modern English.

The insanity model is likewise found in Chaucer (*Franklin's Tale*):

> . . . *that love destroyed so*
> *that wood out of his wit he gooth for wo?*
> (love afflicted him so that for grief he was completely out of his mind)

Linked to the capture model is the notion of freedom, 'love is a thing as any spirit free' (Chaucer), or the lack of it. This appears frequently in medieval literature as in the journey metaphor combined with lack of freedom in Petrarch, 'takes away the path of my liberty' or *'in libertee and eek in mariage'* (Chaucer), implying that marriage is equal to a lack of freedom.

Due to the close links between Chaucer and the poetry of medieval France and Italy, it may reasonably be assumed that, together with Chaucer's creative contribution, some of these Latinate-based models entered Middle English via his poetry. Some of Petrarch's images have an interesting background; the journey metaphor is often symbolised with a seafaring scene: 'yet I do not pray for my freedom, since all other roads to heaven are less true and there is no safer ship in which to aspire to the glorious kingdom'. Likewise, there are many images of gods and mythical figures taken up by the *Decameron*, the *Roman de la Rose* and the *Canterbury Tales*: Venus, Cupid, Jove. Images such as these naturally lead back from the exploration of Latinate metaphor history to the period of Antiquity, a cultural environment which Petrarch wanted to revive in his works.

12.6 Latinate sources in Antiquity

Petrarch wrote in Latin as well as medieval Italian and he became one of the best-known figures in the classical revival, a position which was certainly helped by the fact that he was appointed the equivalent of Poet Laureate in Rome in 1341. He even started addressing his friends by Latin names. This led to some confusion, as with the friend mentioned above who was originally known as Lellus, but who became known as

Laelius in Classical Latin, or Lelius in the late medieval Latin spelling of Petrarch's day (Hornstein, 1948: 69).

Petrarch derived his definition of courtly love from Ovid, adding his own personal experience to it (Thomson, 1959: 324), and an analysis of Ovid's work shows that this was one of the main sources of the medieval courtly love we have been discussing in connection with metaphor. It is in Ovid's work that it is possible to retrace some of the long-term metaphor paths such as LOVE = JOURNEY. In particular, the seafaring image which he used was not only adopted by other medieval writers such as Chaucer but also by later poets such as Shakespeare in the form of 'Elizabethan Petrarchanisms' (Thomson, 1959: 325). The seafaring image was a device for propelling Petrarch's hero (himself) on his voyage of trying to understand and deal with his feelings, thoughts and personal experience, that is, the lover's dilemma. Thomson cites an image from Ovid's *Amores* (II, iv, u. 7–8), likening him to a ship swept along and tossed about by raging water:

> *Nam desunt vires ad me mihi iusque regendum*
> *Auferor ut rapida concita puppis acqua*
> (I am like the stern of the ship led by surging waves)

Boccaccio does not claim to be the inventor of tales recounted in the *Decameron*. They were either directly taken from classical works or from Latin sources circulating during the medieval period. There was a large body of medieval literature available in Latin at the time. Radcliff-Umstead (1968: 171) suggests that the author thereby freed himself in part of the responsibility for the failure of tales to please the reader. In fact, while Boccaccio did indeed adapt his stories from classical sources he also added elements of his own which fitted into life at the time. Parts of the *Decameron* were taken from newly-discovered manuscripts of works by Apuleius who originally wrote in the 3rd century AD (Radcliff-Umstead, 1968: 172). The interesting point about this source is that Apuleius also dealt with illicit love affairs, in this case the tricks wives play on husbands. We can immediately see the link, not only with the types of scenarios in the *Decameron*, but also with Chaucer's *Canterbury Tales*.

Radcliff-Umstead (1968) points out the different types of love conceptualisation in medieval and classical literature. Wives' infidelity has, for example, been viewed from two different viewpoints: (a) moralistic and (b) in the form of rebellious love literature. These viewpoints often appear to be fused in both Boccaccio's and Chaucer's works. The former can be traced back to origins in Greek literature in the story of *Barlaam and*

Josephat in which women of easy virtue were called, in a somewhat misogynous manner, 'devils who catch men'. This work passed throughout Europe after being translated into Latin. In later adaptations, the devilish women became geese, as in the *Narrationes* of Odo of Cheriton, an Anglo-Norman monk writing in the last quarter of the twelfth century. Two relevant points can be made here concerning the evolution of metaphor in this particular example. The first is that, if the pejorative and moralistic tone of 'devils catching men' is lifted, this very ancient image of hunting men (in contrast to the traditional men hunting women) fits into one of Kövecses's present-day models of a hunting image (1988: 73):

She set him a trap
She snared him
He fell prey to her

The second point about metaphor evolution in this example is that the pejorative image of a goose fits into Lehrer's theory of diachronic chaining in the bird semantic field discussed in Chapter 6, in which the goose initiated metaphoric shift in the BIRD = FOOLISHNESS image.

The other attitude towards love, in the form of rebellious love literature, originated in the south of France in the late Middle Ages and spread throughout Europe. One form of amorous revolt was the *comoedia* which was a transitional form between the Latin literary genres of the time and the French *fabliau*. It changed man-hunting by women into comic or farcical situations. By the same token, the type of metaphorical expression such as 'she set him a trap' or 'she snared him' in modern English could be used not only in moralistic tones but also in farcical plays.

Similar scenes were reproduced in different medieval literary works such as a wife's infidelity to an ageing husband in the *Merchant's Tale*, parallel to the same scenario in the *Decameron*. This, again, was imitated by Boccaccio using a *comoedia* with a similar situation, the *Comoedia Lydiae* written in Latin by Matthieu de Vendôme around 1174. The result is that, like metaphoric chaining, the conceptual forms of love went through a chaining process in literary works, often passing through different languages. Such was the case of moralistic attitudes evolving through Ancient Greek, Classical Latin, late medieval Latin, Old French and Middle English. Rebellious love literature originated in late medieval Latin and was transmitted to other medieval languages. The latter was often a reflection on former periods such as the decadent period of the late Roman Empire and moralistic literary views going back beyond this time (Radcliff-Umstead, 1968: 187). This may be summarised as in Figure 12.1.

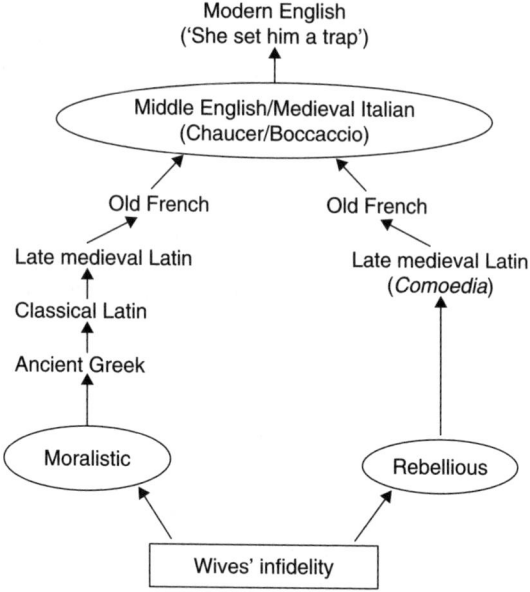

Figure 12.1 Chaining of conceptual forms of love

Without providing an exhaustive list, we shall now look at several specific models which go back to the classical period.

12.7 Metaphor links to the classical period

FIRE

The conceptualisation of love in medieval literature is therefore clearly linked to Latinate sources and many present-day English metaphor models are associated with these origins. If we apply some of Kövecses's list of metaphor mappings of love further to Antiquity, we are able to determine some of the origins attested in the very earliest written forms in European languages.

The controversial FIRE (HEAT) = PASSION and ANGER models seem to be clearly linked to classical sources. Ovid's *Metamorphoses* has an equivalent not only for these models but for many others. Kaufhold (1997: 66–71) describes some of these metaphors in relation to specific characters, such as Tereus who nurtures and sustains the fires of his passion (Latin: *ignes ipse suos nutrit*) with thoughts of Philomela. Procne 'boils over in her seething rage' (*exaestuat*) and 'burns' with anger (*ardet*) at

Tereus' deeds. The figurative fire almost becomes objective reality when Procne feels like burning the royal house with Tereus in it.

Kaufhold's analysis also highlights the fact that many of these metaphor models often combine two characteristics such as FIRE = PASSION with FIRE = FOOD. We have seen that the LOVE = FOOD model is found not only in modern English but also in Chaucer's works. Ovid combines both food and fire: Tereus boils with passion which continues to feed (*nutrit*) his desires. The interesting point about Ovid's mastery of metaphor is that, as the title *Metamorphoses* suggests, his work is a constant play between the literal and the figurative world. In the same way as Procne wishes to burn the royal house after feeling the fire of anger, the fire and food metaphor precedes the preparation of a banquet scene.

Another image of fire used in Ovid's work is a funerary one. In the same way as fire was used more often for religious purposes, within the context of the symbolisation of the flames of hell, during the classical and medieval periods, it was also associated with torches used at funerary settings (*de funere raptas*) (Kaufhold, 1997: 67). The use of this image would thus appear more specific to that time.

WAR

Another difference in long-term metaphor paths between the classical and modern periods concern the LOVE = WAR or LOVE = OPPONENT models. Although these two models use similar images in Kövecses's classification of modern English, for example the metaphor of *fighting* in *he tried to fight off his feelings of love* (LOVE = OPPONENT) and *she fought for him but his mistress won out* (LOVE = WAR) (Kövecses, 1988: 61, 72), Kövecses explains that the opponent and war models use two different situations. The opponent image is placed in the typical model of the love scenario; love can increase to a point of intensity at which a lack of control sets in and there is a subsequent attempt to regain control. The war image, on the other hand, implies that there is not an equal balance of intensity between the partners involved so that a conflict occurs, possibly involving two or three different partners. These metaphors, based on examples illustrated in Lakoff and Johnson (1980), thus involve major themes such as pursuit, combat, advance and so on, entailing capture, conquest or occupation: *she pursued him relentlessly, he is slowly gaining ground with her, she is besieged by suitors* and so on. The war model in modern English is categorised under non-prototypical cases of the scenario.

It would seem that in classical epic poetry war is a typical, or even ideal, model of love. Quoting Fränkel (1945: 28), 'Ovid, a Poet between

Two Worlds', Thomas (1964: 151) claims: '"war with its strenuous exertions is the direct opposite of love with its languid sentimentality: nevertheless, that truism challenged ingenuity to invent reasons why they should not rather be considered as similar". This statement may serve as a basis for a survey of the use of the military metaphor in love poetry, in particular in Ovid's *Amores*, which illustrate the image in its most highly developed and perfected form.' In literary criticism of the immediate post-war period, there therefore seems to be an acknowledgement that two apparently distinct domains of human experience, love and war, are metaphorically intermingled and 'unwarlike though the theme (of love) was, its effect was to induce in the poet the activity of a soldier, and the military metaphor was used to the full' (Thomas, 1964: 152).

The theme of war is immediately apparent in the role of gods of love in Classical Antiquity mentioned earlier and which will be discussed more fully below. The different types of 'idealised' war metaphor used in the past, such as siege tactics, seen in the modern English example of *besieged by suitors*, were also transferred to love poetry of the Middle Ages. Some of these military tactics were, of course, common in actual warfare at that time. Thomas points out that the *Roman de la Rose*, in fact, uses this metaphor model almost exclusively, so that it may be assumed that Ovid's influence was at work here, particularly regarding his poem *Ars Amatoria*. It fits into the romantic model in which love has to be hard to win and is the most valuable possession one can own. Thomas (1964: 158) highlights some interesting love-war situations in *Amores* (translations of the Latin texts supplied by Thomas have been added):

(a) The age for love and war is the same:

> *quae bello est habilis, Veneri quoque convenit aetas:*
> *turpe senex miles, turpe senilis amor (I, ix, 3–4)*
> (The best age for a soldier is also the best for Venus:
> An old man makes neither a good soldier nor a good lover)

(b) The soldier and lover lie on the ground, both keep guard at doors, the one at the door of his general, the other at the door of his mistress:

> *per vigilant ambo, terra requiescit uterque;*
> *ille fores dominae servat, at ille ducis (I, ix, 7–8)*
> (Both lie awake on watch and rest on the ground
> One watches over the doorway of his mistress, the
> other that of his commander)

(c) Both must be prepared to endure long journeys and hardships in quest of victory:

> *militis officium longa est via (I, ix, 9)*
> (The soldier's mission is a long journey)
> *quis nisi vel miles vel amans et frigora noctis*
> *et denso mixtas perferet imbre nives? (I, ix, 15–16)*
> (Who, other than the soldier and the lover, will endure
> The cold of the night and the snow and sleet?)

(d) Both must play the part of a scout, the soldier to spy on the enemy, the lover on a possible rival:

> *mittitur infestos alter speculator in hostes,*
> *In rivale oculos alter, ut hoste, tenet (I, ix, 17–18)*
> (One is sent to spy on the enemy,
> The other keeps his eyes fixed on his rival, who is his enemy)

(e) Both lay siege, the general to the gates of a city, the lover to the door of his mistress:

> *ille graves urbes, hic durae limen amicae*
> *obsidet; hic portas frangit, at ille fores (I, ix, 19–20)*
> (One besieges powerful cities, the other the doorway of his cold-hearted lover; one breaks down city gates, the other doors)

GODS

As we have seen in our discussions of medieval metaphor, the aspect of love has also been described in Cupid shooting arrows at the lover's heart. In Ancient Greece, emotional suffering, like disease, was symbolised as intrusion. This intrusion wounded like a weapon and covered many different aspects of perception besides emotion, such as sensation, disease and pollution (Padel, 1992: 63). The symbolisation of arrows was similar to the thunderbolts sent by the god Zeus as a form of punishment.

Gods played a very important part in Greek mythology. As Padel (1992: 7) puts it:

> As outsiders, we feel our way into the Greeks' perceptions of the world by looking at their gods. Religion was the Greeks' most vivid medium for expressing their sense of their world and their relationships. Each

divinity specialized in a different range of experience and phenomena, and each goddess or god was 'many-named' according to his or her different activities.

The origins of Cupid go back to both Ancient Greece and Rome but this name is only one of several, which sometimes leads to confusion. Two names are given in Ovid's works (*gemini Amores*): Cupid and Amor. According to hypotheses developed by Wlosok (1975: 165–79), Cupid was the older and proper name of the god of love in Roman times and Amor was a literary invention of Latin poetry. Cupid was the name attributed to the Hellenic Eros when he was adopted in Rome together with Aphrodite. However, Cupid does not correspond wholly with Eros since the former was more restricted in its connotations of love while the latter included all aspects. Furthermore, the Greek term *eros* has evolved semantically to signify physical love in European languages whereas *cupido* has not evolved. The interesting point about this development is that in Roman times the reverse situation took place: *cupido* referred etymologically to physical love while *eros* was the more comprehensive concept including, for example, the devotion of the self to the beloved partner, a characteristic feature of the Roman concept of love. It is the delimitations of the conceptual fields of love in Roman times which, according to Wlosok, led to the coining of the term *Amor*. Since the Roman concept *cupido* did not cover all aspects, such as devotion, found in its Greek origin *Eros*, *amor* was adopted. The outcome was that they became the two sons of Venus in Latin literature, a traditional duality which survived into medieval languages, including Middle High German in Wolfram von Eschenbach's *Parzival* (Wlosok, 1975: 179):

> *Manec mîn meister sprichet sô*
> *daz Amor und Cupîdô*
> *unt der zweier muoter Vênus*
> *den liuten minne gebn alsus,*
> *mit geschôze und mit fiure.*
> *diu minne ist ungehiure*
> (Manec my master, says:
> that Amor and Cupid,
> and the mother of both, Venus,
> give love to man
> using darts and fire.
> That love is vast)

We have seen above that the term *Amor* was also used in the poetry of other medieval languages such the *Roman de la Rose*: '*Qu'Amors qui toutes choses passe* . . .'(Since Love, which is stronger than everything) and Petrarch: '*Trovammi Amor del tutto disarmato*' (Love discovered me all weaponless). Although the term is present in medieval languages, *Amor* has tended to disappear in modern European languages The personification of Cupid has survived, as has the goddess of love, Venus. In the example from *Parzival* above, Cupid again illustrates the pain and passion symbol with darts and fire and Thomas (1964) suggests that the warring gods were the origin of the overriding military theme in Ovid's literature of love. The LOVE = WAR model has therefore been present throughout the history of European literature in all its different aspects.

DISEASE

It was seen that some of the typical metaphor models found in Middle English and other parallel languages involved LOVE = PAIN, PROPERTY, LAW, TREASURE and SUBSERVIENCE. Linked to the idea of suffering from pain is the image of disease. The notion of illness occurs, of course, in present-day expressions such as *lovesick*.

It appears that love as a physical affliction is a recurrent theme in the Greco-Roman literary tradition. In Catullus' love poetry, for example, the *Siqua recordanti*, it has been suggested that the author's notion of disease in a failed love affair with Lesbia has also been extended as a metaphor to criticise the social and political conditions of the time (Skinner, 1987: 231-2). Terms such as 'poison' and 'pestilence' are used in implied political rhetoric by Catullus (*In Catilinam* 44, 12) in a speech delivered by Sestius against Antius: '*plenam veneni et pestilential*' (full of poison and pestilence).

Metaphors of sickness are also extended to the domain of friendship. Betrayal of a friend is portrayed by expressions such as '*pestis amicitiae*', the disease of friendship (Catullus, poem 77). Furthermore, the cancer metaphor, as we have seen in the present-day drugs network and Teuchler's three-dimensional model, is also present in Catullus' poetry: '*novo quondam morbo civitas moritur*' (eaten by its cancer, the state ultimately succumbs).

The *cancer* metaphor is one which is used today in a large number of different fields such as civil litigation, gambling, juvenile delinquency, inflation, racism, unemployment and violence (Deignan, 1997: 29). This would therefore point to the fact that it represents a long-term metaphor related to a physiological structure and, logically, would also apply to love and friendship.

Very many love metaphors in medieval and modern English have thus been networked from the classical period. With the information gathered from literary texts, we are now in a position to formulate some specific theoretical constructs regarding the evolution of the network. Our final chapter will therefore focus on pulling the diachronic threads together.

13
Historical Models of Love Metaphors

13.1 Literary paths in metaphor creation

Our discussion of metaphor in European literature points to the fact that this medium has probably played a significant role in the evolution of love metaphors. The influence of writers from different languages and cultures forms channels of conceptualisation in literary forms throughout the ages which fluctuate and vary according to historical periods. Metaphors may continue indefinitely, appear more salient at one period of time than another, become conventionalised or completely die out. Together with the theoretical aspects discussed in Parts I and II, we are now in a position to evaluate the way in which a specific diachronic network has evolved.

One thread of continuity in the networking process involves the models used in literary works which have influenced each other. By studying the works of authors who have written a great deal about love, we are able to trace the different historical paths of this particular model. A comparison of models in Middle English with those researched in modern English enables us to define which are long-term and which tend to be more time-specific or have fluctuating saliency. These two categories can then be traced back to other languages which have used them and which have influenced subsequent literary works. With Chaucer as a starting-point in this research, it is clear that his usage of love models is Latinate-based, stretching back to the Ancient Greek/Roman tradition and forward, in many cases, up to the modern period. The late medieval period, in particular, was influenced by this strand rather then earlier periods in Old English which had more influence from Germanic cultures.

We have seen that, via Chaucer, we are first able to establish immediate links with medieval French and Italian sources such as the *Roman de la Rose* and the poets Petrarch and Boccaccio. Their works may, in turn, be

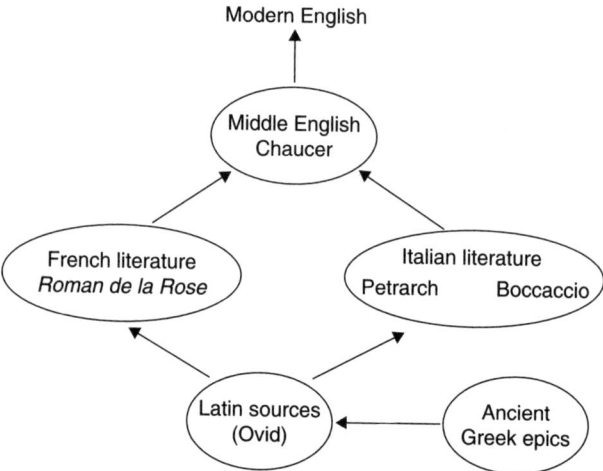

Figure 13.1 Literary paths of English love metaphors with Latinate-based sources

linked to Latin sources, Ovid, in particular, and finally to the Greek epics. This may only represent one thread in the history and origins of English love metaphors but it is probably a major one. It serves as a practical example of how the historical networks which are likely to account for the vast majority of metaphors operate. Figure 13.1 gives an overview of what the literary network looks like.

We shall now extract specific types of metaphor paths from the different examples we have examined and propose practical examples of metaphor continuation, latency, variable saliency and conventionalisation/death. One major example of a long-term, continuous metaphor is the LOVE = FIRE model.

13.2 Long-term models of love

In the fire model discussed earlier, the symbol in one of the examples given by Kövecses, *'she is his latest flame'*, can be traced back to Chaucer's time, *'and lighted your fire'*. This in turn can be found in parallel works from which some of his ideas were drawn, as in *'you will rekindle the burning fires'* (*Roman de la Rose*). It can then be traced to Italian literature: *'but I have been the fire that a lovely look kindled'* (Petrarch) and *'all aflame with passion'* (Boccaccio). The next stage is Antiquity, *'nurtures the fires of his passion'* (Ovid). There are certainly other works in the classical and medieval periods in which these symbols can be found but these poets illustrate

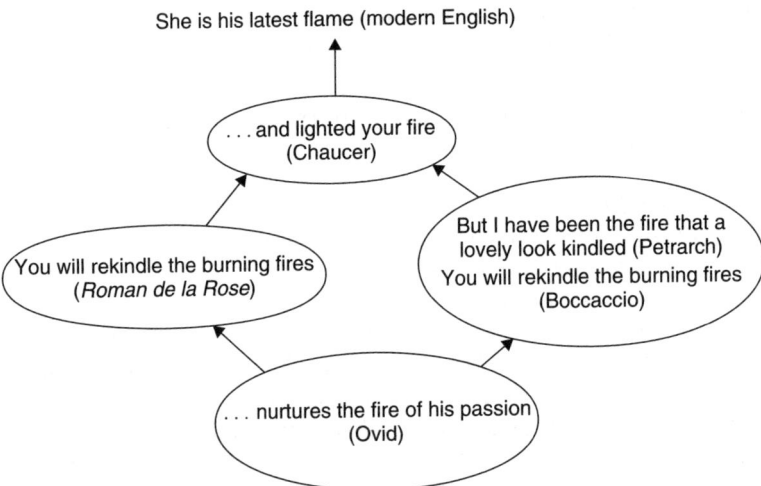

Figure 13.2 The long-term diachronic network of the conceptual metaphor FIRE = LOVE

the type of diachronic progression from one literary period to the next. In the light of the literary periods illustrated above, a diachronic metaphor network of the LOVE = FIRE model may be represented as in Figure 13.2.

The conceptual metaphor of fire appears to have remained alive on a continuous level over a long period of time and is manifest in a variety of different linguistic items today (Kövecses, 1988: 45):

That kindled love in his heart
He was burning with love
My heart's on fire
I just melted when she looked at me
She carries a torch for him

Deignan tends to support this view: 'the metaphor seems to have been established in English for some time, shown by the existence of the words *ardent* and *ardour*. Indeed, these are now so well established as to have lost both their literal sense of "fiery" and any sense of metaphoricity when used to talk about desire' (1997: 34).

Given the rich variety of the fire model in American English today, as well as its high frequency in medieval texts, it is likely that this model has remained highly salient and active during its history. Other similar

13.3 Long-term models of love with variable cultural connotations

At the same time, however, certain physiological models vary in time according to cultural influence. Pain, for example, as we have seen, was an ideal in love during the Middle Ages. It related to courtly ideals of unrequited love and was a noble aim in life and a source of self-esteem, as in Petrarch's poetry. Today, on the other hand, pain in love is usually considered highly undesirable. The result is that, although it is a highly salient, long-term image, it has different cultural connotations according to the historical period. It was likewise seen that pain resulting from love during the pre-Christian period in Ancient Greece tended to be despised, or in other words, was perceived with contempt. Although pain was a highly salient image at all these times, the *types* of saliency fluctuate (Figure 13.3).

It would require more investigation to define fluctuating saliency in greater detail but this example corresponds to Padel's view of changing attitudes towards a metaphoric concept. The model has produced different historical mindsets. With regard to Figure 13.3, it should also be pointed out that the undesirable nature of pain today can also be highly ambiguous. This ambiguity has probably existed throughout the history of physical perception. Deignan (1997: 28–9) observes that words such as *twinge* and *stab*, particularly in describing women's desire in fiction, can actually represent pleasant sensations:

> *I had felt a twinge of desire*
> *A stab of pleasure, or its anticipation, pierced her. She felt weak with desire.*

The difference here is that the borderline between pain and pleasure is a physical phenomenon whereas courtly ideals claim that the esteem of pain is a more spiritual/religious one. Variable parameters such as these raise

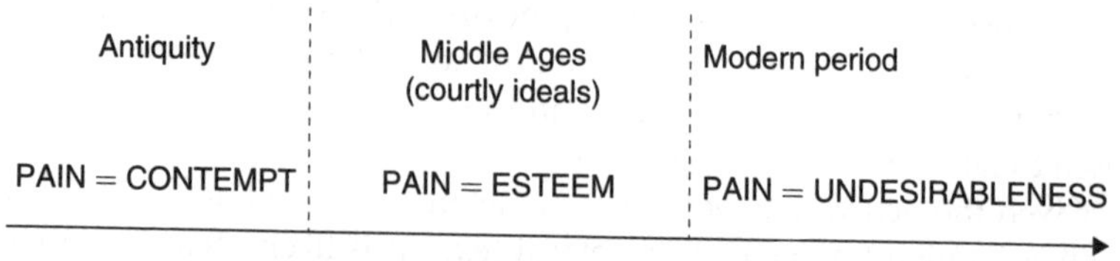

Antiquity	Middle Ages (courtly ideals)	Modern period
PAIN = CONTEMPT	PAIN = ESTEEM	PAIN = UNDESIRABLENESS

Figure 13.3 Variable connotations of the LOVE = PAIN metaphor

the complex issue of time specificity. We shall explore this area with the interrelated aspects of saliency, conventionalisation and metaphor death.

13.4 Time-specificity: models of diachronic saliency

It could be argued that the influence of religion has also had a considerable effect on models such as LOVE = LAW and SUBSERVIENCE. The types of metaphors in this field in Chaucer are probably due to the large impact of Christianity on the evolution of metaphor at that time. The degree of metaphoricity in time-specific models appears to depend on the two parameters of *saliency type* and *saliency frequency*.

The pain model discussed above illustrates the difference: PAIN = UNDESIRABLE is a type of metaphor which is probably highly salient today in the semantic field of love, PAIN = PLEASURE is evidently used in contemporary literature but is probably less salient. Within the present-day LOVE = PAIN base model, there are therefore two different images with the probability of having two levels of saliency at a given period of time. Different perception of the base model also varies with time. The Wife of Bath in the *Canterbury Tales* had a personal view of love and marriage which was different from mainstream ideas. The time scale also infers that duration of saliency levels can vary. A hypothetical model of fluctuating saliency levels can be seen in Figure 13.4.

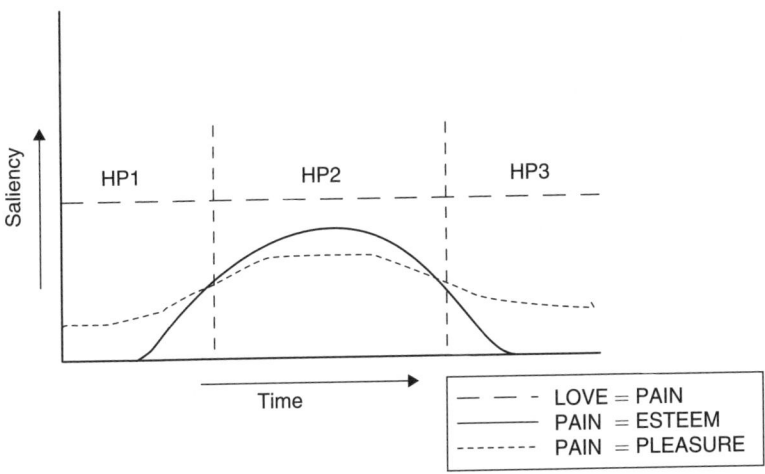

Figure 13.4 Fluctuating diachronic saliency in the pain model

Pain as a component of love has existed since time immemorial, so this model would presumably remain at a high and constant level of saliency. The PAIN = ESTEEM mapping equation, however, definitely appears to be time-specific, related to medieval courtly love. In this case, the metaphor might have come into existence just before or around the beginning of the medieval period and disappeared during the modern period. PAIN = PLEASURE is a model which, if in some way it has a physiological base, might have always existed. However, its saliency of frequency would probably vary. If it is combined with PAIN = ESTEEM, as in the medieval period, its frequency might have been higher at that time. This last point is hypothetical and would have to be investigated with relevant data. However, the model does give an idea of how different saliency parameters operate on the time scale.

13.5 Conventionalised love metaphors

If we turn to conventional metaphors, some of the examples of love metaphors listed by Kövecses (1988: 18) in the unity metaphor could be regarded as conventionalised. These were also common in the medieval period. The level of metaphoricity is, however, subjective. *We belong together* or *they are inseparable* do not sound particularly metaphoric. On the other hand, *she is my better half* does appear to have a higher level of metaphoricity.

The examples we have seen in Chaucer such as, *and thanked God that he might have her completely so that no man might share in his bliss*, would have appeared fairly conventionalised to a contemporary of Chaucer. The long-term unity conceptual metaphor no doubt has a large number of conventionalised metaphor paths which lost their metaphoric qualities a long time ago, even though they must have originally started as metaphors. Whether there is a ratio between conventionalisation and categories of conceptual metaphors, for example, a more basic notion in a particular field such as unity in love, is difficult to evaluate. It is, however, likely that conventionalisation starts very early in the history of a large number of metaphor paths. A typical scenario of historical conventionalisation probably involves the fact that a common conceptual metaphor retains a large number of conventional metaphors over a long period of time, if not indefinitely, but continues to generate new metaphors. The unity metaphor *we are one* probably existed during the medieval period and no doubt represented a conventionalised state at that time, whereas *she is my better half*, based on the same conceptual metaphor, is undoubtedly more recent and sounds a lot less conventionalised.

Historical Models of Love Metaphors 217

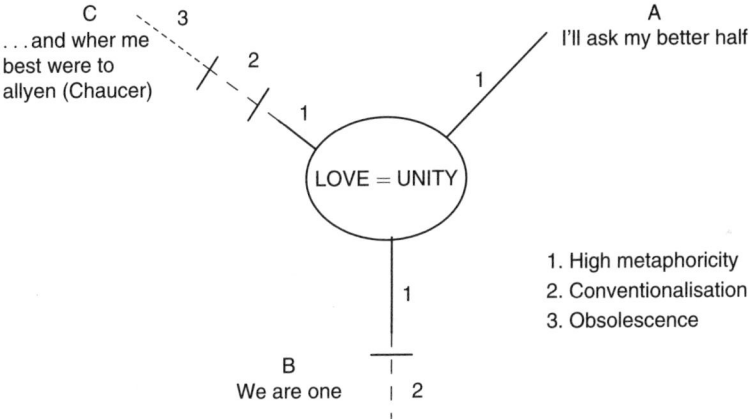

Figure 13.5 Conventionalisation in the LOVE = UNITY model

The aspect of historical conventionalisation therefore comprises a base model which networks metaphor paths in varying stages of conventionalisation. The individual linguistic items in the path may then pass on to a stage of obsolescence or metaphor death. Again, these stages tend to be subjective, as debates by linguists on the subject have shown, but a hypothetical model illustrates the point (Figure 13.5).

The expression A, *I'll ask my better half*, in the LOVE = UNITY model in modern English tends to have a degree of metaphoricity about it whereas B, *we are one*, appears to have reached a conventionalised stage. However, the Chaucerian expression C, *and wher me best were to allyen* (and where it would be best to **ally myself**) probably went through a stage of conventionalisation in the medieval period but is obsolescent today. Again obsolescence raises the issue of metaphor death.

13.6 Metaphor death in love

The LOVE = UNITY model has thus remained a long-term one but its offshoots in the form of metaphor paths have undergone different stages of conventionalisation and metaphor death. A distinction again has to be drawn between conceptual and linguistic models. Some conceptual models also appear to die out. This would be the case of the LOVE = LAW concept or, at least, it is far less salient today. It was seen that it produced metaphors such as *statute* and *debt*, in quasi-legal terms. The interesting point about these metaphors is that the former has died out whereas the latter, financial

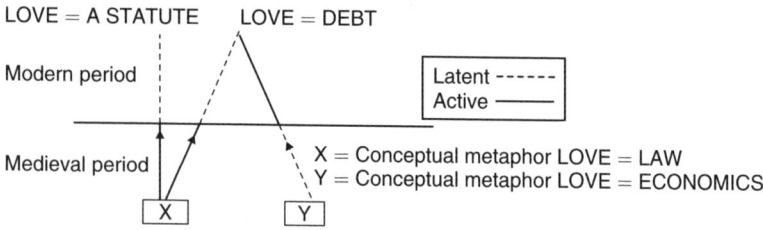

Figure 13.6 Metaphor death and conceptual switching

aspect, still exists, although it is derived from a different source. In the medieval period, the two were linked to religion and courtly love, whereas the financial issue today is linked to the notion of investing in a relationship, parallel to investment in the business world.

This is an example where we can see that one conceptual metaphor's paths may die out but, instead of being regenerated from the original conceptual base, the same image can re-surface from another base concept. The switching of base concepts is similar to the collocational switching we have discussed with reference to images being transferred to other emotions. Such was the case of the diachronic pattern SWELL = ANGER > SWELL = PRIDE in the evolution of English metaphor. In the case of *debt*, its origins have changed from the LAW model, as in Chaucer, to the LOVE IS AN ECONOMIC EXCHANGE model (*I'm putting more into this than you*) in modern American English (Kövecses, 2000: 26) (Figure 13.6).

The conceptual metaphor X, LOVE = LAW, produced the debt metaphor in the Middle Ages which became obsolete (or latent) in the modern period. The reverse happened with the LOVE = ECONOMICS conceptual metaphor which was activated in the modern period and produced a switching of the DEBT metaphor from LAW to ECONOMICS. In contrast, however, the STATUTE metaphor, based on the LAW base concept, became obsolete in the modern period and therefore died out completely.

13.7 The overall picture

If we now summarise how figurative language, and in particular metaphor, evolves through time, we are in a position to offer the following general principles that are relevant for a large number of items.

Within the modern cognitive framework, which broaches mainstream trends in recent theories on metaphor creation, it appears that core concepts, linked to our experience of the human environment, network clusters of figurative items to a base image. During the course of time, many of these clusters follow regular paths of evolution according to the conceptual context of a given culture. A distinction has to be made between underlying conceptual metaphors and the surface, or linguistic items themselves. Both may appear and disappear but the linguistic items in individual languages can be of very short duration. Some of these constructs, however, can last for a very long time, particularly conceptual metaphors such as the LIFE IS A JOURNEY image.

This raises the issue as to whether some, particularly long-term, metaphor networks are actually universal, or at least cross-linguistic, in nature. A sample of European languages reveals that, in the case of the drugs scene, this does appear to be the case. Certain images such as spatial orientation, which correspond to Lakoffian proposals of universals, do appear in all languages studied in this particular semantic field. The kinds of common images found in European languages cannot lay claim to being universals in all cultures but a number of assumptions may be made. Further research is currently being carried out on widely differing cultures to find out whether there are true conceptual universals.

At the same time, different cultures produce varying underlying conceptual metaphors which create varied types of metaphor networks. This is also apparent in culturally related languages such as the Indo-European field. A useful test for this can be made by translating figurative items between European languages. It is particularly the linguistic items themselves which differ, even if there are a large number of shared conceptual metaphors. Analyses of specific semantic fields reveal that one language very often tends to be more predominant in one group of metaphor clusters than in another language. This would suggest that the 'snowball effect' often observed in networking is more language-specific in that particular image. This leads to translation constraints and culture-specific metaphor.

This study suggests that there is an ongoing diachronic networking process in metaphor evolution. Metaphors are conceptually linked to pre-existing ones and can be traced back in time. Underlying core concepts act as building blocks for subsequent metaphor paths which may pass through different stages of activity and latency. Even if a figurative item becomes obsolete, it may be regenerated at a later stage due to the conceptual networking process. Culturally related languages such as English and French reveal common paths in basic concepts such as flat, smooth, dry, wet, round, square, tight, loose and so on. However, activation may take place at different historical periods unless there is cultural overlap due to borrowing. The theory of diachronic networking is also supported by other related studies such as chaining in semantic fields.

The basic structure of networking is, however, complicated by additional issues such as saliency structures and the status of metaphor death. A large number of items, as demonstrated by the numerous studies undertaken on the subject, consist of conventionalised metaphors. These are no longer really considered as metaphors by the general language community of the historical period in question, even though a clear metaphoric mapping procedure originally took place. There has been a lot of debate on this matter and many linguists do not agree on what actually constitutes a dead metaphor. Many conventionalised metaphors would still be considered as metaphors by some but not by others. Certain conceptual metaphors have the capacity to be regenerated at a later date whereas other truly dead metaphors do not.

In addition to these features, a metaphoric symbol does not necessarily die out but switches over to another concept, thereby involving the process of collocational switching in base concepts, metaphoric images and linguistic items. A symbol may continue to live on in another conceptual form. This often accounts for synchronic variability and further constraints in the translation of figurative language.

Disagreement as to what actually constitutes the level of metaphoricity also raises the issue of saliency, involving not only fluctuating frequency but also saliency types. Despite the complexities of metaphor death and saliency, it can be said that there are clearly time-specific metaphors in the same way as there are culture-specific ones.

In order to examine the hypothesis of diachronic networking within an empirical framework, we have investigated one particular network by tracing its metaphoric items back in time. English models of love in literature were analysed, starting with a comparison of the late Middle Ages and working back to their origins in Antiquity via contacts with other medieval European languages. It could be seen that similar models were linked to each other through the strand of Latinate-based paths of Chaucer, Petrarch and Boccaccio. These originated in Latin and Greek works. The result was the discovery of a number of long-term and time-specific models in the overall network.

Time-specific metaphors can sometimes match up with culture-specific ones in other languages but they may be located on different time-scales. This seems to be the case of parts of the body being fundamental to human thought and feeling. This raises all sorts of questions about universals: what are the diachronic metaphor universals and do they evolve in the same way? Are there, for example, frequent unidirectional changes in body parts?

A further dimension to diachronic networks is that, although the same image may be used throughout the centuries, the image may not only acquire a different semantic use but also a different attitude to it. This leads to changing historical mindsets as time passes. Long-term threads in the metaphor path may remain, but the original reasons for its conception disappear.

Despite the variations, it can be seen that our common cultural heritage has produced vast numbers of common metaphor networks which have evolved through time. Many of the shared metaphor building blocks of this cultural heritage have produced regular patterns of metaphor paths. By tracing these paths back in time, we are not only able to uncover common denominators in the core concepts of metaphors, we are also able to find many of their origins in the earliest written records of Antiquity. Historical manuscripts bear witness to this complex of interrelated thought. For this reason, we are able to suggest that there are regular principles in the evolution of figurative language due to a process of diachronic conceptual networking.

This would imply, contrary to the often despairing attempts in the past of trying to find general principles in semantic change, that figurative language is an area which does offer us the opportunity to establish regular theoretical models in the evolution of meaning. Conceptual networking would appear to be a fruitful avenue of research in this venture.

References

Aitchison, J. (1992), 'Chains, nets or boxes? The linguistic capture of love, anger and fear', in W.G. Busse (ed.), *Anglistentag (Proceedings 1991)*, *Düsseldorf*, Tübingen: Max Niemeyer Verlag, pp. 25–38.
—— (1996), *The Seeds of Speech. Language Origin and Evolution*, Cambridge: Cambridge University Press.
Allan, K. (2003), 'A diachronic approach to figurative language', in J. Barnden et al. (eds), *UCREL Technical Papers*, Vol. 18, Lancaster: Lancaster University Press.
Aristotle (1927), *Aristotle: The Poetics*, trans. W. Fyfe, Cambridge, MA: Harvard University Press.
—— (1932), *The Rhetoric of Aristotle*, trans. L. Cooper, New York: Appleton-Century-Crofts.
Bailey, R.W. (1991), *Images of English: a Cultural History of the English Language*, Cambridge: Cambridge University Press.
Baker, M. (1992), *In Other Words. A Course Book on Translation*, London: Routledge.
Barcelona, A. (ed.) (2000), *Metaphor and Metonymy at the Crossroads: a Cognitive Perspective*, Berlin and New York: Mouton de Gruyter.
Beidler, P.G. (1973), 'Chaucer's *Merchant's Tale* and the *Decameron*', *Italica*, 50 (2): 266–84.
Berlin, B. and P. Kay (1969), *Basic Color Terms: Their Universality and Evolution*, Berkeley: University of California Press.
Boardman, P.C. (1977), 'Courtly language and the strategy of consolation in the *Book of the Duchess*', *English Literary History*, 44 (4): 567–79.
Buck, C.D. (1949), *A Dictionary of Selected Synonyms in the Principal Indo-European Languages*, Chicago: University of Chicago Press.
Burnley, J.D. (1980), 'Fine Amor: its meaning and context', *Review of English Studies*, n.s. 31 (122): 129–48.
Burns, E.J. (2001), 'Courtly love: who needs it? Recent feminist work in the medieval tradition', *Signs*, 27 (1): 23–57.
Butturff, D. and D. Butturff (1971), '*Le Roman de la Rose* and the sophistry of love', *The French Review*, Special Issue, No. 3, Medieval and Renaissance Studies: 52–8.
Charteris-Black, J. (2004), *Corpus Approaches to Critical Metaphor Analysis*, Basingstoke: Palgrave Macmillan.
—— and T. Ennis (2001), 'A comparative study of metaphor in Spanish and English financial reporting', *English for Specific Purposes*, 20: 249–66.
Chickering, H.D. (1977), *Beowulf. A Dual-Language Edition*, New York: Anchor Books.
Clubb, L.G. (1960), 'Boccaccio and the boundaries of love', *Italica*, 37 (3): 188–96.
Coffman, G.R. (1945), 'Chaucer and courtly love once more – The *Wife of Bath's Tale*', *Speculum*, 20 (1): 43–50.
Cotton, E.G. and J.M. Sharp (1998), 'Figurative language in the evolution of the Spanish verb', *Metaphor and Symbol*, 13 (3): 205–29.
Cruse, D.A. (1986), *Lexical Semantics*, Cambridge: Cambridge University Press.
Culpeper, J. (1997), *History of English. Language Workbooks*, London: Routledge.

Deignan, A. (1997), 'Metaphors of desire', in K. Harvey and C. Shalom (eds), *Language and Desire*, London: Routledge, pp. 21–42.
——, D. Gabrys and A. Solska (1997) 'Teaching English metaphors using cross-linguistic awareness-raising activities', *ELT Journal*, 51: 43–51.
De Rougemont, D. (1972), *L'amour et l'occident*, Paris: Librairie Plon.
Dictionnaire historique de la langue française (1998), A. Rey (ed.), Paris: Le Robert.
Draaisma, D. (2000), *Metaphors of Memory: a History of Ideas about the Mind*, Cambridge: Cambridge University Press.
Duden (2006), *Das Herkunftswörterbuch. Etymologie der deutschen Sprache*, 7, third edition, Mannheim: Duden.
Dury, P. (1999), 'Etude comparative et diachronique des concepts ecosystem et écosystème', *Meta*, 44 (3): 485–503.
Economou, G.D. (1965), 'Januarie's sin against nature: *The Merchant's Tale* and the *Roman de la Rose*', *Comparative Literature*, 17 (3): 251–7.
Edwards, R.R. (1996), 'Source, context and cultural translation in the *Franklin's Tale*', *Modern Philology*, 94 (2) 141–62.
Ekman, P., R.W. Levenson and W.V. Friesen (1983), 'Autonomous nervous system activity distinguishes among emotions', *Science*, 221: 1208–10.
Emanatian, M. (1995), 'Metaphor and the expression of emotion: the value of cross-cultural perspectives', *Metaphor and Symbolic Activity*, 10 (3): 163–82.
Fabiszak, M (1999), 'A semantic analysis of emotion terms in Old English', *Studia Anglica Posnaniensa*, 34: 133–46.
Fein, Ellen and Sherrie Schneider (1995), *The Rules: Time-tested Secrets for Capturing the Heart of Mr. Right*, New York: Warner.
Fillmore, C.J. (1975), 'An alternative to check-list views of meaning', *Proceedings of the 1st Annual Meeting, Berkeley Linguistics Society*, University of California, Berkeley, 123–31.
—— (1982). 'Frame semantics', in Linguistic Society of Korea (ed.), *Linguistics in the Morning Calm*, Seoul: Hanshin, pp. 111–38.
Forceville, C.J. (1996), *Pictorial Metaphor in Advertising*, London: Routledge.
Fränkel, H. (1945), 'Ovid, a poet between two worlds', Sather Classical Lectures.
Galway, M. (1938). 'Chaucer's sovereign lady: a study of the Legend and related poems', *Modern Language Review*, XXXIII: 145–99.
—— (1945). 'Chaucer's hopeless love', *Modern Language Notes*, 60 (7): 431–9.
Geeraerts, D. (1989), 'Prospects and problems of prototype theory', *Linguistics*, 27: 587–612.
—— (1990), 'The lexicographical treatment of prototypical polysemy', in S.L. Tsohatzidis (ed.), *Meanings and Prototypes: Studies on Linguistic Categorization*, London: Routledge, pp. 195–210.
—— and S. Grondelaers (1995), 'Looking back at anger: cultural traditions and metaphorical patterns', in J.R. Taylor and R.E. Macular (eds), *Language and the Cognitive Construal of the World*, Berlin: Mouton de Gruyter, pp. 153–80.
Gevaert, C. (2001), 'Anger in Old and Middle English: a 'hot' topic?', *Belgian Essays on Language and Literature*, Belgian Association of Anglicists in Higher Education, University of Liège, Belgium, pp. 89–101.
—— (2002), 'The evolution of the lexical and conceptual field of anger in Old and Middle English', in J. Diaz (ed.), *A Changing World of Words: Studies in English Historical Lexicography, Lexicology and Semantics*, Amsterdam and New York: Rodopi, pp. 275–99.

Gibbs, R.W. (1994), *The Poetics of Mind. Figurative Thought, Language and Understanding*, New York: Cambridge University Press.
—— (1999), 'Researching metaphor', in L. Cameron and G. Low (eds), *Researching and Applying Metaphor*, New York: Cambridge University Press, pp. 29–47.
Goatly, A. (1997), *The Language of Metaphors*, London: Routledge.
Goldwasser, O. (2003), 'Lovers, prophets and giraffes. Metaphor and categorisation in Ancient Egypt', paper given at the Fourth International Conference of Researching and Applying Metaphor, University of Manouba, Tunis.
Goosens, L. (1990), 'Metaphtonomy: the interaction of metaphor and metonymy in expressions for linguistic action', *Cognitive Linguistics*, I (3): 323–40.
—— (2000), 'Patterns of meaning extension, "parallel chaining", subjectification and modal shifts', in Barcelona (2000), pp. 149–69.
Gorbachev, M. (1988), *Perestroika. New Thinking for our Country and the World*, New York: Harper and Row.
Hardy, T. ([1874] 1974), *Far from the Madding Crowd*, London: Macmillan.
Harris, R. (1976), 'Comprehension of metaphor: a test of a two-stage processing model', *Bulletin of the Psychonomics Society*, 8: 321–4.
Haser, V. (2000), 'Metaphor in semantic change', in Barcelona (2000), pp. 171–93.
Heaney, S. (1999), *Beowulf* (in translation), London: Faber and Faber.
Heine, B. (1997), *Cognitive Foundations of Grammar*, Oxford: Oxford University Press.
Hieatt, A. and C. Hieatt (1976), *Chaucer: Canterbury Tales. A Bantam Dual-Language Book*, New York: Bantam.
Hodgson, G.M. (2002), 'Darwinism in economics: from analogy to ontology', *Journal of Evolutionary Economics*, 12: 259–81.
Holman, H. (1951), 'Courtly love in the Merchant's and the Franklin's Tales', *English Literary History*, 18 (4): 241–52.
Hornstein, L.H. (1948), 'Petrarch's Laelius, Chaucer's Lollius?', *PMLA*, 63 (1): 64–84.
Ibrahem, A. (2000), *Egyptian Gods and the Solar Eclipses:* http://www.eclipsechasers.com.
Izard, C. and S. Buechler (1980), 'Aspects of consciousness and personality in terms of differential emotions theory', in R. Plutchik and H. Kellerman, *Emotion: Theory, Research and Experience*, Vol. 1: *Theories of Emotion*, New York: Academic Press.
Jager, E. (1990), 'Speech and the chest in Old English poetry: morality or pectorality?', *Speculum*, 65 (4): 845–59.
Jespersen, O. ([1909] 1949), *A Modern English Grammar*, London: Allen and Unwin.
Johnson, M. (1987), *The Body in the Mind: the Bodily Basis of Meaning, Imagination and Reason*, Chicago: University of Chicago Press.
—— (1992) 'Philosophical implications of cognitive semantics', *Cognitive Linguistics*, 3: 345–66.
Johnson, M.G. and T.B. Henley (1988), 'Something old, something new, something borrowed, something true', *Metaphor and Symbolic Activity*, 3(4): 233–52.
Johnson-Laird, P.N. (1983), *Mental Models*, Cambridge: Cambridge University Press.
Kaufhold, S.D. (1997), 'Ovid's Tereus: fire, birds, and the reification of figurative language', *Classical Philology*, 92 (1): 66–71.

Kay, C.J. (2000), 'Metaphors we lived by: pathways between Old and Modern English', in R. Roberts and J. Nelson (eds), *Essays on Anglo-Saxon and Related Themes in Memory of Lynne Grundy*, King's College London, Centre for Late Antique and Medieval Studies, pp. 273–85.

Kay, P. and W. Kempton (1984), 'What is the Sapir-Whorf hypothesis?', *American Anthropologist*, 86 (1): 65–79.

Kittay, E.F. (1987), *Metaphor: its Cognitive Force and Linguistic Structure*, Oxford: Clarendon.

Kittredge, G.L. (1912), 'Chaucer's discussion of marriage', *Modern Philology*, IX: 435–67.

Kövecses, Z. (1988), *The Language of Love*, London and Toronto: Associated University Presses.

Kövecses, Z. (1995), 'American friendship and the scope of metaphor', *Cognitive Linguistics*, 6–4: 315–46.

—— (2000), *Metaphor and Emotion: Language, Culture and Body in Human Feeling*, Cambridge University Press.

Labov, W. (1973), 'The boundaries of words and their meanings', in C.-J.N. Bailey and R.W. Shuy (eds), *New Ways of Analysing Variation in English*, Washington DC: Georgetown University Press.

Lakoff, G. (1972), 'Hedges: a study in meaning criteria and the logic of fuzzy concepts', in *Papers of the 8th Regional Meeting, Chicago Linguistic Society*, University of Chicago, pp. 183–228.

—— (1987), *Women, Fire and Dangerous Things*, Chicago: University of Chicago Press.

—— and M. Johnson (1980), *Metaphors We Live By*, Chicago: University of Chicago Press.

—— and M. Turner (1989), *More than Cool Reason: a Field Guide to Poetic Metaphor*, Chicago: University of Chicago Press.

Langacker, R.W. (1988), 'Review of Lakoff (1987)', *Language*, 64: 384–95.

Le Goff, J. (1989), 'Head or heart? The political use of body metaphors in the Middle Ages', in M. Feher (ed.), *Fragments for a History of the Human Body*, 3, New York: Zone, pp. 13–26.

Li, X. (2005), 'Etude de la métaphore dans une perspective trans-culturelle en anglais et en chinois', unpublished Master's dissertation, University of Provence, France.

Lehrer, A. (1985), 'The influence of semantic fields on semantic change', in J. Fisiak (ed.), *Historical Semantics and Historical Word-formation*, Berlin: Mouton de Gruyter, pp. 283–96.

Locke, J. ([1690] 1979), *An Essay Concerning Human Understanding*, ed. P.H. Nidditch, Oxford: Clarendon.

MacCormac, E.R. (1985), *A Cognitive Theory of Metaphor*, Cambridge, MA: MIT Press.

Matsuki, K. (1995), 'Metaphors of anger in Japanese', in J.R.Taylor (ed.), *Language and the Cognitive Construal of the World*, Berlin: De Gruyter, pp. 137–51.

Meillet, A. (1958), *Linguistique Historique et Linguistique Générale*, Paris: Honoré Champion.

Naciscione, A. (2004), 'The pattern of instantial stylistic use of phraseological units as a mental technique', in *Proceedings of the International Conference 'Rencontres Linguistiques Mediterranéennes & Europhras'*, Ecole Normale Supérieure, Tunis, pp. 2–13.

—— (2006), 'Figurative language in translation: a cognitive approach to cognitive terms', in A. Veisbergs (ed.), *Pragmatic Aspects of Translation. Proceedings of the Fourth Riga International Symposium*, Riga: University of Latvia, National Language Commission, pp. 102–18.

Newmark, P. (1985), 'The translation of metaphor', in W. Paprotté and R. Driven (eds), *The Ubiquity of Metaphor*, Amsterdam: Benjamins, pp. 295–326.

Ortony, A., G.L. Clore and A. Collins (1988), *The Cognitive Structure of Emotions*, Cambridge: Cambridge University Press.

Oxford Dictionary of English Etymology (1993), ed. T.F. Hoad, Oxford: Oxford University Press.

Oxford English Dictionary (2006), ed. J. Simpson, third edition, Oxford: Oxford University Press.

Padel, R. (1992), *In and Out of the Mind. Greek Images of the Tragic Self*, Princeton, NJ: Princeton University Press.

Prokosch, E. (1938), *A Comparative Germanic Grammar*, Baltimore: Linguistic Society of America.

Paris, G. (1883), 'Lancelot du Lac, II: Conte de la charrette', *Romania*, 12: 459–534.

Quinn, N. (1991), 'The cultural basis of metaphor', in James W. Fernandez (ed.), *Beyond Metaphor. The Theory of Tropes in Anthropology*, California: Stanford University Press, pp. 56–93.

Quinn, N. and D. Holland (1987), 'Culture and cognition', in N. Quinn and D. Holland (eds), *Cultural Models in Language and Thought*, Cambridge: Cambridge University Press, pp. 3–40.

Radcliff-Umstead, D. (1968), 'Boccaccio's adaptation of some Latin sources for the *Decameron*', *Italica*, 45 (2): 171–94.

Radman, Z. (1997). 'Difficulties with diagnosing the death of a metaphor', *Metaphor and Symbol*, 12 (2): 149–57.

Reddy, M.J. (1969), 'A semantic approach to metaphor', in R. Binnick et al. (eds), *Papers from the Fifth Regional Meeting of the Chicago Linguistics Society*, University of Chicago, pp. 240–51.

—— (1979), 'The conduit metaphor. A case of frame conflict in our language about language', in A. Ortony (ed.), *Metaphor and Thought*, Cambridge: Cambridge University Press, pp. 284–324.

Resche, C. (2006), 'La métaphore dans le domaine économique: lieu d'interface entre langue et culture', in R. Greenstein (ed.), *Langues et cultures, une histoire d'interface*, Paris: Publications de la Sorbonne, pp. 13–43.

Richards, I. (1965), *The Philosophy of Rhetoric*, Oxford: Oxford University Press.

Ricoeur, P. (1978), *The Rule of Metaphor*, London: Routledge and Kegan Paul.

Rosch, E. (1975), 'Cognitive representations of semantic categories', *Journal of Experimental Psychology*, 104 (3): 192–233.

Santamaria, J.A., V. Martino and E.K. Clemons (2004), *The Marine Corps Way. Using Maneuver Warfare to Lead a Winning Organisation*, New York: McGraw Hill.

Schäffner, C. (1997), 'Metaphor and interdisciplinary analysis', *Journal of Area Studies*, 11: 57–72.

Schank, R. and R. Abelson (1977), *Scripts, Plans, Goals, and Understanding: an Inquiry into Human Knowledge Structures*. Hillsdale, NJ: Erlbaum.

Schnell, R. and A. Shields (1998), 'The discourse on marriage in the Middle Ages', *Speculum*, 73 (3): 771–86.

Schultz, J.A. (2002), 'Love-service, masculine anxiety and the consolations of fiction in Wolfram's "Parzival"', *Zeitschrift für Deutsche Philologie*, 121 (3): 342–64.
Searle, J.R. (1979), 'Metaphor', in A. Ortony (ed.), *Metaphor and Thought*, New York: Cambridge University Press.
Silverman, D. and B. Torode (1980), *The Material Word: Some Theories of Language and its Limits*, London: Routledge and Kegan Paul.
Skinner, M. B. (1987), 'Disease imagery in Catullus, 76, 17–26', *Classical Philology*, 82 (3): 230–3.
Smith, E. and D. Medlin (1981), *Categories and Concepts*, Cambridge, MA: Harvard University Press.
Smith, M., H. Pollio and M. Pitts (1981), 'Metaphor as intellectual history: conceptual categories underlying figurative usage in American English from 1675 to 1975', *Linguistics*, 19: 911–35.
Stearns, M.W. (1942), 'A note on Chaucer's attitude towards love', *Speculum*, 17 (4): 570–4.
Steen, G. (1994), *Understanding Metaphor in Literature: an Empirical Approach*, London: Longman.
—— (2002), 'Towards a procedure for metaphor identification', *Language and Literature*, special edition, '*Metaphor Identification*', 11 (1): 17–33.
Stern, G. ([1931] 1968), *Meaning and Change of Meaning with Special Reference to the English Language*, Bloomington: Indiana University Press.
Sweetser, E. (1987), 'Metaphorical models of thought and speech: a comparison of historical directions and metaphorical mappings in the two domains', in J. Aske, N. Beery, L. Michaelis and H. Filip (eds), *Proceedings of the Thirteenth Annual Meeting of the Berkeley Linguistics Society*, New York, pp. 446–59.
—— (1990), *From Etymology to Pragmatics. Metaphorical and Cultural Aspects of Semantic Structure*, Cambridge: Cambridge University Press.
—— (1992), 'English metaphors for language: motivations, conventions, and creativity, *Poetics Today*, 13: 705–24.
Taverniers, M. (2002), *Metaphor and Metaphorology. A Selective Genealogy of Philosophical and Linguistic Conceptions of Metaphor from Aristotle to the 1990s*, Ghent: Academia Press.
Taylor, J.R. (1989), *Linguistic Categorization: Prototypes in Linguistic Theory*, Oxford: Clarendon Press.
Teucher, U. (2003), 'The therapeutic psychopoetics of cancer metaphors: challenges in interdisciplinarity', *History of Intellectual Culture*, 3 (1): 1–15.
Thomas, E. (1964), 'Variations on a military theme in Ovid's "Amores"', *Greece and Rome*, 11 (2): 151–65.
Thomson, P. (1959), 'The "Canticus Troili": Chaucer and Petrarch', *Comparative Literature*, 11 (4): 313–28.
Tourangeau, R. and R. Sternberg (1982), 'Understanding and appreciating metaphors', *Cognition*, 11: 203–44.
Traugott, E. (1985), '"Conventional" and "dead" metaphors revisited', in W. Paprotté and R. Driven (eds), *The Ubiquity of Metaphor*, Amsterdam Studies in the Theory and History of Linguistic Science, Current Issues in Linguistic Theory, 29, Amsterdam: Benjamins, pp. 17–56.
—— (1989), 'On the rise of epistemic meanings in English: an example of subjectification in semantic change', *Language*, 65 (1): 31–55.

—— and R. Dasher (2002), *Regularity in Semantic Change*. Cambridge Studies in Linguistics, Cambridge: Cambridge University Press.

Trésor de la langue française (2002), ed. J. Deudien, Paris: CNRS (Centre National de la Recherche Scientifique).

Trier, J. (1931), *Der deutsche Wortschatz im Sinnbezirk des Verstandes. Die Geschichte eines sprachlichen Feldes*, Heidelberg: Winter.

Trim, R. (1997), 'How universal is metaphor? The case of drugs in European languages', *Lexicology. An International Journal on the Structure of Vocabulary*, 3/2: 244–72.

—— (2005), 'Tracing regular metaphor paths in the history of a language: evidence from divergence in the dryness concept between English and French', in Z. Maalej (ed.), *Metaphor, Cognition and Culture*, selected papers from the Fourth Conference on Researching and Applying Metaphor, University of Manouba, Tunis, pp. 79–95.

Ullman, S. (1957), *The Principles of Semantics*, New York: Barnes and Noble.

—— (1962), *Semantics: an Introduction to the Science of Meaning*, Oxford: Blackwell.

Van den Broek, R. (1981), 'The limits of translatability exemplified by metaphor translation', *Poetics Today*, 2/4: 73–87.

Vico, G. ([1744] 2002), *The New Science*, edited and translated by Leon Pompa, Cambridge: Cambridge University Press.

Whorf, B.L. (1956), *Language, Thought and Reality*, Cambridge, MA: MIT Press.

Wierzbicka, A. (1986), 'Human emotions. Universal or culture-specific?', *American Anthropologist*, 88 (3): 584–94.

—— (1992), *Semantics, Culture and Cognition. Universal Human Concepts in Culture-specific Configurations*, Oxford: Oxford University Press.

Wilkins, E.H. (1963), 'Boccaccio's early tributes to Petrarch', *Speculum*, 38 (1): 79–87.

Wlosok, A. (1975), 'Amor and Cupid', *Harvard Studies in Classical Philology*, 79: 165–79.

Yu, N. (1995), 'Metaphorical expressions of anger and happiness in English and Chinese', *Metaphor and Symbolic Activity*, 10 (2): 59–92.

Index

activation, metaphor 111ff.
allusion 20
ambiguity 92
   disambiguity 93
amelioration, semantic 97
analogies 12
Anomaly View 13
assertive verbs 145
attestations, dictionary 112
attributes 9

base concepts 19
basic-level structures 22, 30
binary concepts 116
body metaphors 46ff.
building blocks, metaphor 110

chaining, metaphor 25
   lexical 18
change, semantic 3, 91
checklist theories 14
chronological metaphors 190
clichés 11
clusters, conceptual 9
cognates 101
cognitive domain 20
cognitive linguistics 9
collocational switching 122
colour metaphors 56ff.
   basic colour terms 57
   focal colours 22
Comparison Theory 13
conceptual equivalence 63ff.
   links 5, 19
   metaphors 5, 28
   networking 33ff., 109ff.
   switching 218
   systems 7, 54
conceptualisation 5, 54
   abstract 101, 104
   channels 211
   concrete 101, 104
   deontic 102

epistemic 102
hyperonymical 126
reconceptualisation 151
conceptualising capacities 54
conduit metaphors 10–11
connotations, cultural 211ff.
   variable 214
contact, language 112
context 151
continuous metaphors 122
conventionalisation, historical 217
conventionalised metaphors 9, 145, 216ff.
convergence, divergence 89ff.
core concepts 93
corpus data 145
creation, metaphor 16, 90, 211ff.
creative metaphors 26, 65ff.
cross-language patterns 28
cultural contact 89
   distance 29
   influence 137
   models 50ff
   overlap 66, 68
   transfer 51
cultural-specific patterns 49ff., 152
culture 9

dead metaphors 9, 11, 141ff., 217ff.
diachronic regularity 4, 99ff., 109ff.
dialectal metaphors 66
domains-interaction theory 16
domains, source and target 10
dormancy 110ff.
dormant networking hypothesis 111

emotions, fundamental 68–9
   structure of 170ff.
etymology 19
   re-etymologisation 143
euphemisms 97
evolution, historical 9
   metaphor 151

extensions, metaphor 20
  recurrent meaning 91

fields, semantic 91ff.
  chaining of 104ff.
figurative structures, simple and complex 104
fixed-reference meaning 14
flexibility, meaning 13
framework semantics 14, 20
fuzziness 14

generalisation, semantic 97

hedges 16
hierarchical ordering 93
hieroglyphics 4
homonymy 95ff.
  diachronic 97
humoral theory 55

icons, computer 7
idealised cognitive models 19
idioms 12
imagery 151ff.
image-schematic structures 22
interpretation, metaphor 5
interactionist view 13–14
irony 12, 98

latency 150–1
laws, semantic 3
lexical forms 7
lexicon 112
  relexicalisation 122–3
linguistic forms 28
linked concepts 19
literal meaning 18ff., 145
long-term metaphors 5, 122ff., 214ff.

mapping, mental 4
mental states 99
models, mental 22
metalanguage, semantic 68
metaphoricity 9
metaphorisation process 101–2
metaphtonymy 12
metonymisation 102
  metonymy 11ff.

mindsets, historical 152ff.
  religious 160ff.
modality, epistemic and root 99
monosemy 92

narrowing, semantic 97
networking, diachronic 90, 109ff.
  conceptual 19
  cyclic 150
  historical 5, 167ff.
  semantic 18, 91ff.

objectivism 13
obsolescence 90
original metaphors 11
origins of metaphor 4

paths, metaphor 109ff.
pectorality 127
pejoration 97
perception 7
performative verbs 145
personification 12, 47–8
phraseological units 20ff.
physiological effects 55
polysemy 91ff.
  figurative 95
  prototypical 93
  random 95
pragmatics 151
predominance, language-specific 79
prototype metaphor 15ff., 95
proverbs 12
psychology 14
puns 20

radial categories 18
regeneration, metaphor 147
regional metaphors 66
replacement, semantic 97
retrieval, metaphor 110

saliency 64, 137, 215
  diachronic 138ff.
  fluctuating 215
  frequency of 215
  language-specific 66
  parameters of 216
  time-specific 215

scenarios, ideal   25, 175
metaphor   21ff., 32ff.
  non-prototypical   26
  typical   25
scripts   20
semantics, diachronic   91
  generative   14
semiotics   7
shift, semantic   3, 101
short-term metaphor   122
signs   8
similes   12
snowball effect   72, 219
spatial orientation   23ff., 31
spatio-temporal terms   145
speech acts   99
stock metaphors   11
symbols   8
synaesthesia   12
synonymy   94

tenor   13
thematic structure   145
thought processes   83
time dimension   9
time specificity   66, 125ff., 152
translatability   65ff.
  translation   63ff.
  translation constraints   219
tropes   11
truth conditions   14

unidirectionality   99
universal metaphors   25, 28ff.

vagueness   92
vehicle   13

Whorfian hypothesis   83ff.

zeugma   12, 20